Alone

Also by Pip Granger
and published by Corgi Books

NOT ALL TARTS ARE APPLE
THE WIDOW GINGER
TROUBLE IN PARADISE
NO PEACE FOR THE WICKED

Alone

PIP GRANGER

CORGI BOOKS

TRANSWORLD PUBLISHERS
61–63 Uxbridge Road, London W5 5SA
a division of The Random House Group Ltd
www.booksattransworld.co.uk

ALONE
A CORGI BOOK: 9780552155366

First publication in Great Britain
Corgi edition published 2007

Copyright © Pip Granger 2007

Pip Granger has asserted her right under the Copyright, Designs and
Patents Act 1988 to be identified as the author of this work.

This book is a work of non-fiction based on the life, experiences and
recollections of the author. In some cases names of people, places,
dates, sequences or the detail of events have been changed solely to protect
the privacy of others. The author has stated to the publishers that, except in
such minor respects not affecting the substantial accuracy of the work,
the contents of this book are true.

A CIP catalogue record for this book
is available from the British Library.

This book is sold subject to the condition that it shall not,
by way of trade or otherwise, be lent, resold, hired out,
or otherwise circulated without the publisher's prior
consent in any form of binding or cover other than that
in which it is published and without a similar condition,
including this condition, being imposed on the
subsequent purchaser.

Addresses for Random House Group Ltd companies outside the UK
can be found at: www.randomhouse.co.uk
The Random House Group Ltd Reg. No. 954009

The Random House Group Limited supports The Forest Stewardship
Council (FSC), the leading international forest certification organisation.
All our titles that are printed on Greenpeace approved FSC certified paper
carry the FSC logo. Our paper procurement policy can be found at:
www.rbooks.co.uk/environment.

Mixed Sources
Product group from well-managed
forests and other controlled sources
www.fsc.org Cert no. TT-COC-2139
© 1996 Forest Stewardship Council
FSC

Typeset in 11.5/15pt Times New Roman by
Falcon Oast Graphic Art Ltd.

Printed in the UK by
CPI Cox & Wyman, Reading, RG1 8EX.

6 8 10 9 7 5

For Joyce, my dear old friend

Acknowledgements

This book is a memoir of my childhood and the things that made me what I am. It is neither a history, nor an autobiography. Telling the story means that I have to include personal events from other people's lives, but I have no wish to bring back distressing memories for those involved, so I have changed the names of almost everyone in the book, and altered any details of their lives not vital to the story. Several minor characters are composites of various different people: they all have fictitious names. If anything here reminds you of actual people you know or knew, I can assure you it is a coincidence.

I would like to thank: my husband, Ray, who is a constant support and an absolute star; my dear friend and first reader, Jill Nicholson; my editor, Selina Walker; my agent, Lizzy Kremer; and all those who beaver away behind the scenes at Transworld, especially Judith Welsh, Sam Jones, and Diane Meacham for my beautiful cover.

CONTENTS

PROLOGUE

Hard to Bear

I sat very still and held my breath, in case the two men standing close by heard my breathing, or the rustle of dried leaves beneath my brand new, navy blue Clark's sandals.

'Night, Reg. See you down Walfamstow tomorrow?'

'Yeah. I'll see you there, Eddie. Me dad's just got himself half a dog, and it's running in the 4.30.'

'I hope he bought the front half!'

Reg chuckled. 'Wouldn't matter. Bleeder seems to be running on three legs whichever way he's facing, doesn't stand a snowflake's, but me dad and his mate reckon he's young, he'll come on in time. Personally, I think that if he was an 'orse, he'd be dog meat by now . . .'

Their voices faded away. I heard the bolt on the public bar door shoot home, closely followed by the one in the saloon. The Bear was closing, so it had to be gone eleven by the time those very last customers had stumbled into the night and crossed the narrow lane to stand beside my hiding place. I peered through the leaves of the dog rose and watched as the lights in the pub across the road went out one by one. It seemed to be hours before the place was closed up, but eventually the last bedroom light winked out and I was left utterly alone in the night.

At least, I thought I was alone. I must have dozed off, all wrapped up in an old eiderdown, because the next thing I knew I was jerked wide awake by a sound so inhuman that it turned my skin clammy and my mouth dry. Every hair on my body seemed to stand to attention, like so many little antennae searching out the direction of the danger. The sound came again, a long, low, grumbling, rumbling growl, followed by a rattle and then a huge, gusty sigh. I was rigid with fear, convinced that I was about to be eaten alive by whatever was out there. I was under no illusions. Anything that had a growl that deep and a sigh that loud had to be really, really big. It would have no trouble at all getting through the dense hedge into my secret den. All it had to do was to barge hard, and the dog rose and honeysuckle would part company from the field maple and hawthorn that hid it from the world outside, and I would end up being something's supper. I sat and waited for the end to come, hardly able to breathe. My heart was hammering so hard in my ears that it drowned out the stealthy footsteps I knew were coming closer.

I suppose I was too dopey with fright to think straight, but it took me ages to realize that the beast in the night was in fact the poor old bear that lived in the garden of the pub, banged up in a cage and so in no position to invade my camp. I knew the bear quite well, as it happened. In fact, I had spent many a Saturday and Sunday lunchtime with that bear, waiting in the pub's garden for my mother. I knew that he liked Smith's crisps sprinkled with just a little salt. This doesn't mean that I had ever got close to him – not within his reach, anyway. I had always chucked the donated crisps, still in the crinkly packet – which he chomped up, then spat out – through the bars from a safe distance. He might have looked like my teddy, only with much darker fur, but I knew that he would eat any child that was careless enough to stray within his reach, because my brother Peter said so, and so did everyone else. Anyway, he had a crazed look in his eyes. That look meant that I always kept a deeply respectful distance between him and me.

I don't remember if I ever got back to sleep that night, but I do know that I crept out of my hiding place as soon as the very first glimmer of light filtered through the leaves. The relief was enormous. It had been a scary old night, and I wanted to get home and safely into my bed before my mother woke up. First, though, I nipped over the road to say good morning to the bear and give him the remains of a Marmite sandwich that I'd snatched from the kitchen counter on the way out of the back door the night before.

We stared at each other for a while in the chill morning air as he munched, and I thought about how sad he looked in that tatty old cage. Silently, I promised him that I would give up hamsters and pet mice immediately and for ever, and never visit a zoo again. Then I ran back over the lane and across the dew-soaked grass to our house in Wincanton Avenue.

Sliding quietly in through the unlocked back door, I tiptoed past the living room, where a strange man was snoring loudly on the dragon rug that Mother had designed and hooked during the long winter evenings a year or so before. Odd bods sleeping it off in various parts of the house was a fairly regular occurrence, so I didn't give him a second thought. He was sound asleep, and therefore relatively safe, and he hadn't been sick, so there was no cleaning up for me to do.

Reassured on these points, I carried on up the stairs, taking great care to skip the steps that creaked. I made my way, silent as a wraith, to my bedroom at the front of the house. I had to be safely in bed before my mother woke up: I was pretty sure that she had no idea I'd been out all night, and I wanted it to stay that way.

I had discovered my camp opposite the Bear almost as soon as my mother, brother Peter and I had moved into the Wincanton Avenue house, when I was about six and Peter was ten. By that time, we were already good at assessing the need to make ourselves scarce, and knew that it was always handy to have a bolt hole to disappear to when things got tricky. We had hideaways all over the place, some that we shared and some that we didn't. We needed them because home was a cross between an active volcano and a leaky boat. It was volcanic because our mother was inclined to blow every now and then, and when she did it was a good idea to be out of the way of the flying debris, which could come in the form of vitriolic sarcasm or an actual dinner plate. Better still, if we could sense the storm brewing, or read the signs right, remembering previous 'morning after the night before' days, we could ride out the eruption at a safe distance, tucked away in the garden shed, up a tree somewhere or in one of our camps.

Dog rose den, though, was all mine. Peter never came there, even though it was virtually on our doorstep. I don't think it was ever talked about; it was just taken for granted between us that we each had to have a private place. There was a four-year difference in our ages, after all, which is aeons when you are very young, and he didn't want his baby sister slung round his neck all the time. As it was, when I first started school he was chief-in-charge of walking me home and staying with me until Mother got in, which meant that he couldn't hang around with his mates until he was freed from sister-sitting duty.

The leaky boat aspect of our home life was due to the fact that Mother could be just a tad flaky at times. It was the 1950s, separation and divorce were shameful events and society did little or nothing to support single mothers, especially if it was felt that they'd brought it upon themselves. After all, enough husbands and fathers had perished in the war, and it was an utter disgrace if a woman and her children carelessly managed to misplace theirs! Like a lot of things in the age of austerity that hit post-war England, compassion was rationed to those who really deserved it; widows did, orphans did, but divorcees didn't – it was as black and white as that.

With life being so tough, Peter and I understood that we had to be as little trouble as possible; that we had to smooth Mother's way where we could; and, above all else, that we had to keep schtum about anything that might upset or anger her. We knew that she'd been lumbered with us, and so we had to make the job as easy as we could. We knew that if our little boat sank, we'd wind up in the Cottage Homes along with all the other unwanted children.

Our life together must have always been difficult, I now realize. I have only to remember all the stories surrounding my birth to get some inkling of that. It was, apparently, nothing short of a miracle that I was born at all. And once I had got here, it was a case of one family crisis after another, in what, at the time, felt like a seemingly endless stream.

PART ONE

Cries in the Night

1

A Bit of a Bloody Nuisance

It was dark and it was cold as my mother dangled helplessly by her bra strap from the wing mirror of the little black MG and listened to the stream as it gurgled its way under the bridge to the sea.

Instinct told her not to move, or to struggle, in case the strap or the mirror snapped and plunged her into icy water, or dashed her on the rocks she imagined far below. So she waited, her heart hammering in her ears, hoping for help to come. Her poor shocked and fuddled brain couldn't keep track of time. They had been crossing the bridge when the MG crashed into the parapet, and she'd been thrown from the car by the force of the collision. She could never say how long she hung there, listening to the river, her heart and the ominous creaking of the mangled MG: it might have been a few moments, or it might have been hours. By the time my father, the driver of the car, came to and hauled her to safety, she had resigned herself to yet another miscarriage. There had already been several, and she supposed one more wouldn't make a lot of difference. She'd grown used to it; at least, that's what she told herself.

'But you were a determined little bugger,' she'd say, when she related this story to me. 'You weren't about to let a little thing like a car crash stop you in your tracks. You were going to come into this world, come hell or high water, and come you did!' – but not before fate stuck its foot out once again five months later.

On 25 July 1947, Mother fell down the stairs at home and went into labour a month early, just hours before she was due to join her own mother for a birthday tea.

On hearing the news, Grandma grew excited. 'You just hang on until after midnight, darling,' she suggested. 'Another grandchild would be the best birthday present you could ever give me.'

For once, Mother was dutiful. She 'kept her legs firmly crossed,' as she indelicately put it, and I was born in the early hours of the 26th.

Things didn't go smoothly even then. Despite having survived the two accidents, Mother almost bled to death immediately after the special, and wildly dramatic, delivery of Grandma's birthday present. Father, running true to form, had somehow managed to fall out so spectacularly with the local doctor that the man refused point-blank to attend my birth for fear of being physically assaulted. History doesn't relate what the argument was about, but the upshot was that a military doctor had to be summoned from a nearby army camp to deal with the sudden and urgent – thanks to the stairs – business at hand. Sadly, his knowledge of childbirth was largely theoretical, as his only medical experience had been ministering to the needs of the men at the barracks. His woeful lack of practical experience led to the 'bloodbath', as my mother so graphically described it, that almost killed her.

As he saw my mother slipping away, the army doctor, urged by the midwife, called the more experienced GP in desperation and pleaded with him to come to the rescue. Having asked for, and received, a solemn promise that my father would not be present, the local doctor arrived just in time to deliver a single, hefty prod in the appropriate place to bring the afterbirth safely away. Even so, it was touch and go for Mother for a while until, through the fug, she over-heard the midwife saying that she'd never seen 'such an ugly little scrap' as me. It was then that Mother decided that she'd better live, because she was the only person ever likely to be able to love me. Mother always related this birth story – complete with gory details involving buckets of blood and my four-year-old brother, Peter, being dragged into this dreadful scene, so reminiscent of an abattoir, to say goodbye to his mum – to show that I had been a bit of a bloody nuisance, both literally and figuratively, right from the very start.

Neither of my parents was a stranger to the demon booze. In fact, not to tart it up at all, they were alcoholics, the pair of them. They were deeply involved in a passionate relationship that rose to tremendous, exciting highs and plunged to terrible and often frightening lows, and they were both just as deeply involved with the alcohol that fuelled it. I expect that explains the crash, the fall down the stairs and the violent disagreement that so unnerved the doctor that he temporarily abandoned his Hippocratic Oath in favour of keeping out of Father's way. It also explained why our home life was so very different from that of most other people that I knew.

England in the 1940s and 1950s was no place to be marching, dancing or staggering to a different tune. Two world wars within living memory had left the country reeling, bankrupt and with a desperate need to rebuild all that had been lost. It took quite a while for it to dawn on people that things would never go back to the same old order – which in a great many cases was just as well – but that wasn't obvious when all that most people longed for was a return to normality. Sadly, the population was not to get its just reward for the battering it had taken for some considerable time. In fact, things like rationing got a whole lot worse before anything got better. Fuses were short, life was drab and there was little room for a feckless little family like ours.

Mother and Father had met at the Unity Theatre, a left-wing playhouse that was part of a movement that had been formed in association with the Left Book Club. The movement's aim was to further the cause, education and well-being of working men and women who were suffering so very badly during the terrible economic Depression of the 1930s. These lofty aims were supported not only by many of London's intellectual bohemian set, but also by such well-known faces as Michael Redgrave and the black American singer and actor, Paul Robeson, who had fled to Britain to escape the racism that plagued him in the USA.

Everyone mucked in at the Unity; amateurs and professionals acted side by side, sets were painted by anyone who could hold a brush, lighting was dealt with by any competent sparks who happened to be about and the whole place was kept clean and tidy by anyone who walked through the door. In fact, the first time Mother met Paul Robeson was in the Unity's Ladies' loo.

'I heard this incredibly deep voice singing "Old Man River", so I followed it to its source and found Paul Robeson, his face all covered in white spots like a reversed Dalmatian. He was whitewashing the Ladies' and singing while he worked. He was such a nice man. Everyone liked Paul.'

A combination of idealism and the terrors of a world war proved to be a powerful aphrodisiac for my parents, and, shamefully for the times, they wound up becoming lovers at their very first meeting.

As Mother often said, 'There's nothing like the threat of imminent death for loosening knicker elastic, I can tell you. Lots of people dropped their drawers who wouldn't have dreamed of it a few years before.'

She never said if she was one of the newly converted drawer-droppers or an old hand. I suspect the latter, frankly: Mother enjoyed sex and made no bones about it.

Sex without marriage was still frowned upon by the vast

majority of people, war or no war, and many couples took the precaution of entering into hasty marriages that they lived to regret in more peaceful times, rather than carrying on an illicit relationship and risk producing a bastard – an appalling prospect. However, Mother was unable to marry Father straight away, because she had already galloped up the aisle in one such hasty ceremony. Her first husband was called Grenfell, and he was abroad in 1941, when Mother and Father met, fighting for king and country. It would take Mother several years to free herself of her unwanted spouse and to marry her second husband, Douglas, our father. In fact, my brother, who was born in 1943, attended their wedding. My poor grandparents must have been mortified, although they would also have been relieved that a marriage had taken place – at last.

By 1944, Hitler's determination to pulverize London with flying bombs had got way, way out of hand and was making the business of living tricky in the extreme, as well as dangerous and frightening. For my mother, a walk to the shops to queue for the family's meagre rations meant manoeuvring Peter's battleship of a pram – they came really large in those days – round craters great and small, dodging exposed gas mains, side-stepping gushing water pipes twisted into weird and sometimes wonderful sculptures and negotiating tons of broken glass glittering in the giant mounds of shattered concrete, brick and stone that littered the streets. Strangely, baths always seemed to find their way to the top of the rubble, and were usually intact, the same way that stairs seemed to survive to climb towards nothing.

It was simply one of those crazy facts of wartime life. That's why people who couldn't, or wouldn't, go to an air raid shelter often cowered beneath the stairs or huddled in the bath.

All of these hazards made daily life an obstacle course for everyone going about their lawful, or indeed unlawful, business. Most depressing of all were the sad little reminders of lives once lived and then blown apart. There were a lot of those. It might be a teddy bear with one well-sucked ear, lost and lonely in its pile of broken bricks and mortar, or a large pair of bloomers blasted off their washing line and lying forlorn in a patch of rosebay willow herb, or 'fireweed'. This was always the first plant to colonize a new bomb site, as if it settled with the plaster dust that drifted back to earth once a raid was over, giving survivors and rescuers alike a truly ghastly pallor.

The worst thing of all was to happen upon a house that had just been hit by a doodlebug, because of the chance of finding a shattered body or two, or the odd limb missing its person. It all added to the gloom and doom that seeped into the psyche and reminded everyone who passed that, next time, it could be them. All these sights contrived to turn a simple stroll into an endurance test for both mind and body. They gnawed away at the spirit, and finally drove my mother and father to look for something better and safer for their brand new baby boy. It was all very well risking their own lives by staying in the capital, but a baby was a different matter altogether.

So they moved away from the Smoke to Wantley Cottage

in Cuckfield, Sussex, not far from Haywards Heath, the town where my mother's parents lived. Later, they moved into another house in the village, Northern Breach, where I was born. Mother and Father took his widowed mother, Emily Alice, along with them to care for Peter, while Mother went out to work as a teacher to augment the family income.

Most women and children had to move to pastures new by themselves, but the move as a family was made possible because Father had escaped active service on account of his limp. Father's left leg had been attacked by polio when he was thirteen, and was left weaker and shorter than his right one.

Father was deeply ashamed of his left leg, and went to enormous lengths to explain it away as an injury rather than admit to having had polio. He was so ashamed of it that, according to Mother, they had been married several years before she even caught a glimpse of it. He always contrived to undress in the dark, or in another room, anything rather than expose it, although as I remember it, it wasn't badly deformed to look at. Before my brother's birth and the move to Sussex, Mother and Father had been regular swimmers at the Hampstead Heath ponds, a hangout for the bohemian, arty, intellectual set to which they belonged. Even there, Mother said, Father managed to hide his poor leg. She said he was very inventive about it, distracting people's attention just long enough to allow him to slip into or out of his trousers, or delaying his immersion with a last few drags on his fag, until everyone else was halfway across the pond with their backs towards him.

His shame must have been very great, but its cause is still a mystery to me. Polio was something that people simply didn't talk about in those days. Perhaps they were afraid to name the thing that they most feared, in the same way that the Victorians didn't like to talk about TB, or 'consumption'. For some weird reason, Father seemed to associate polio with poverty, which also harks back to the TB of Victorian England, which really did run riot where diets were poor and overcrowding in tenements was endemic. What had made Father so conscious of his humble origins I really couldn't say, except perhaps that the class system was an even more serious business for the English then than it is now, especially if you were born into the lower end of it – which he was.

An incident that occurred at the time illustrates just how badly the lower classes could be treated. Once Father was diagnosed with the dreaded polio, an ambulance was called. It's hard to appreciate, now that polio has been virtually eradicated, just how deeply it was dreaded. At the onset of the disease, there was no way to tell just how severe it would turn out to be; it could kill, leave the sufferer in an iron lung or leg irons for life, or relatively mildly crippled like my father. Years later, the scene that followed the arrival of the ambulance was described to me by a very old woman called Ethel, a friend and neighbour of Emily Alice, my grandmother, who was there at the time.

'The ambulance came and they loaded Douglas into the back. Emily went to climb in with him, but they wouldn't let her. Mothers weren't allowed, you see. She'd just lost her husband, only weeks before, and she was so frightened of losing her only child too, poor dear. She started to cry and carry on something terrible, pleading with them, but they wouldn't have it. In the end, she got down on her knees right there in the middle of the street, begging them to take her along with him, but they still weren't going to let her go with them.

'That's when I came out, me and the rest of the neighbours,' Ethel continued with satisfaction, 'and we told 'em straight that the poor woman had only just lost her husband to cancer and that they had her only relative in this world in the back of their ambulance and that it would be wicked, really wicked to leave her behind. In the end they took her, either because they felt sorry for her or because they thought us women would rear up and belt 'em one: we did outnumber 'em about three to one. After all, if she'd been Lady Muck, they'd never have tried to stop her or given her any argument, they'd have jumped to it right quick. It's only because she was a charlady from the backstreets of Kilburn that they came over all official.'

Shamefully, Ethel's assessment of the situation was almost certainly true. There was definitely one rule for the upper crust and another, and much crueller one, for the lower orders of the day. It was as if the poor didn't have finer feelings, or, if they did, they simply didn't matter. It's possible that Father's sense of shame came from that dreadful incident, along with his incredible drive to 'better' himself.

Mother always ascribed the beginning of Father's life-long habit of telling whoppers to the need to cover up for his leg. Personally, I think it was also partly due to the fact that he was a writer by inclination. In my experience, writers rarely let anything as mundane as the truth get in the way of a good story. There's always a cast of hundreds in the retelling of an incident, never the two women, one man and his flatulent dog who were actually there. Also, his own father seems to have been something of a liar, so maybe Father simply didn't have the blueprint for being straight-forwardly honest.

Over the years I have come to think that Father must have had a desperately unhappy relationship with his own father, a man he never, ever talked about. His lifelong tendency to tell porkies may have begun with the fear of punishment, as well as having had a bad example. My grandfather was sixty when Father was born, and it's possible that a combination of being too old to tolerate a young child, jealousy at having to share his young wife with a son she adored and a stern, Victorian attitude made him a frightening and loathed figure to his son.

There was an up-side to Father's hated polio, though. It meant that not only did he get turned down for active service at the outbreak of World War II, but he also received a modest, but incredibly useful, petrol allowance. This allowance was often augmented by dodgy petrol coupons run up on a busy little printing press located in a backstreet somewhere in the Smoke, or liberated from an official stash at the Ministry warehouse by a suitably corrupt clerk with extra-large pockets. Naturally, Father made it his business to slip the printer or the clerk a few bob for the valuable coupons and so stretched his mileage a little further. Father enjoyed a freedom of movement not open to the majority of his contemporaries. He made the most of it; he was never one to allow an opportunity to pass unexploited, a handy skill he'd honed during the Depression that had dogged the 1930s.

Both of my parents were creative, passionate and volatile by nature. Adding booze, and plenty of it, to this mixture, it often became a case of 'light the blue touchpaper and stand well back', but, for a time at least, they seem to have thrived on it. Perhaps the only real wartime casualty in the family was Mother's relationship with my brother, Peter.

She always said, 'Almost as soon as he made his appearance, he was snatched out of my arms and handed over to Emily Alice to care for, and I was sent back to work so that your father could concentrate on his so-called writing career and I could keep everyone.'

I know it made her both bitter and sad. She was bitter not only because she resented being the main breadwinner, but also because she wanted to be a 'great' writer herself, and felt that she had been granted little time to spare and no peace and quiet in which to concentrate on furthering her ambition.

She also found that Peter never really felt like her own child, something that made her feel guilty and sad for the rest of her life. Today, we'd say that she wasn't given the opportunity to bond with her son, but that was a notion that wasn't understood at the time: she just knew that it felt all wrong, that Emily Alice was more of a mother to Peter than she was 'allowed' to be. What made it sadder, in my view, is that Emily Alice died of cancer just weeks before I was born, which meant that Peter both lost his 'mum' and gained a rival at roughly the same time. If you add to that the trauma of watching his other mother almost die in childbirth, I can't help but feel it created a scar that troubled him always. He certainly had some bitterly negative feelings about our mother that I only learned about towards the very end of his own life. I was quite shocked at the depth of those feelings when he told me, and it was only after his death that I was able to work out what probably led to them.

To begin with, living in Cuckfield was a blessed relief to everyone. What's more, Mother and Father had the support of her parents and Emily Alice to help them along. Mother was always very fond of Emily Alice, and the feeling was, surprisingly, reciprocated. I say surprisingly, because Emily Alice was well known among her friends for being a very possessive woman, who adored my father. Everyone was astonished that she was able to share him with another woman – any other woman. But she did.

She once walked in on Father and Mother having a screaming match, and immediately, without stopping to find out what the row was about, jumped on my father, grabbed his hair, and shouted, 'Don't you dare to talk to my daughter-in-law like that!' She was, according to witnesses, genuinely devoted to my mother, and the three of them seem to have been able to live quite happily under the same roof, which, given the personalities involved, seems nothing short of a miracle to me.

Emily Alice was, by all accounts, a fiery little woman. She was under five feet tall and Welsh in origin. Apparently I take after her in appearance and in some aspects of my personality, although nobody ever said which aspects. Given that the three of them seem to have been very close, I find it surprising that I have never even seen a photograph of her, and despite repeated requests from me, very little information about her was passed on.

Perhaps, once again, it's something to do with the times. Perhaps people didn't talk too much about the dead, because after two world wars, the flu epidemic after World War I and the high mortality rate that was an everyday part of Victorian life, my parents' generation and their parents' generation didn't talk much about the dear departed, working on the theory that it was morbid to dwell. It was simply a part of the famous English stiff upper lip that everyone was so proud of at the time.

By my first birthday, my looks had improved enormously. So much so, in fact, that, during my party, Mother's friend Rosemary suddenly exclaimed, 'Good God, look at her, she's *pretty*!' And Mother always said that, sure enough, when she'd looked past the chocolate that covered my face from eyebrows to chin, I was indeed pretty.

Nobody ever explained how I'd managed to smother myself in chocolate, as sweets were still so heavily rationed as to be virtually unavailable. I suppose it was Father again, wheeling and dealing like crazy to get hold of a bar of the precious stuff for his favourite girl.

It was only days after this that we were evicted by our landlord, a Church of England vicar, for non-payment of rent. We wound up back in London, in a rest centre in Kensington. That's when Mother was forced to go back to work, having insisted at my birth that she wasn't relinquishing the care of her second child to anyone else. She'd done that with Peter and it had cost them both dear; she refused point-blank to do it again.

The lack of Mother's teacher's salary during the first year of my life was one of the reasons we couldn't pay the rent. Another was that what little money there was tended to wind up in the coffers of the local boozers and tobacconists. Anyway, we were evicted, and Mother wound up working again. With Mother and Peter out at school all day, I was left in the care of Father. Thus began my long love affair with Soho, and my precious 'Marts toast, Daddy' years.

2

No Rest for the Wicked

The reek of carbolic soap, Jeyes Fluid, unwashed bodies, cigarettes, Evening in Paris perfume and over-boiled cabbage are what come to mind when I think about the Rest Centre, and I wonder if that particular blend of honks constitutes an actual memory or not. As I was just a year old when we wound up there in 1948, I have my doubts, but then again, they do say that smells trigger recollections better than any of the other senses, so they must linger long in the memory.

Ceaseless noise is another thing that pops up when I try to think back. Coughs, snores and sobs in the night, laughter tinged with that sharp edge of hysteria that goes with endless stress, the shrieks of children playing, the clatter of feet on bare boards and stairs, and voices raised in anger, or complaint, or calling for wandering kids to come and have their necks washed, followed by the ritual whine of protest: 'Aw, Mum, must I? You washed it *last* Sunday and it ain't dirty yet, honest.'

There was a time when to be poor and homeless was almost a criminal offence, for which men, women and children were banged up in the notorious workhouses of the nineteenth and early twentieth centuries. Winding up in the workhouse was considered so shameful that many people preferred to live and die in the gutter. The authorities were so keen to discourage the workshy that they made conditions in workhouses as wretched as possible, hardly more comfortable than the hedgerows or streets that they were supposed to shelter people from. They were not called 'workhouses' for nothing, either; inmates had to earn the right to forfeit their freedom of choice, their self-respect and their dignity. The work was menial and hard and the hours were long, and they had the unmitigated cheek to call it 'charity'.

That notorious slave-master Hitler, creator of Auschwitz, Dachau, Buchenwald and the rest, where so many hapless souls were worked to death, played a part in changing the British attitude to the homeless. So many thousands of people lost their homes and all their possessions to his bombs that it was difficult for anyone to suggest that the indigent had brought it upon themselves. The piles of rubble and the bomb sites told a different story. But the memory of the old times was there, all the same. I remember having 'the old workhouse' pointed out to me with a shudder, in several towns across Britain during the 1950s and '60s. They were always forbidding, grim buildings, and several had been turned into mental hospitals or orphanages once their role as workhouses was over.

The Rest Centre we moved to in London's Kensington was, according to Mother, a lot better than those awful places, but privacy was still at an absolute minimum, and indignities still had to be endured. Later, Mother told me that, as there were so few family rooms, families were split up, with men and boys housed in one section of the building and women and girls in another. Families earned one of the coveted private rooms by the simple method of staying long enough to work their way up to the head of the queue. Some of the family rooms even had the luxuries of their very own sink and a gas ring, which were two things that everyone longed for.

Being so tightly packed into the available space meant that such nasties as head lice, worms, ringworm or scabies spread as fast as crabs in a brothel amongst us inmates, and that's where the indignities came in. There were regular inspections by 'Nitty Nora' and her colleagues whether we needed them or not. Worming pills and potions were doled out in the form of a piece of chocolate or chewing gum, but they fooled no one; the taste was awful.

I'm not sure why we ended up in a rest centre in Kensington when we were evicted from a cottage in the heart of Sussex. I think it may have had something to do with Mother's work as a teacher. There was a shortage of qualified teachers in poor, Blitz-battered old London after the war, while Sussex probably had enough, so that suitable posts were hard to come by there.

Apart from the availability of work, there were other compensations for being temporarily housed in a London rest centre. Two of them were Vera and Iris. They were 'working girls', but they didn't grind out their living in Woolworth's, a laundry, a factory or an office – they did night work in the dark and dreary streets of post-war London. When they weren't pounding the wet, winter pavements in their flimsy, peep-toed 'tart's shoes' and murmuring 'Fancy a good time, lovey?' to likely-looking punters, they lived at the Rest Centre along with us and their own children. The pair of them became good friends to us, and Peter played on the local bomb sites with their children.

Theirs was a common enough wartime tale: an ill-considered knee-trembler with a GI, who literally came one day and went the next, left them with little bundles of joy and no obvious means of support. As Victorian morality remained alive and well long after the old Queen had gone to her just reward, there was often little sympathy for the girl who had loose knicker elastic, slack morals, the bad taste to 'get herself' in the family way and, even worse, the poor judgement to want to keep her child. Most such by-blows were quietly put up for adoption. Those who kept their children really needed the support of their families to manage. Vera and Iris had no such support. Iris was an orphan, thanks to the Blitz, while Vera's family disowned her as soon as the bulge began to show.

However, despite their misfortune, they were a jolly pair, who enjoyed a drink, a dance, a fag and a laugh. Mother grew very fond of them. Not only did she share their love of a good time, but she was also very aware that she too had

had 'a little bastard'. She had been lucky enough to have supportive parents and a man who both stuck around and had a mother who was ready, willing, able and, indeed, eager to care for her baby. What's more, by the time I was born, she was married to the actual father of her children. She became fast friends with Iris and Vera. They helped each other out with childcare, lent each other fags and money when they were able, and generally helped to keep each other's spirits up.

When I was eighteen months old, Mother and Father were allotted one of the coveted family rooms, which provided both a modicum of privacy and that luxury of luxuries, the private sink. The room was shabby, but then, everywhere was shabby because materials for repairs, furniture and general home-making were still so scarce that you stood a better chance of getting a full set of hen's teeth than you did of getting a new bit of lino, carpet or a set of curtains. The furniture was supplied, because so many had lost everything to the Blitz – or, in our case, the bailiff – but it was battered, scratched and sparse. There was a double bed for Mother and Father, an army surplus folding bed for Peter and a twenty-fifth-hand cot, held together in places by bits of string and twisted wire, for me. Most of our clothes were stuffed into one small utility chest of drawers, which meant that they came out too creased for Mother to wear to work, so a change of clothes meant an early stint at the communal ironing board before she set out.

One of the alcoves that flanked the boarded-up fireplace was given over to a hanging rail that took a few dresses, our one threadbare winter coat each, Mother's good 'interview' suit, Father's two jackets and several pairs of his elderly trousers. A faded bit of chintz was hung on sagging curtain wire to hide our makeshift wardrobe from view. The other alcove housed the coveted sink and a small, rickety two-tier table with a gas ring on top and three chipped cups, two saucers, four plates, the couple of jam jars we used as glasses and the one that held our few bits of cutlery. On the floor, beneath the sink, and hidden behind yet more sagging and faded chintz, was our one saucepan, one frying pan, and a colander.

Packets of tea, sugar (when available), margarine and any other stores were kept in a cardboard box or two, stuffed out of sight under the bed. The kettle lived permanently on the ring unless Mother was trying to whip up an illegal, but cheap, simple meal of stew, boiled eggs or homemade soup. Cooking was not allowed in the rooms, but sometimes funds were so low that eating out at an ABC café or getting a meal from the local chippy was not an option. The authorities supplied the gas ring to make tea and heat water for washing and shaving. They knew that to deprive a Brit of a reviving cuppa was a cruelty too far and would probably lead to a general uprising of thoroughly cheesed-off inmates.

Our room had a large, draughty sash window that overlooked the bomb site where Peter and the other older children habitually played. It was an incredibly dangerous playground, as, among the fireweed and buddleia, there lurked mounds of shattered brick, broken glass, twisted, broken, jagged pipes and splintered wood, complete with vicious, rusty nails that stuck out ready to snag, scratch or puncture the unwary. Peter's precious flannel shorts, his knitted jumpers, shirts and baggy socks bore witness to the bomb site hazards, as did his arms and legs, but nag as she might, neither Mother, nor any of the other mums, could keep their kids away from it. It was the only handy place to go to get away from the noise, smell and air of depressed defeat that hung about the dingy rooms and corridors of the crowded Rest Centre.

Once again, what had started out as a blessing (with running water and gas ring), ended up being the cause of yet another catastrophe. The longed-for privacy led to yet another pregnancy, and it could not have come at a worse time. We were homeless, practically penniless – despite Mother's teaching salary – living in one room and now, horror of horrors, the family breadwinner had a bun in her oven. Once the baby began to show, Mother's bread-winning would be over, at least until after the baby was born.

In the late 1940s, children were definitely not supposed to know where babies came from, and an obviously pregnant teacher might just give her pupils a hint. It wasn't all that long since women had been required to leave their teaching posts as soon as they married, as it was considered improper for married women to work in any of the professions.

Legal abortion was not available then, nor for many years after. The only options women had when they found themselves with an unwanted baby on the way, were to go through with the pregnancy and have the child adopted, go to a backstreet abortionist and pay them to do the deed, with wildly varying fees and degrees of skill, hygiene and basic anatomical knowledge, or simply to put up and shut up, and resign themselves to another mouth to feed and another body to house and clothe. None of these was open to Mother if she were to continue to keep us all in the style to which we had become accustomed, so the 'do it yourself' method, using a knitting needle and a bottle of gin, was all that she felt she was left with.

Then, to add to the general joys, Father disappeared.

'What do you mean he's buggered off?' Vera demanded, angry but not even remotely shocked. Nothing men did surprised her, or so she told my mother: she was, after all, a 'five bob and find your own railings' brass, and she had met and serviced all sorts in her time.

'I mean that Doug has buggered off. The bastard emptied my purse before he went. He left a note, said he couldn't face living here with a new baby and no money coming in, and that he was sorry.'

'Sorry! Sorry! I'll make the bastard sorry if I catch hold of him, he'll be singing soprano before he can say "balls", take my word on that.'

So it was that Mother supplied her own knitting needle – a size eight, or so she said – but Iris and Vera kindly supplied the gin, Father having stolen our last farthing.

'Book the bathroom for a hot bath as early as you can on Saturday morning, so the water's still as hot as you can get it,' advised Iris, who had some experience of the process. 'It opens things up a bit and relaxes your muscles and that helps. Me and Vera'll look after the kids while you get the job done. We'll keep an eye on you an' all, make sure you're OK.'

'Does it hurt?' Mother asked.

'Not much, as long as your aim's all right. Don't rush it. Take it slow, that's my advice, sort of feel your way in,' Vera told her kindly. 'After's no worse than your usual contractions and, as the baby's still small, there's plenty of room for it to slide out easy.'

'That's right,' Iris chipped in. 'And boil your needle first, that's best, but let it cool down before you use it, or you'll burn yourself.'

Mother followed their instructions to the letter the following Saturday morning, fortified by vast quantities of gin, but things did not go smoothly. By the early hours of Monday morning, Mother was at death's door again. This time it was septicaemia that almost did for her, despite her boiling the needle as instructed. Alarmed at her condition, and fearful that the authorities would hear her delirious moaning, Vera called an ambulance.

While she hovered between life and death in the local hospital, Vera and Iris fought like wildcats to thwart the authority's plan to take Peter and me into care. 'You're not taking 'em, I tell you,' insisted Vera, her voice rising in fury. 'Joan's not coming out to nothing. That bleeder of a husband of hers has gone, and I reckon she'd curl up an' die of mortification and just plain misery if she lost her kids as well. We'll take turns looking after the poor little buggers until she's fit to come back to 'em.'

'Yes, and we'll look for that toe-rag of a dad of theirs while we're at it. I don't s'pose he'll be hard to find. A quick blimp round the boozers down Soho way should turn him up,' Iris assured the warden. 'You'll only have to get them out of the home again if he comes back here to look after 'em. Hardly seems worth your trouble.'

Their arguments swung it, at least temporarily, but the warden insisted 'Find the father fast or off they go', so Iris and Vera started their search for Father immediately. Between times, they took it in turns to see to the children – their own and us – while the other went to work.

It didn't take them long to find our father. He was, as pre-dicted, propping up the bar at The French House in Soho's Dean Street. Everyone in the know called it 'The French' because it had a French landlord and the Free French met there with their leader, Charles de Gaulle, during the war. The name on the sign was the York Minster, but only strangers ever called it that.

It was Vera who found him and dragged him back to us at the Rest Centre, threatening him all the while, 'I'll castrate you with a rusty razor blade if you try to leg it again, you double-dyed swine, you. The kids need you, Joan needs you, and me and Iris need you. We have to get back to work. So, if you have it away on your toes again, you'd better leave the bleeding country, because if any of us finds you, it'll be you in hospital next time, learning to walk like a cowboy what's lost his 'orse.'

As it turned out, it wasn't Father who was rushed to hospital within minutes of his return, it was me. I suffered a fractured skull, and I was swiftly admitted to the hospital where my mother lay dying. Father's story was that I was sitting on a low bed, playing with my toes, when he walked in. Apparently, my joy at seeing him was so unconfined that I flung out my arms wide to him, yelled a delighted 'Daddy!' and promptly fell on the floor and cracked my head. Realizing that the injury was serious, Father and Vera rushed me to hospital in a taxi, courtesy of Iris, who'd had a good night and was in funds. Iris stayed behind to keep an eye on the other children and to rest up a bit after her strenuous night's work. I was admitted to the children's ward immediately.

Once Father was certain I was in good hands, Vera dragged him down to the ward where Mother lay unconscious. He was unable to see her, it not being visiting time, but a nurse did tell him how his wife was doing – not at all well, apparently.

Vera nodded towards a uniformed figure sitting in the corridor reading a newspaper. 'What's old Andrews doing there? He's a bit off his beat, ain't he?'

'He's waiting to see if your friend comes round, so he can charge her with performing an illegal abortion on herself,' said the nurse.

'He what?' Vera roared, only to be shushed by the nurse, who looked around nervously in case anyone had heard.

Father was all for punching said officer on the nose, but Vera was firm. 'Don't you dare! Joan and the kids don't need you in clink, and unless you're going to get off your arse and earn the money to pay the fine that you'll get as well, you'd better stay put. *I'll* deal with Andrews,' she said and strode off to do just that. It didn't take long.

'What did you say to get rid of him?' Father asked once they were finally heading back to the Rest Centre.

'Not a lot. I just told him that I'd tell his missus that he was one of my regulars, that he always settled for a bung of a few bob or a bit of the other – or both, the greedy sod – rather than charge me with soliciting. That brought about a change of attitude in double-quick time, I can tell you.'

Mother always swore that it was a whispered conversation between nurses about my head injury that brought her back from the brink.

'You needed me, and anyway, I was so furious with your father that I couldn't wait to get out so that I could give him the tongue-lashing that he so thoroughly deserved.'

It appeared that everyone believed Father's story of my fall from the bed, but I have wondered about it since. Personally, I think it was far more likely that he was drunk, and that he inadvertently dropped me. Naturally, he would lie about it, sure in the knowledge that if Vera didn't get him with the threatened rusty razor blade, then Mother certainly would have done.

Mother finally recovered from the abortion, and was neither charged nor even interviewed by the police, thanks to her friend Vera. Father, meanwhile, was chastened by the whole thing, and stayed put to look after me while Mother went back to school and teaching. Shortly after Mother was safely returned to us, Vera was finally rehoused on a new estate somewhere in Essex, while Iris married a widower from Streatham and settled down to look after him, his three young children and his widowed mother. As Vera said at the time, it might have been easier for her to stay on the streets, but then again, maybe not. Sadly, over time, Mother lost touch with her friends, but she never forgot them, or their kindness to her and, indeed, her children.

3

Marts Toast, Daddy

In the late 1940s and early '50s, if you had a heart's desire, a simple yen or an urgent need for anything – a pair of double bed sheets, a Siamese kitten, Spanish guitar lessons, a French chef, a mandolin in good condition, a cleaner, a second-hand boiler, two dozen soup plates, a violin or hand-made buttonholes – then it paid to join the cluster of people reading the scruffy envelopes, slips of paper and yellowed postcards that festooned the newsagent's window in Old Compton Street, in Soho. If you wanted an actual news-paper – any newspaper, from *The Times* to *La Vie Parisienne*, *Heraldo de Madrid*, *Hellas*, the *New York Times* or the *Times of India* – then all you had to do was step through the door, slap your coins on the counter and choose from the huge variety of newsprint on offer in the tiny little shop, which was called, I believe, Moroni's.

I first experienced this world after Mother and I had been

discharged from hospital. Things settled into an uneasy truce at the Rest Centre; Mother went back to teaching, while Peter continued going to the local school, and I was left in the care of Father.

We soon developed our own routine. Once up and dressed, we'd make our way to the tube station, with me riding on Father's shoulders to speed things up a bit. We'd rattle our way on the Bakerloo Line to Piccadilly Circus, drop into Moroni's for a packet of fags, the *News Chronicle* and a brief chat as to who was about that day. While Father was talking, I'd examine the myriad foreign newspapers, paying special attention to anything that had a different kind of script. Sometimes, we'd make up names for the ones that Father couldn't read to me; I remember that we liked to alliterate, and came up with the *Constantinople Clarion*, the *Macao Messenger*, the *Turkish Trumpet* and the *Siberian Siren*, among others. On a good day, Father would pretend to read one of the front pages to me, weaving fantastical tales of dragons stalking the Singapore streets, munching humble coolies and rich silk merchants alike for their breakfast – although they naturally preferred the fat merchants, as poor coolies were tough and on the stringy side.

I loved my father's stories, and his remarkable ability to enter into an imaginary world at the drop of a fag-end, and I gather that other people loved it, too. Father was one of those rare human beings who could inspire devotion in women, men and children alike when he chose, but his hair-trigger temper could also inspire real fear in almost equal measure. For some reason, most people were prepared to overlook the temper, or forgive him for it at least. I suppose he must have had more than his fair share of charm: as a child, I was unable to see just how it worked on people. I simply know that it did.

I understand that Adolf Hitler and the Ugandan dictator, Idi Amin, had that same quality of animal magnetism. Hitler, despite his somewhat ludicrous appearance, had a sexual attraction that brought women (and some men) to him by the cartload, but, having gained their abject devotion, Adolf didn't seem to know quite what to do with them: whereas my father, and Idi Amin, certainly did.

Our favourite café, in Berwick Street market, was always our second stop after the newsagent's. Our menu never varied. It was always 'marts toast, Daddy' (or tomatoes on toast to the uninitiated) for me, while Father made do with gallons of weak, milky tea, several Player's Navy Cut, a good cough and a glance at the newspaper headlines.

The café was a typical Mama and Papa enterprise. Betty was in charge of taking orders, schlepping teas and waiting tables, and her husband, whose name I never knew, did the cooking. He had been in the catering corps during the war, and there was little or nothing he didn't know about supplying plentiful amounts of food to hordes of hungry punters at reasonable prices. It wasn't a big place, just a dozen or so small tables and a counter with a large urn bubbling away on it. The urn ensured that the two large windows that flanked the door were permanently steamed up in winter, less so in summer when the street door could be left open.

Betty must have had green fingers, because flourishing lemon-scented pelargoniums, spider plants and busy lizzies were crammed into every available inch of space on the windowsills, and the greenery acted as a living curtain. Watching the market traders and their punters through all those leaves made me think I was in a steamy old jungle somewhere, rather than in the very heart of London. Sometimes, if the sun was out, there was a brief period in the day when it was at exactly the right angle to shine through this tracery of leaves and make pretty patterns on the faces of the noshing punters.

Behind the counter there were two glass shelves, one on each side of the door that led to the kitchen at the back. The shelves held bits and pieces of pretty, colourful china that had taken Betty's fancy over the years and that had, by some miracle, managed to survive the Blitz, the nemesis of so many beautiful, but oh-so-breakable, things. There was also a long row of peachy, green and amber-yellow fluted sundae glasses in a variety of shapes: long and boat-shaped, tall and slender, or squat and round. These had not seen active service since the onset of rationing, but were patiently waiting the return of the sunny days of the knickerbocker glory, peach melba and banana split. I had never had any of these treats in my life, and had no idea what these weird-sounding desserts were, but I was more than willing to find out. Sadly, like the jewel-like sundae glasses, I simply had to wait in patience until sugar rationing was over. Given Betty's mouth-watering descriptions of 'dollops of vanilla ice cream, slices of peach' (or 'banana', whatever that was), 'lashings of syrup' (ditto), 'fruit jelly', 'sprinkles of hundreds and thousands' (ditto again) and 'a nice wafer or two', the waiting in patience bit was not so easy.

'Do you want to give me a hand wiping down the tables, lovey?' Betty would ask me when the place was quiet after the morning rush. 'It'll give your dad a chance to focus and read his paper and it'll help me no end. You're a good little table wiper, you are.' Sometimes, as a special treat, I was allowed to dry the teaspoons when Betty was washing up. The china was on the restricted list, though, in case I broke a plate or one of the thick, white cups that were not that easy to replace in the age of austerity. The kitchen was out of bounds as well, because of the many dangers of scalding liquids, hot steam and ferocious gas rings.

My reward for services rendered would be a sugar cube from Betty's carefully hoarded stock under the counter. The punters didn't get sugar cubes, they got granulated from a hefty, glass sugar basin with a spoon in it. It sat on the counter next to Betty's huge teapot. That way, Betty could keep an eye on the precious white stuff and pick out the brown lumps that formed when a customer stirred their tea with the sugar spoon by mistake. The brown lumps were not wasted; they were dropped on to a dry saucer, ready for use in Betty's and her old man's tea.

If it was a busy day, then one of the locals would undertake to amuse me while Father lined up behind his eyes. This could often be something of a challenge if he'd been drinking the night before – which he usually had. If none of the customers was interested in keeping me amused, then I would press my nose to the damp window and watch the hustle and bustle of the market outside. I loved the way the traders weighed out their spuds and tipped them expertly from the big, silver scoop thing into waiting oilskin bags held out by the customer. I liked to watch as they picked over onions, carrots or beetroots looking for the best stuff for their regulars – and their worst for casual customers or ones they didn't like. I caught on fast that the dodgy veg was always brought from the back of the stall, while the good stuff was on display at the front.

On the rare occasions that Mother managed to persuade Father to do some shopping, I would never let any of the traders fob us off with the back-of-the-stall veg. I would become quite indignant if they tried. 'Can we have our carrots from the front, please?' I'd pipe in a voice that carried. 'We can't afford to throw anything away, you know, or to cut out the rotten bits.'

Nine times out of ten, the trader would chuckle throatily and point out, with a grin and a roll of friendly eyes, that Father had 'a right one there'. Sometimes they'd drop one or two extra onions or spuds into our bag, 'for her cheek'. I've always loved markets, and I suspect it stems from the many happy hours I spent hanging around the stalls in Berwick Street or in 'our' café, watching the passing scene.

Once breakfasted, we'd be ready to face whatever the day had in store for us. It was in Soho that I first encountered the scents of garlic, spices, freshly ground coffee, vanilla and French perfume wafting on the wind from the various establishments crammed, rouged cheek by unshaved jowl, in Soho's narrow, bustling, soot-encrusted, but strangely fragrant streets.

A leisurely stroll from Berwick Street into Rupert Street would soon bring the exotic smell of curry spices drifting to my eager nostrils from the kitchen of the Koh-i-Noor. Once we'd walked up Old Compton Street from Wardour Street, past the Algerian Coffee Shop that roasted and ground its own coffee, I could detect the delicious smell of garlic cooking in butter or olive oil as we turned into Greek Street, and got a whiff of the French restaurant, L'Escargot Bienvenu. I loved the wooden sign that hung above the restaurant's green shutters, a charming painting of a round and cheeky-looking snail with its head nosing towards the soil. Above that, there was a plaster cast of a man joyfully riding another horned snail as if it was a horse. I decided that the man had to be very small indeed, even smaller than me, to ride a snail. Privately, I thought he must have been some kind of fairy, but with his wings hidden from view under his coat. I was so disappointed to discover, years later, that my fairy was, in fact, the restaurant's founder, Monsieur Gaudin.

Parmigiani's and Lena's Store, the former on the corner of Frith Street and Old Compton Street and the latter in Brewer Street, were Italian delicatessens, and rich sources of olfactory and visual bliss for me. Both stores had a wonderful amalgam of food smells, combining garlic, vanilla, coffee and chocolate with about a zillion other subtle herbs and spices. I'd drool at the first sniff. Anywhere else in England was more likely to be redolent of over-boiled cabbage, fried Spam, horribly sweet horse meat and snoek, which was a South African relative of the barracuda, I believe.

The huge harlequin bolted to the first-floor wall above Parmigiani's gave it the edge over Lena's Store as far as I was concerned: I was fascinated by its sheer size and the colour it lent to the grey, sooty street. The harlequin's costume was made up of diamond shapes in primary colours so bright that it glowed even on the dullest of days.

I soon came to love Soho and its bustling streets, filled with men and women from all over Europe and beyond, living, working and playing together with an acceptance that few, if any, other places in 1950s England could offer. This period was the start of a lifelong love affair with Soho, its delicatessens, restaurants, cafés and eccentrics.

It has been a wellspring of inspiration to me. Initially, it provided such a welcome change from the Rest Centre, where the hopeless misery of destitution and homelessness seemed to permeate the very walls. Later, after we had finally been rehoused, it provided a refuge from the sprawling Essex housing estate where I was shunned for coming from a family that was too different to be tolerated. Soho and its people specialized in tolerance: they'd been practising it since the eighteenth century, and they're still at it today. Later still, as it turned out, it proved to be a rich vein that I could mine for my own novels about Soho in the Fifties, but we didn't know that then.

Wherever we went in Soho, I was greeted with wide

smiles and sometimes sweets, and even hard cash. I often had a many-sided threepenny bit, a shiny sixpence or even a big half-crown pressed into my hand by shifty-looking lounge lizards, glamorous dancers from the Windmill, costermongers from the market and even an Italian opera singer wearing spats and carrying a gold-topped cane. Plump Italian ladies or smart French ones would clap their hands and exclaim, 'She is a princess, a little English princess, so like little Anne.'

Those days that I spent 'up west' with my father, just him and me, were to be the only times that I had him to myself. When it was just the two of us, he was rarely angry or frightening. In fact, he sometimes displayed a childlike sense of fun that I adored. I can still remember the warmth of his large, square hand holding mine and having to run to keep up with his uneven gait as we made our way through the labyrinth of streets and alleys on our way 'to meet a man' at the snooker hall or to Pitta's in Old Compton Street for a plate of cheap nosh and a few laughs with its theatrical clientele.

Father was supposed to be pursuing a career as a writer, but living in the Rest Centre and being in sole charge of a toddler made this difficult, so he contented himself with going to cafés, bars and dives to enlarge his acquaintance among Soho's literati and artists, as well as its businessmen and spivs. The rationale for this, I'm sure, was that it was all material for when he finally got to sit at his typewriter once again.

*

Father had begun his writing career during the war. Having been a lad on the make during the Depression in the 1930s, he knew that it paid to keep an eye firmly fixed on the main chance. He became something of an expert at spotting an opportunity, golden or otherwise, and he'd seen one as World War II had loomed. He guessed that paper would be at a premium once hostilities got under way, as this had happened in World War I and he was pretty sure it would happen again. Our little island was unable to produce enough of it, and importing the raw materials became more and more difficult, with the seas surrounding it being patrolled by prowling German warships and U-boats. So, he scraped together some money and bought a warehouse full of the stuff.

Sure enough, it wasn't long before newspapers were a shadow of their former selves, with far fewer pages, packed tight with smaller print. The various ministries gobbled up stocks of paper by issuing written orders, coupons, instructional leaflets, travel passes and posters by the ton. The ministries were such voracious users of the precious material that there was little left over for such non-essentials as toilet paper and books. Newspapers only got a look-in because they were handy for propaganda, mis-information, morale-boosting, wrapping fish and chips and, of course, toilet paper.

During the war, escapism became more and more necessary to servicemen posted far from home and civilians who spent their nights cowering in tube stations and air raid shelters. Cinemas did a roaring trade once the government caught on that keeping them closed for the duration was not an option. Even theatres made sure that, when possible, the show went on, although many remained boarded up for the whole six years.

'Everyone had a radio though, and we all tuned in,' Mother explained to me in later years. 'Not only to hear the latest news, because we stopped trusting that. So much wasn't reported, you see, so that the Germans couldn't crow when they made a direct hit on something important, and of course, there was lots of deliberate misinformation too, to fool Jerry about our military plans. But we all liked a good laugh, and some dance music, and the radio was great for that.'

For some, though, none of these things were available. Men on the front line couldn't nip to the flicks, listen to *ITMA* or take in a show, and neither could the folks at home when the Blitz was raining high explosives and incendiary bombs down on them. Portable escapism in the form of books became highly desirable at such times, but sadly, they were in seriously short supply.

'That's when your father, with his warehouse full of paper, his gammy leg and his precious petrol allowance, came into his own. He became a writer, publisher, printer and distributor of cheap and cheerful books.'

What he produced was pulp fiction. Some of his books, and the books written by his willing friends – and Mother – made it on to the convoys of ships that sailed the treacherous Atlantic Ocean, to entertain His Majesty's Navy and the brave merchant seamen who did their best to keep

Blighty supplied with essentials. Little or nothing of this material survived the war, because pulp fiction, by its nature, is pulped to be reused. But it meant that Father, and indeed Mother, had a track record as a writer, and, once the war was over, both had ambitions to return to it.

So Father and I hung around the cafés, bars, restaurants, drinking clubs and the snooker halls, making friends, contacts and acquaintances as we soaked up the atmosphere of what's called London's 'infamous square mile', although it is actually much smaller than that.

One of the most colourful of Father's friends was Legionnaire Jim, a man who had, apparently, been thrown out of the Foreign Legion. 'He joined the Legion because he was on the run after murdering someone, and it wasn't safe for him to hang about in England,' Father explained to Mother one night when we got back from the West End. Hanging was the punishment for murder until the mid-1960s, so I can understand Jim's reluctance to linger on these shores. Family history does not relate who he killed. I suspect that it was a West End gangster or another crook, though, because that was the company that Jim habitually kept.

'And you're taking my baby into the company of cut-throats and murderers are you?' asked Mother archly.

'Give it a rest, Joan, and listen. As I was saying, he joined the Legion but got slung out again in double-quick time. The rumour is that he killed a sergeant and was thrown out for being too vicious, even for those murdering bastards. Now that's saying something, that is.'

'Yes, it's saying that my little girl has no business being dragged into the company of a man like that,' Mother spat, tired after a long week at school. 'Have you got no common sense at all?'

'It's all right. He likes her, he tells her stories.'

'What kind of stories?'

'Cowboys and Indians, stuff like that.'

'Well, keep her away from him, stories or no bloody stories,' Mother told him. But Father ignored her and we carried on seeing Jim. In fact, I was determined to marry Jim when I grew up. He may have been very nasty indeed to other men, but he was very nice to me.

It was while we were in Soho that Father came up with his next big money-making scheme. The pulp fiction had more or less seen the family through the war years, but it had dried up after peace broke out. The money from it was long gone, and there was an urgent need to find something else. Mother's salary only went so far, and having two prodigious thirsts to service, as well as two children to keep, it went almost as soon as it came. Our straits were dire indeed, and living in the Rest Centre was doing absolutely nothing for domestic harmony. Something had to be done!

That's when Father entered the smutty book trade. It's a bit excessive to call the books that he bought and sold pornographic, certainly by today's hardcore standards. They were more along the lines of erotica, erudite tomes on sexual matters – including a big, fat dictionary of fetishism – and foreign publications of such books as *Tropic of*

Cancer, *The Story of O*, *Lady Chatterley's Lover*, *Venus in Furs* and various books by the Marquis de Sade, all of which were banned or restricted under the draconian obscenity laws of the time.

At first he borrowed money to buy stock, at a little below premium rates. He then flogged it where he could, usually to unsuspecting servicemen or visitors who were looking for a little sin in Soho, but he had bigger ambitions. It was always a family joke that Father was so innumerate that he had to use his fingers to count, and that for anything over ten, he'd have to whip off his shoes and socks to count his toes as well. Although he was not quite that bad, it was certainly true that numbers were a bit of a mystery to him – until he decided that he needed a pilot's licence to fly to the Continent and further his new-found career. It made economic sense to import his own books, thus cutting out at least one of the middle men. When it was in his interests, he found he could use a slide rule, read maps, plot courses and work out longitude and latitude like a pro. It was amazing.

I have no idea how he could afford to pay for lessons, but learn to fly he did at a funny little aerodrome somewhere in the sticks, in Surrey or Sussex, or maybe Kent. It wasn't much, just a Nissen hut for a club room where pilots could gather to drink, spin yarns about their derring-do and wait for the weather to lift. There was a pump with a long handle for pumping the aviation fuel through a length of hose into the waiting tanks of the planes, some concrete runways, a squat tower with windows all round, a tall radio mast, a few bright orange windsocks, another Nissen hut stuffed full of spare parts and some hangars to tuck up the aircraft when they weren't in use.

I can smell that clubhouse even now. It reeked of booze, cigar and cigarette smoke, leather, polish, Parma violets, oil and men. At one end was a bar with a shelf of bottles behind, a couple of beer pumps on the scratched and ringed surface and a few barstools to complete the picture. There was also a blackboard to one side of the shelf. This had names, numbers and weather conditions scrawled on it. The information on the blackboard varied, depending who was in, what they owed for drinks and the current state of the weather.

Sylvia, the source of the scent of violets, ran the bar and made sandwiches when the weather kept everyone grounded for long enough for bellies to rumble and complain about the lack of sustenance. She also baby-sat me when Father was in the air, but all I can remember about her was lots of dark, wavy hair, very red lips, a throaty laugh, a curvaceous figure, a voice like a Billingsgate porter – with language to match – and, of course, the heady smell of Parma violets. Sylvia was engaged to George, the owner of the flying club. He was ex-RAF, and had the rich, fruity accent of the very posh delivered from under a luxuriant moustache that made Jimmy Edwards's look puny in comparison. Birds could have nested in it. George was very proud of that 'tache, to judge by the way he stroked and caressed it. If it had been a cat, it would have purred.

The couple had been on the verge of matrimony for many years, but the rumour was that his folks disapproved of

Sylvia so violently that they threatened to disinherit him. So they bided their time and lived contentedly in a small bungalow opposite the entrance to the aerodrome. Every now and then, George would make a sortie to the family seat to smooth parental feathers and dodge the débutantes his mother had lined up for him to consider for a stroll down 'the jolly old aisle'. He'd leave Sylvia at home in the bungalow when he made his visits, but he never stayed away for long.

'I miss the old girl,' he'd explain to one and all, and slap her behind and make her squeal as he said it. Apart from that, both their lives revolved around the club and each other.

There were tables and chairs dotted about the clubhouse and on the walls, large maps covered in heavy, scratched and yellowed sheets of plastic that added to the smell of the place. There were also propellers fixed to the walls, memorials to planes that had gone to the great hangar in the sky, lost but not forgotten. Each had a story attached: one belonged to an Auster, flown by 'that silly bugger Reggie "Pongo" Bagshot, who pranged it when he ploughed into that field on the Isle of Wight. His poor old crate would have been tickety-boo if he hadn't hit that bloody bull. Farmer was livid, the bull was none too happy, either – and the cows were desolate.'

The contrary British weather was responsible for many an hour spent in the club room listening to yarns, lies and grumbles about 'the sodding weather'. The winds were too strong, or coming from the wrong direction; or there was fog, low cloud, a storm brewing – the list of hazards seemed endless, but somehow these worries never put the pilots, licensed or budding, off their stroke.

As soon as George's plummy voice boomed over the Tannoy, there was a general scraping of chairs as the men – and one or two women – rose as one and headed for the runways and hangars. Soon there'd be a cacophony of coughs and splutters as one engine after another turned over and caught. The air would be redolent with the smell of aviation fuel and hot engine oil, there'd be men with earphones and what looked like ping-pong bats waving their arms about and a hoarse cry of 'Chocks away!' And a Tiger Moth, Gypsy Moth or an Auster would rattle along a runway and soar into the air, carrying my father and his instructor with it.

Later, when Father had enough flying hours and had passed his navigational tests, he would leave his instructor on the ground and I would be in the passenger seat, soaring up towards the beautiful blue skies and scudding, cotton-wool clouds. Once up there, I'd look down and marvel at the tiny houses and the mosaic of green, yellow and brown fields and pity the titchy people, scurrying around like so many ants, because they were stuck on the ground while I was way up in the sky, looping the loop with my daddy.

4

The Knee-High Smuggler

I rustled and crackled like a crumpled old Smith's crisp packet as I walked across the tarmac with my teddy in one hand and my father's solid, square hand holding the other. I was hot and grumpy, because I'd been made to wear my liberty bodice even though it was summer-time, and thick liberty bodices were meant for the cold days of winter. Everyone knew that; except, apparently, my father. But I quickly discovered that there was a method to his madness. He'd stuffed large, white, five-pound notes between me and my bodice when my little pink plastic shoulder bag could take no more. That's why I crackled when I moved.

Later on in my life of crime, I was provided with a specially doctored teddy that could take even more of the precious, and rather beautiful, banknotes. I remember those notes well. They were the size of a doll's tablecloth and had lovely flowing handwriting telling the bearer how much the Bank of England said they were worth. I think that the paper they were made of had at least some linen in it, because they felt so crisp, and the sound they made when handled was most satisfying. However, they were significantly less pleasing when stuffed down a person's liberty bodice, as they tickled and scratched something awful and made the wearer hotter and crankier than ever.

I had the sense not to make a fuss, though. I had learned to my cost that annoying my father was never a good idea: no match was needed to ignite his temper, a spark would do, as he had no fuse, not even a short one. What's more, I sensed that what we were doing was our secret, and I wasn't to let anyone know about it, especially if they were wearing any kind of uniform. It's funny how the children of the bent take that lesson in with their mother's milk. It's like a sixth sense.

Post-war England was stony broke, and travellers were forbidden to carry more than about twenty pounds out of the country. A measly twenty-odd quid was nowhere near enough lolly for Father's new enterprise, which was why I had become a walking bankroll. Nobody would think to search a curly-haired, blue-eyed moppet of three or four for currency when she was out for a jaunt with her daddy. And so it was that we made the first of our many trips to Le Touquet in France.

Poor Peter was green with envy. Like all boys at the time, he was besotted with aircraft, flying and all things aeronautical. The war and the heroics of the Royal Air Force had seen to that. As soon as we were out of the Rest Centre and into a council house in Essex, Peter would spend many happy hours in his bedroom, fiddling with bits of balsa wood, glue, white tissue paper, varnish, elastic bands and little tins of smelly, shiny paint, creating Spitfires and Messerschmitts to dogfight once again. He'd rumple up his counterpane to be the White Cliffs of Dover, and his bed-side rug would become the English Channel as he re-enacted skirmishes between the RAF and the German Luftwaffe. He became a master of sound effects: he could do spluttering engines, exploding bombs and rattling machine guns as the action demanded.

If there was no other boy available to be the German half of things, then I was dragooned into action, which thrilled me to bits, because I so rarely got to play with other children that even playing with my older brother was a huge treat. It was so much of an honour for me to be allowed to play with Peter that I didn't seem to mind being shot down in flames over and over again. We both understood that it wasn't on for the Royal Air Force to land in the drink: that was the Germans' job. I, being the younger and 'only' a girl, was always cast as the enemy.

Naturally, as soon as a lad with murky knees that lurked just beneath the hem of his grey flannel shorts showed up, I was tossed aside and ordered to go and play with my dolls, or something equally boring. Which is why I harboured a secret satisfaction at being the family's chief mini-aviator and currency smuggler. For once, I was top dog and mistress of the skies, while poor Peter was chained to his desk at school, struggling with handwriting practice and his three times table.

*

It was market day in Le Touquet, and Mother had joined Father and me on one of our 'business trips' to France. Sometimes all four of us made the journey across the Channel, but Peter wasn't with us on this occasion. Which may have been just as well, because, although he was dead keen, Peter was not a good traveller and there was always the risk that he'd ruin the precious stock by vomiting on it. Even men in grubby raincoats, hungry for second-hand sex, drew the line at paying hard cash for a stained, crusty and smelly copy of *Lady Chatterley's Lover*.

For once, it was a happy day; both parents were more or less sober, and inclined to view the world and each other with a benign eye. We strolled in the sunshine between stalls piled high with wonderful food. Stall after stall displayed colourful fresh fruit and vegetables, deliciously smelly French cheeses, long sticks of bread and fabulous fish and shellfish nestled in crushed ice. As we walked past, our eyes on stalks and our mouths watering, I was filled with wonder. For the whole of my life, England had had food rationing, and so I'd never even seen a lot of the produce before, let alone eaten it. My parents were in transports of delight, and deep in food nostalgia. They kept asking each other if they remembered when 'you could get a succulent steak, followed by apple pie and cream, for one and threepence?' or extolling the virtues of the knickerbocker glory that Betty had told me so much about, and I listened, fascinated. We were having a lovely time.

We wanted to take it all home with us, but one big problem was weight. We simply couldn't buy everything in sight, because the three of us, plus the precious books, cigarettes and brandy we were taking back with us, were about as much as our flimsy little plane could carry. The second problem was lack of lolly: we'd spent almost all of the money we'd smuggled out of England on our contraband, so funds were tight. We just had to be content with gawping at the produce and sampling tiny little bits of what we could afford, eating it on the hoof.

Mother and Father were just discussing the last time they'd seen 'a bit of cheese that size' when Mother stopped dead in her tracks and gaped at some peculiar yellow, bent things on a fruit stall.

'Bananas!' she breathed, as if she had just seen God. 'Look, bananas!' I looked, but couldn't see what the fuss was about, because I thought that the almost mythical fruit came in a sundae glass, as Betty had told me, and I was so disappointed to gaze at the yellow mound and note the absence of 'dollops of vanilla ice cream', not to mention the sprinkle of hundreds and thousands. 'We've got to get some,' Mother told Father. 'The kids have never had a banana, and I can't wait to see their faces when they taste one.'

Mother, the only French-speaker in our party, began negotiations with the stall holder as Father counted up the money we had left, and in the end they managed to buy what they called 'a hand' of ten bananas. This confused me slightly, because although the bananas did look a bit like big, yellow fingers, all the world knew that a hand held only five digits. But then there was no telling about the way grown-ups saw things, and anyway, everyone was in such a good mood, and I knew better than to argue the toss.

We found a bench and sat down, with me firmly sandwiched between them, and Mother solemnly handed me a banana which I politely stuck in my mouth, although I was still hankering for the ice-cream and hundreds and thousands. If they said it was edible, then I had to believe them, but I have to say, it tasted a bit strange to me, sort of waxy and hard and pithy. My parents thought this was hilarious, and rocked with laughter until tears ran down their cheeks. I'd taken a reluctant bite and was trying to chew it before they collected themselves enough for Mother to notice what I'd done. Still chortling, she showed me how to peel the thing. It was like opening a birthday present, and my first bite, *sans* skin, was like being transported to heaven. It was wonderful, truly wonderful. I was all for gromphing another one, being something of a little porker, but Mother was firm: we were taking them home to share with Peter, and that was final.

Once at the aerodrome, with all of our illicit loot safely stashed under my seat, we were soon trundling along the runway ready to take off for the trip home. There was never any looping the loop, hedge-hopping, victory rolls or fancy stuff on return trips, in case our cargo was dislodged and damaged, so the flight was uneventful.

Once we landed safely in England, a cheery Customs

officer stuck his head into the cockpit and asked, 'Anything to declare?'

And, for once, Mother was able to say, with complete honesty, 'Yes! We've bought a hand of bananas.' And she reached back to where I was sitting, grabbed the paper bag with the fruit in it and waved it triumphantly at the official. The officer duly peered inside the bag. There was a moment's confused silence, then he began to laugh, and his eyes twinkled merrily as he drew out the contents and dangled them in front of Mother's startled face.

'As far as I'm aware, there's no duty or restrictions on these, madam,' he informed her. During the journey I'd quietly scoffed the lot, and all we were left with was a hand of empty skins.

For the most part, I preferred going to France with Father on my own. First off, if Peter was aboard we couldn't do any fancy stunts on account of his weak stomach and his tendency to make for the door to get out, even when we were high above the clouds. Also, the combined honk of vomit and aviation fuel is not a happy one. Then there was the problem, if Mother came too, of keeping our parents out of the bars.

Drinking was one of the things they liked to do together, but sadly, when they guzzled booze it led to domestic strife very quickly. Sometimes it was just a bit of a squabble, but the trouble was, you could never be sure when the bitching would boil over into actual violence, and then it was a toss-up who clouted who first.

Once, when all four of us had flown over by way of a celebratory trip, the fight was so severe that gendarmes were called, and we all spent most of the night in custody while we waited for my parents to sober up and calm down. We were in a café that was also a bar, and while Peter and I enjoyed our cheese omelettes and chips, our parents were downing a substantial liquid lunch to celebrate finally being allocated a council house, on a brand new estate in Essex. Father wasn't that thrilled to be moved out so far from town, but Mother had already found a new job, fairly near to our new house, so she was ecstatic. At last, a home of our own! However, the celebration became increasingly fractious with each gulp of wine. That was the trouble with having boozy parents: celebrations, parties and even holidays would soon turn into battles royal when alcohol was introduced into the proceedings. And of course, it always was. The irritable wrangles that day suddenly escalated into open warfare when one of the waitresses approached us with a wide smile, her arms outstretched, and exclaimed, 'Douglas!' in a surprised and delighted tone.

'Angélique,' Father replied, a tad more cautiously.

Angélique spoke rapidly in French, but as only Mother understood her, she had to act as interpreter and her face grew more and more thunderous as the conversation progressed.

'She says she is delighted to see you again.' Mother listened some more. 'She says she has never forgotten that day when you dropped out of the sky and made an emergency landing in her father's cow pasture.'

'I told you about the emergency landing . . .' Father began, but Mother wasn't listening to him, but to another burst of rapid French from Angélique. This was followed by what was obviously a series of questions from my mother; we could tell by the way her voice rose at the end of sentences, in that note of enquiry that questions in any language seem to have. Angélique answered them happily, smiling all the while, obviously unaware of the dangerous changes taking place in Mother's expression. However, Father, Peter and I noted the signs and I, for one, almost went off my lunch as my fear grew. Even though the delicious omelette and chips had turned to ashes in my mouth, I ploughed steadily on with them, knowing that it was always a bit of a toss-up when we would get to eat again. Mealtimes could be very fluid in our household, or missed altogether, depending on Mother's condition and the state of our rocky finances. Therefore, it paid to gromph when the opportunity arose, and to not be a fuss-bucket about it, either, the way that children so often are. If we complained, our nosh would wind up in the bin and we simply went without, which cured Peter and me of being faddy very quickly.

'What's she saying?' Father asked anxiously.

'Wait!' Even Angélique's smile wavered as that single word exploded like a pistol shot and she finally noticed the tension that was building at our table, and the worrying glitter in Mother's eyes.

With a murmured, 'A bientôt,' Angélique beat a hasty

retreat back to the kitchen. Mother took several deep breaths before telling us what mademoiselle had said.

'It seems that my excellent French has led her to believe that I am the cousin who has been translating her letters to you, and who has been replying on your behalf. She thanked me profusely.' Mother smiled tightly and her eyes glittered with pent-up rage. 'She says that I write a beautiful and very romantic letter, and that her parents are looking forward to you coming to stay again soon.'

'I can explain . . .' Father began, but Mother interrupted before he could get any further.

'I bet you can, you, you . . .' – Mother paused as she searched for inspiration – 'You incestuous bastard!' she hissed venomously. 'Have you explained to Angélique that you have two children by your "cousin" and that, being married already, you are in no position to be courting her?' Mother took another hefty swig from her glass before she continued. 'So that's where you disappeared to when you took off for the weekend! And there was me, silly cow, thinking you were trying to find some work. When will I ever learn never to believe a single word you say?'

For a moment, the silence at our table was deafening, then Mother calmly picked up the carafe of water that had come with our meal and hurled the contents into Father's face. Before anyone else could react, Father's hand connected with Mother's cheek with such a resounding slap that everyone in the café stopped talking and stared at us. When Mother picked up a bottle by its neck, and was obviously preparing to clout Father with it, the *patron* strode over and intervened, grabbing the bottle before it could land on its target. He spoke urgently and Mother translated; it seemed that we were being asked to pay up and leave. Without another word, or a glance right or left, Mother hustled Peter and me out of the place and left Father to pay the bill. We waited outside for him to join us, and when he did, all hell broke loose. Mother swung a heavy bag of smutty books at Father's head, and although he ducked, he didn't duck fast enough. The bag caught him a glancing blow on the shoulder, and books scattered everywhere.

'Now look what you've done, you stupid bitch!' Father yelled and punched her on the nose. Blood spurted all over her best green blouse. I began to howl with shock and fear, and poor Peter stepped between them in an attempt to put a stop to the violence. He was shoved roughly aside and landed with a thump in the gutter where he was narrowly missed by a man on a bicycle who, in swerving to miss him, almost got hit by a truck. The cyclist joined in the quarrel, gesticulating wildly. Our parents ignored him, their attention fixed solely on each other.

Mother pulled back her arm and delivered an uppercut between Father's legs, which doubled him up in such agony that it made him heave, and while he was bent over, losing his stomach contents, she landed a blow on the back of his head with her heavy handbag. Father sagged to his knees, surrounded by books. Mother was just prevented from delivering the *coup de grâce* by a muscular gendarme who grabbed the chair she'd snatched from one of the tables on the pavement and had raised high, ready to crash down on Father's bowed head.

By this time, Mother's rage, misery and humiliation were so complete, all reason had fled, and she hauled out and socked the gendarme in the chest with her clenched fist. He was not pleased. Mother was promptly slapped in irons, or, more accurately, handcuffs. The gendarme fished his whistle out of his top pocket and blew a shrill blast to summon reinforcements when it looked as if Father was about to stagger to his feet and rejoin the fracas in defence of the wife who had just tried to batter his brains out. There's no rhyme nor reason when it comes to drunks in their cups.

When another gendarme appeared on the scene, Father was also put in handcuffs, despite his strenuous efforts, and we were all marched away. Once we reached the gendarmerie, Mother and Father were put into adjoining cells, separated, presumably, to avoid any more bloodshed.

Nobody spoke English, and neither Peter nor I spoke much French beyond 'Bonjour' and, in my case, 'Une glace chocolate – er, please,' because, once I'd tasted it in France, chocolate ice-cream had become my favourite thing in all the world, but my French didn't run to 's'il vous plaît' at that time. So, Peter and I held hands and stood in the middle of the room where the gendarmes hung out and eyed the officers warily, while they in turn tried to mime questions, instructions and suggestions at us, but to no avail. We were so scared that our brains had shut down. All we could do was stand there. In the end, amid many a Gallic shrug of frustration, one bright spark thought of getting a translator and hurried off to find one. He returned with a plump lady with large, dark eyes, enormous bosoms, a very ample rump and a ready smile on her very red lips.

''Ello, little ones,' she began, with an encouraging and sympathetic smile. 'My name is Madame Bernard. I keep the charcuterie a little way along the street. I understand that your people are in the cells for a little time, until they are in command of themselves once again. What are your names, little ones?'

Now, we had had it drummed into us by Father that you never told the police or Customs anything, so, as one, we clamped our mouths shut and just looked at her, too terrified to speak. Madame Bernard rattled off quite a long speech in French to our captors, who nodded enthusiastically at what she said.

'I 'ave told the gendarmes that the gendarmerie is no place for such petits enfants, er, for such small persons. That, naturellement, you are very afraid. I will take you with me to my 'ome, for a little food and drink, and I will keep you with me until the gendarmes liberate your mère et père. You may 'ave to stay the night, but do not worry, you will see your people in the morning, or, per'aps, much sooner than that. Would you like to come with me?'

Peter and I looked at one another, united in greed. We didn't tell her about the omelette and chips we had just downed, and we simply nodded.

'Bon! Let us go.'

Still Peter hesitated. 'Can we tell Mummy and Daddy where we're going? They'll worry,' he whispered.

Madame Bernard nodded her understanding and spoke to the man that I had decided was in charge. He, in turn, held out a huge, beefy, red hand to Peter and led him to the cells, while I waited with Madame and a small circle of policemen. We all looked at one another without a word. Peter may have found his tongue, but I hadn't. I used the opportunity to take in my surroundings instead. It was quite a large room, with lots of chairs, a table and walls plastered in notices, posters and pictures of people, men mostly, with lots of French words printed under them. The place smelt strongly of dark, French tobacco, strong coffee and the vinegary smell I associated with wine that had been left lying about for a spell. How I knew that particular smell I cannot say, because wine never hung about in our house long enough to become vinegary. I can only assume that I knew it from when it had been drunk and had come up again, or from my trips to Soho, to Le Touquet and to Paris.

Peter returned and whispered in my ear, 'They're all right. They said to go with the nice lady and that they'll see us later.' And so we allowed ourselves to be led away to the flat above Madame's charcuterie.

I was so tired by this time, and so nervous at being left with a complete stranger, that I burst into tears as soon as we entered Madame Bernard's cramped and gloomy flat. Madame was very kind, but although I was used to being left in the care of grown-ups, I did usually know them, if only a little bit. I didn't know Madame Bernard at all. I was in such a funk that I hardly took in my surroundings beyond noting heavy dark furniture, and gloomy paintings of dead birds, dead fish and heaps of fruit in ornate, gold-coloured frames. I can't even remember what that sweet woman gave us to eat. All I remember is Peter hissing at me, 'Stop being such a sissy' and Madame gathering me on to her ample lap and shushing me soothingly, assuring me that I would see my 'mère' and 'père' very soon. I didn't like to tell her that I wasn't sure that I wanted to see them, especially if they were still fighting.

A young gendarme came and collected us shortly after our croissant the next morning. Luckily, in France it was not an offence to be in possession of a couple of khaki kitbags full of erotic literature, otherwise our troubles would have been far greater than they were, because our stock would have been confiscated and we needed the money badly. We had a new house to furnish and the rent to pay. When the nice head gendarme was satisfied that no more blood was likely to be shed, he had the books returned to my father, popped some nuggets of nougat into Peter's and my pockets, offered Mother, the one who understood French, some sage matrimonial advice, and sent us on our way.

It was only much later that I wondered who had been translating Angélique's letters and writing the replies, and realized that it must have been one of Father's cronies from the French House in Soho.

It astonishes me now that we survived those trips. After all, Father drank heavily, and yet he was flying a light aircraft and, once we landed, driving like fury to get back to Soho to distribute the loot among his investors. He didn't restrict himself to books, booze and French fags, either. If funds allowed, then perfume and wristwatches also crossed the Channel with us. Sometimes, I'd dabbed so many perfume samples behind my ears while Father did business with the shop assistant, and had so many watches stuffed up my jumper, that I smelt like a scent factory and ticked like a ruddy time bomb.

I must have been an effective 'smuggler's beard', though, because the Customs officials on both sides of the Channel got to know me well, and we were rarely challenged. In fact, the French Customs officers grew fond enough of me to slip me little treats – a chocolate croissant, some nougat, a paper twist of sugared almonds, a ripe peach or a small, mouth-watering pastry – while a colleague dealt with the entry or exit stamps in our passports.

If, by some mishap, we were held up by Customs on the English side of the Channel, then a bottle of brandy, a hundred fags, a few books or a small wad of banknotes usually sorted the problem out very quickly. The English in general were tired of austerity, and that included some of our Customs officials. Also, if they suspected what we were up to, I believe they were deeply reluctant to arrest a man with a little girl in tow. Some of these men were parents themselves, I expect, and didn't want to subject me to the humiliation of having my father arrested before my very eyes for a few smutty books and the odd half-ton of fags.

Once we'd landed and cleared Customs, we'd take off

again and return the plane to the flying club. Then we'd unload the booty, taking care to slip Sylvia and George some smokes and a bottle of something for their private stash, then zoom along the country lanes on our way back to Soho to distribute the booty. We both knew that Mother was likely to be less cross and out of sorts at being stuck at work all day while we were off gallivanting in France, if we returned to the Rest Centre (and later, to our council house in Harold Hill) with lots of lovely fivers, a carton of fags and a bottle of something alcoholic. Mother wasn't interested in perfume.

After the shameful banana incident, I always made sure we had a treat for Peter too, either comics bought in Soho with some of our profits, or some little sweet treat bought in France. To this end, we would save some fags and booze from the stock and did our best to track down Father's pals, Campanini, Legionnaire Jim, Ron and Frank, because they usually paid cash on the nail. Only when we had some cash did we finally venture home.

It was a strange way of life for a little girl, I realize now. Most small girls played with dolls with their friends, but I had no friends, because I always spent my days with Father; he and his pals didn't seem to know any other children, and therefore, neither did I.

At the time, it felt normal to me, if lonely, and it was only when I started school that I realized that no one else led my kind of life. It was there that I honed my watching skills. It was as if I hoped to learn by observation what that elusive 'normal' was, and with luck, make a passable imitation of it. If I could do that, then I might, just might, be accepted at last. And if not, then I was going to have to get used to the idea that, just like my parents, I was odd and different and I was going to have to get used to being on the fringes – forever an outsider looking in.

5

Pots

One of the main aims in a child's life is to be exactly like their friends and neighbours. It's not their fault, they're just made that way – plus it is always safer to blend in with one's background. And it's not just children, either; many adults feel the same way. As any redhead will testify, if you can't be picked out from the crowd, you can get away with more, it's as simple as that. Sadly, my family might just as well have been a tribe of flaming copper-knobs, because there was absolutely no question of us blending in with our new neighbours.

'I don't want to live on some godforsaken housing estate in the sticks,' Father announced when he heard that we had been allocated a house on a large council estate in Harold Hill, and so were able to leave the Rest Centre at last.

'Well, we can't stay here, so unless you have a better plan – and the money to pay for it – Essex it is. There's a permanent job waiting for me at a new school. I went for the interview last week and I heard this morning that I'd got it. A permanent post means holiday pay, which will be handy.'

Poor Mother must have been heartily sick of trying to rely on Father to provide some stability and pay the rent. A council house and steady teaching work must have felt like absolute heaven to her.

'Looks as if you got the whole thing sewn up while my back was turned,' said Father, bitterly, but he didn't carry on the argument.

It was the early 1950s. I am not entirely sure why we wound up in Essex, but I suspect that it had something to do with the fact that new housing was desperately needed in and around London to replace the large swathes of the capital that had been destroyed in the Blitz – and there was plenty of available building land to the east.

Another consideration was that Ford, in Dagenham, and many other large manufacturers, were based in the area. The factories, which had been turned over to war work, geared up to start producing as soon as the fighting was over and reliable sources of raw materials became available again. Britain was on its uppers, and needed to export to refill the coffers that six long years of war had emptied.

As manufacturing restarted, demobbed servicemen and London's dispossessed moved out to Essex to take up jobs and the new homes provided. And, of course, there had been a baby boom after the war, when the servicemen returned to the arms of their wives and girlfriends – with inevitable results. This meant that Essex's brand new residents had children who were reaching, or had already reached, school age, which in turn meant there were lots of new schools that needed teachers to staff them.

It all sounded ideal, but what Mother had not envisaged was that our faces would not fit, that life on a housing estate would be Father's definition of absolute hell and, as a result, he would become even more unreliable. That said, I don't think it occurred to either of my parents to attempt to blend in. They revelled in being rugged individualists and even if they hadn't, they'd have had little choice in the matter.

Luckily, we lived far enough away from Mother's new job for our unorthodox home life not to impinge on her work, but it did make things very difficult for me. I wasn't used to playing with other children for one thing, and this made me shy, awkward and, in some ways, curiously grown-up. I had spent my young life hanging around with at least one murderer, as well as a good sprinkling of smugglers, spivs, gangsters, eccentrics, singers, writers, actors, dancers, prostitutes and homosexuals, which was a universe away from playing with dolls and skipping ropes in the street with other little girls. I suppose that such worldliness in one so young must have been very alarming to parents who were so much more conventional than mine. Having a mother and father who stuck out like angry rhinos in a playpen did not help at all, and the other little girls in our street were kept well away from me by mothers who were anxious for their daughters to grow up into respectable wives and mothers.

Peter fared better, partly because boys enjoyed more freedom of movement than girls, so their mums probably didn't always *know* that they were playing with him. Besides, his access to fast cars and aeroplanes made him a really desirable pal to have, and it was well worth risking parental wrath for the chance to swan about in a motor and, better still, to fly in a Tiger Moth. Few working people owned cars in 1950s England, and I don't think I ever met anyone – apart from the people at the flying club, that is – who flew light aircraft and indulged in victory rolls above the roofs of their houses. But Father did. That was enough to bring every small boy in the area to our doorstep – and to help keep every small girl away.

'Life was hard for many women in the Fifties,' my mother explained to me in later life. Her hazel eyes became sad as she stared back into the past. 'During the war years, we may have been scared out of our wits by bombs and war news on the radio, but compared to the pre-war days, we knew such freedom.' She went on to tell me how many women had gained pilot's licences and had flown aircraft – not in battle, but from one aerodrome to another, so that the planes were where they were needed. She was absolutely right, it was a far cry from the lot of women in the 1950s.

'And a lot learned to drive as well, and many girls found themselves driving ambulances and staff cars in all sorts of places that they never dreamed they'd see,' she said wistfully.

In the war, single women were, in fact, moved all over the place as land girls or factory workers and, if well educated, as code breakers at Bletchley or clerks in the War Office, or some other ministry. Some French-speakers were trained as wireless operators and agents and dropped behind enemy lines to help the French Resistance with their efforts to knobble the Germans. Initially, the powers that be reckoned that nobody would suspect a woman, but they were wrong there: the mortality rate among wireless operators, men and women, was very high.

'It was such dangerous work, you see. Jerry only had to get a fix on your radio, or some bastard decided to betray you to the Gestapo, and it was the firing squad at dawn, after you'd been tortured for any information you might have, of course. Being a female didn't save you. Oh no, it only meant that the chances were you'd be raped before they shot you. There were lots of women in the services too, Wrens, WAAFs and the rest, but unlike the "special forces" they didn't see combat or engage with the enemy.'

I listened with rapt attention. I always found the period just before and after I was born absolutely fascinating, even when I was young. 'But all that changed in 1945,' my mother continued. 'The men came home looking for jobs, they needed us women to be chained to the bloody kitchen sink and flat on our backs in the bedroom again. We were supposed to provide home comforts for our returning heroes, and to breed like mad to replace the lads lost in combat. The government wanted to make sure that the numbers of boys was kept up, you see, so that the poor little sods could grow up to defend the realm, in case we got ourselves embroiled in yet another war. As for girls, they were to be trained up for their domestic duties.'

Propaganda to this effect was peddled in newspapers and

especially in women's magazines, which extolled the virtues of being homemakers and mothers. 'We were expected to clean all day and then to have tidy hair, a clean frock and our slap on, so we looked attractive for our man when he got in from his day's graft.' Mother paused briefly and let out a humourless laugh. 'Not that your father ever troubled with the grafting part.'

On top of all that, Fifties wives were expected to have a meal on the table and their old men's slippers warming before the fire. To be honest, I never remember Mother doing those things, but then, she was the breadwinner, and even if she had tarted herself up, warmed slippers and the rest, there was no guarantee that Father would come home to reap the benefit. No wonder she didn't trouble.

'We were supposed to forget all about our war work, all that lovely freedom and the lolly that we had earned in our own right. We were to blot it right out of our minds. It was back to having the housekeeping doled out to us as if we were children and being banged up in the house as if it was a prison.'

It was hardly surprising that, in this climate, Father's fast cars and light aircraft tended to leave the local little girls cold. Smelly old engines were very definitely boys' stuff. So, unlike the boys, the girls did not flock to our house; they stayed away in droves.

My mother was a creative woman, and having a proper house to turn into a home by collecting new (to us, at least) furniture, running up curtains and cushion covers, and hooking new rugs, must have been a real treat for her, even if the other housewifely duties left her cold. It had been such a long time since she'd had a place to call her own. Then there was a garden to whip into colourful shape as well. The women in my mother's family were all keen gardeners. A family joke was that the most common view of a Marriott female was her bum sticking up out of a flowerbed as she planted, weeded or tidied, and Mother was no exception. Neither am I, I'm pleased to say.

Mother's initial happiness with our new home and the opportunities it afforded to let her creative streak rip would, tragically, not last. Booze and Father saw to that.

Alcoholism is as progressive a disease as an untreated cancer, and my parents' drinking was growing steadily more excessive, expensive and destructive. By the time they moved to Essex, their marriage was hanging on by a frayed thread, and it wasn't long before Mother's efforts at home-making were being undermined by booze-fuelled rows. Father seemed to take particular delight in destroying the things that Mother had just made, and he thought nothing of tearing precious curtains and cushion covers to shreds, grinding cigarette butts out on her homemade rugs and hurling our new china, collected piece by treasured piece as Mother could afford it, at newly decorated walls. He would disappear for days on end, too, increasing Mother's fears that he was sleeping with other women – which he undoubtedly was. Needless to say, Mother's initial euphoria evaporated, and bitterness and deep depression took a firm hold. Her drinking escalated still further in her attempt to stem the waves of misery that threatened to engulf her.

I think that she must have been desperately lonely as well. Not only were we shunned by our neighbours, but Mother was at work all day, so there were few opportunities for her to have a natter over the fence, to help friendly relations along. I suppose she must have made friends among her teaching colleagues, but inviting them home was absolutely out of the question, because she never knew what state Father would be in, if he was about. And anyway, she had her own, secret addiction to service as soon as she got through the door.

'I couldn't bring anyone home who was likely to report back to school that I drank like a fish and fought like a fish-wife with my husband. I would have lost my job and would never have got another in teaching. Anyway, if I brought a woman home, chances were that unless she had two heads, that lecherous bastard of a father of yours would have made a pass at her. The swine could not help himself.'

Of course, the loud and sometimes violent domestic brawls didn't help Mother and me to make friends either. Domestics were supposed to happen quietly behind closed doors. Yelling loud enough to wake dead Pharaohs was not the norm: muttering caustic asides between gritted teeth was the usual British way of strife. And women were meant to be ladies at all times.

A stream of Anglo-Saxon invective pouring forth from painted lips was unheard-of, except, perhaps, among the upper classes, where it was seen as another unfortunate eccentricity due, probably, to all that inbreeding. It certainly was not supposed to happen on a respectable council housing estate in Essex. It happened a lot in our house, though, when Mother suspected Father of straying again, or when he had systematically destroyed something she had worked so hard to buy or to make. On those occasions Mother could, and did, swear as fluently as Father. This was another good reason why the local girls and their mums avoided us, in case being foul-mouthed was catching.

'Anyone would think we had the damned plague,' Mother would complain sometimes when Peter was off playing and Father had disappeared again, leaving us alone to amuse one another. Not that Mother was much of a one for playing with her children. After a hard day at school, she was pretty tired of kids, any kids, but her own in particular. Evenings and weekends were for catching up on chores and her reading and, of course, for drinking, so I was left pretty much to my own devices.

Boys were made of tougher stuff, and they were not, for the most part, tied to apron strings in the way that girls were. It didn't do to be too protective of boys. They had, after all, to grow into men, possibly fighting men at that. Everyone was afraid that too much feminine influence might turn them into 'nancy boys', and that would never do. Homophobia was rampant in those far-off days and anyway, homosexuality among males was illegal: practising gay men, or even accomplished ones, could be imprisoned. There were no such laws for lesbians, because it didn't occur to the Victorian lawmakers that ladies, or even women, would do such a thing.

The old double standard flourished in the tucked-up, thin-lipped, grey, miserable, austerity-ridden society of 1950s England, and my family was way, way, way out of step.

'You fucking whore!' Father's voice jerked me out of sleep. I lay huddled under my thin, army surplus blankets in the dark and waited for the sound of smashing china and crashing furniture. They didn't come straight away.

'No, darling,' Mother answered in a relatively reasonable, but slightly slurred voice, 'merely a talented amateur.'

'What do you mean by that?'

'Just stating the bald facts, darling, nothing more.'

I heard a hard slap. 'I said, what do you mean by that? Who've you been with?'

'You bastard!' An almighty crash, followed by the tinkling of glass. Another fight had begun.

'You could've fucking killed me! That thing was solid pewter, you could've caved my head in.'

'What a pity I've got such bloody awful aim, then. And what do you mean, "Who have *I* been with?" Chance would be a fine thing. While you're off straddling your tarts I'm stuck here night after night baby-sitting your bloody kids.'

'They're your kids too.'

'So they are, more's the pity. I should have had my head examined the night I met you.'

I stuck my fingers in my ears, squeezed my eyes shut and disappeared under my bedclothes, trying hard not to cry. I hated it when my parents argued. I don't know how long it was, but some time during this particular row, I felt someone poke me in the side. I pushed the blankets back and opened my eyes to see Peter standing by my bed in the gloom.

'You OK?' he asked.

I nodded, but it wasn't true. I wasn't OK. I was shivering and terrified, as I always was when they got tanked up and fought so furiously.

'Are you OK?' I asked in my turn.

Peter also nodded. 'Shall I tell you a story?' he asked, and I agreed that he should, eager to shut out the misery being played out downstairs and to hear how the brave pilot, Peter Pots, slew the Hun single-handedly over the English Channel.

The family always called Peter 'Pots', a nickname he'd had since he was tiny and learning to live without nappies. Instead of asking for 'Peter's pot' when he felt the call of nature, he asked for 'Peter pots', and from that moment on, his fate was sealed. I still think of him as 'Pots' and I often write a character called Potts into my books as my private memorial to him.

We crept down the next morning to find the wind and the rain blowing through what remained of the living-room window. Further inspection showed that something had crashed into the metal frame so hard that it had snapped under the impact. We went outside and crunched across the broken glass to see what could possibly have done all that damage. It was a heavy pewter plate, with a crumpled edge that showed it must have been thrown like a discus to snap the metal window frame like it had. Father had been right: had it connected, it would have killed him.

The inspection over, we went back inside, embarrassed by the hostile, and occasionally pitying, stares of passers-by who had also had their sleep interrupted by the furious battle in the night. Peter made us breakfast and we ate in tense silence as we waited for our parents to surface. Only Mother did, looking like death warmed up. Father had buggered off, God knew where, and had left Mother to look after his 'bloody kids', and to face down the curious and disapproving neighbours. We didn't see our father for some considerable time after that. The funny thing is, I can't remember for the life of me who looked after me during that period, it's a complete blank, but somebody must have, because I was still too young to go to school. Perhaps it was Mother's school holiday, and we didn't need Father. Which is probably just as well, because it wasn't too long after that that he left us for good.

It must have been during this period that Peter and I were sent away on holiday to Hastings, to stay at a bed and breakfast place with our father's much older half-brother, Will. Will usually lived in one dingy room in a sooty boarding-house in Willesden, so the Hastings trip was his summer holiday. Father was missing, and Mother wanted a break from childcare, so Uncle Will, a lifelong bachelor, obliged by offering to take us off her hands for a week or so. Will tended to hang around our little family rather a lot. It gave him a sense of belonging. Anyway, Peter and I decided that we really didn't want to stay with him any longer.

'What do you say to going home?' Peter whispered in the dark after Will had tucked us up in bed. I nodded my agreement. I didn't like it with Will and I didn't like the place we were staying in much either. The landlady seemed to have nine million rules governing the behaviour of children, all of which boiled down to, 'Thou shalt not have fun, make any noise, run about or stay in your room after nine in the morning.' What's more, there were no toys or books to amuse us, just Will: to us, he was an old man and, being a bachelor, he had no idea how to play with kids.

While Will was still snoring in his bed the next morning, we quietly got dressed. When we were ready, Peter stealthily retrieved our return train tickets and a crisp, ten-bob note for food, tube and bus fares, from our uncle's wallet and we tiptoed silently across the room and out of the door. Once on the landing, we legged it down the stairs and out on to the street. The relief of getting away from Will and that horrid, dark house so redolent of cabbage and cats' pee was wonderful, and a feeling that I can still remember today.

It was a bright, breezy morning and I had the fresh, clean smell of the sea in my nostrils. We walked as quickly as we could to the station, looking back all the while in case Will had woken up and was in hot pursuit. He hadn't, and he wasn't. Once at Hastings station we asked someone which platform we needed to get a train to Waterloo. The man told us, then looked suspicious and asked us where our mummy was.

'She's at home,' I piped up.

'Where's home?' the man asked.

'Harold Hill,' I told him helpfully, while Peter gave me a sharp kick in the ankle.

'What are you doing here all by yourselves, then?'

'We're not by ourselves, our uncle's with us,' Peter told him.

'I see no uncle.'

'That's because he's waiting for us on the platform. He said we could pretend to be great explorers and that he'd wait for us on the platform,' Peter explained. 'Can we go now, he'll be ever so worried?'

'Yes, all right, you cut along and be quick about it, the London train's due any minute now,' the relieved man told us. So 'cut along' we did, and pretty sharpish at that. We wanted to be safely on the train in case Will woke up and found us, our tickets and his ten-bob note missing.

We made it to Waterloo, and then had to take a tube train to Embankment, where we changed to the Circle Line to take us to Liverpool Street station. Once there, we boarded yet another train that took us to Romford and from there we caught the familiar bus home. I am astonished that we managed such a mammoth journey all by ourselves, when neither of us was tall enough to see above the ticket counter at the tube station. But manage it we did, thanks largely to my brother's memory and impressive resourcefulness.

We were asked several times what we were doing travelling about all on our own, and each time Peter came up with a plausible story. Sometimes he said our uncle was in the toilet and would be back soon; or he'd use the explorers again, and he'd wave his hand vaguely to indicate that our uncle was somewhere 'over there'. He must have been convincing, because we were allowed to carry on unmolested and we made it all the way home safely.

Mother was shaken rigid when she got in from the pub to find us calmly sitting at the kitchen table scoffing jam sandwiches that we'd made for our lunch. We'd left Hastings before we'd had a chance to get any breakfast, and although we'd bought some chocolate from a vending machine at Liverpool Street, we were still starving.

'What're you doing here?' she demanded.

'We didn't like it there,' Peter explained.

'Why didn't you like it there? What was wrong with it?'

We'd rehearsed our story on the way home, so Peter was glib as he told her what a misery Will had been and how we preferred to stay at home.

Mother sighed heavily. 'And what about me? Did it occur to either of you that I might like a little time on my own?' She didn't wait for a reply but answered her own question, 'No, of course it didn't, you selfish little sods. So where's Will now?'

'We left him there.'

'I beg your pardon? What do you mean, you "left him there"? Where did you leave him?'

'In bed at that house, the one that smelt of cats' pee, cabbage and rotten old socks,' Peter explained carefully. We had agreed not to mention that Will scared us when we were left alone with him. We simply did not have all the words to explain, and anyway, we were afraid that our father might kill him if he knew how weird Will was. We didn't want our father hanged for murder, and we didn't want to push our mother further off the rails. To be honest, I don't think we'd reasoned it all out as clearly as that. We simply knew that trouble was best kept to ourselves, and that some secrets were best kept away from our emotionally fragile and volatile grown-ups. To this day, I have blanked out exactly what Will did to us to make us so afraid of him, and perhaps, in a way, that is best. I only know that when he eventually died, it was a huge relief to both Peter and myself, and we were not even remotely sorry to see the back of him for ever.

'Does he know that you've buggered off?'

We both shook our heads but kept our lips buttoned. It was obvious that Mother was getting cross and we didn't want to get into even more hot water when we were already up to our necks in it.

We were saved by the bell, because at that moment the telephone rang. It was Will asking if Mother had heard from us or the police at all, because he'd misplaced us somehow.

'Don't worry, the little sods have turned up here,' she told him.

Peter and I looked at one another, utterly relieved to be back. Even though home was rocky at best, at least it was familiar. We knew the rules, and we knew how to survive there.

When Peter died – more than a dozen years ago now – I was devastated. I still miss him, but to be honest, I suppose I love and miss the boy he was when we were young, because I never really knew him as a man, or even as a teenager. Peter was sent away to a public school when I was nine, and in a sense, I lost him then. He married very young and emigrated to Canada – largely to get away from the family, I'm sure.

I still have my treasured memories of him walking me to and from school or puffing out his little chest and taking on anyone he caught bullying me. I shall always remember the comfort that he brought on nights when the fights downstairs woke us up and either I crept into his room, or he into mine, and he'd tell me stories. My favourites were about the bloodstream, when the white cells rushed to defend the body against invaders and huge battles ensued. In those stories, the white cells always won, and nobody ever died – except the invaders of course, and they didn't count.

I started writing my novels when Peter was dying, in order, I think, to nail down the few, short years that we spent together. Although I was unaware of it when I was writing, I realize now that the character Luigi is, to young Rosie, what Peter was to me. My brother Pots was, when we were children, my brave protector, my best, and sometimes only, friend, my hero and my witness.

In reality, I lost my brother fifty years ago when he went away to school, and again when he married and emigrated to Canada, but when he died, I knew, once and for all, that he was gone for ever. I love and miss him more than I can say.

6

Heartbreak House

The first inkling I had that something was terribly wrong was a heart-rending cry in the night. The scream had a primal quality that had me sitting bolt upright in bed even before I knew that I was awake. The hairs on the back of my neck and the ones on my arms all stood to attention as the howl of misery came again. I was too afraid to investigate, and sat rigidly to attention, waiting for the animal that had made those awful noises to come and gobble me up.

What I heard next was much more familiar: it was the sound of breaking glass as something hit the wall downstairs. Then came Mother's voice, loud and furious. 'What makes this one different from all the other whores you've spent all our money on?'

Father's voice rumbled in reply. 'Calm down, you'll wake the kids.' I think that that was more scary than the screaming. Screaming I was used to, but the sweet voice of reason, especially issuing from my father's lips, was rare indeed. It meant that whatever was going on between them was serious, very serious.

Peter arrived silently, torch in hand, and asked in a whisper if I was all right. I nodded and we waited for the drama downstairs to be played out.

'Get out, just get out!' Mother screamed so loudly that I was sure the Eskimos in Alaska would start packing up their igloos immediately, eager to obey.

'I can't leave you like this,' Father answered, with more than a trace of worry in his voice, 'and I can't leave the kids with you in this state either. For Christ's sake, pull yourself together.'

'Pull myself together?' Mother gasped. 'Pull myself to-bloody-gether! You bastard. Why should I pull myself together so that you can feel better, you pox-ridden prick? Brace yourself for some bad news, Doug – I DON'T GIVE A DAMN HOW YOU FEEL! I don't care if you rot in hell for ever. In fact, the sooner you take yourself there, with that syphilitic hag you've dug up from God knows what tenth-rate brothel, the better. Meanwhile, until then bugger off – just BUGGER OFF!'

'Put the knife down, Joan, or I'll have to take it away and I may have to hurt you,' Father warned.

'Then you'd better do just that, hadn't you? Because if you don't, I'll kill you. I swear I'll kill you, and then I'll hunt down your latest tramp and I'll kill her as well.'

Father's voice was surprisingly gentle. 'No you won't, Joan, you don't have it in you. But you must calm down, you'll wake the kids.' Little did he know that they'd already woken virtually everyone north of the Equator, and one or two million souls south of it as well.

Something hit a door with an ominous thud.

'Bloody hell!' Father roared, all patience and understanding gone. 'You could have killed me with that. You just missed me by inches.'

'PITY!' Mother screamed, and we heard a tremendous clatter as she yanked at what sounded like the cutlery drawer, presumably looking for another suitable weapon. It flew out of the dresser and crashed to the floor, scattering knives, forks and spoons all over the kitchen lino. 'Now, I told you to get out. If you don't go, right now this minute, this one will be aimed lower down and with luck and decent aim, you'll be singing castrato. How will your tart like that, eh?'

There were the scuffling sounds of a brief struggle, then silence for a good few minutes. Peter and I looked at each other, eyes like radar dishes, then in silent agreement we crept to the top of the stairs in an attempt to make sure that neither of them was lying dead in a pool of blood. We could see nothing, so Peter put his finger to his lips and mouthed at me to stay put. He was going to do a recce to see what was what. I nodded, too frightened to move from my spot deep in shadow. Peter tiptoed down the stairs to the dark hallway and along the passage towards the back of the house and the kitchen, where all the noise had been coming from. Before he could reach a point where he could see into the room, there was a hailstorm of cups, saucers, plates and glasses, and he was forced to beat a hasty retreat to the top of the stairs once more.

We waited. With the contents of the china cupboard exhausted, saucepans and frying pans followed. An enamel colander hit the front door, bounced and landed on the Welcome mat. This was followed by the kettle, still full of boiling water.

'You're insane, do you know that?' Father yelled as he retreated under the bombardment. 'I could be scarred for life, you maniac.'

'Good! It would serve you right. And if I'm mad, guess who drove me to it? I wish I had never clapped eyes on you, let alone any other part of my anatomy. I really must have been mad. Look what you've brought me to, two brats and no hope of escape now. Just get out. Go to your whore and don't ever come back, do you hear me? NOT EVER!'

'Right! I'll do just that! And for the record, she's better between the sheets than you ever were, you middle-class nutcase.'

'OUT!' Mother roared, shattering eardrums in Outer Mongolia. 'I should have known better than to take up with a low-life, lower orders guttersnipe like you. My father said no good would come of it, and he was right. No bloody good has come of it. Life with you has been worse than my worst nightmares. Get out, you useless prick, just get out and stay out.'

We saw Father storm down the hall to the front door and yank it open so hard we thought it would have to come right off its hinges, but it held, just. Mother was close behind him with the carving knife that she had retrieved from the kitchen door.

Father hesitated just long enough to see the wicked blade, and decided it really was time to go, and fast, with no pithy parting shot. He stumbled slightly and just made it through the door before the knife whistled past his head and sailed out into the dark night to land with a clatter on the concrete path.

Mother slammed the front door behind our father so hard that we heard it rattle the windows in our bedrooms.

Peter and I scuttled hastily back to my room. We heard the engine of Father's car throb into life outside, and looked out of the window just in time to see it draw away from the kerb. I could have sworn that there was someone in the passenger seat, and I thought for a moment that Mother had gone with him, leaving us all alone in the night. But she hadn't. Once all was quiet once again, she began to sob as if her heart was breaking. I suppose that it was.

Peter and I looked at one another, wondering what to do. We weren't used to crying; yells and curses, yes, but not those sobs. We went carefully down the stairs and stood for a moment in the doorway of the kitchen, taking in the scene. The littered floor glittered with cutlery, broken china, glass and dented saucepans. There was a large gash in the door, where the carving knife had sliced deep into the wood. And there our mother sat, a picture of abject misery, with her head in her hands, her shoulders heaving as each gut-wrenching sob was torn from her.

Without a word, we crossed the room – negotiating the wreckage carefully, so as not to cut our bare feet – and then stood each side of the hunched shape and rested a hand comfortingly on her shoulders. How long we stood like that before she noticed us, I couldn't say, but it felt like hours.

Eventually, the heaving slackened off a bit and she dropped her hands to reveal a tear-soaked, snot-sodden, stricken face, eyes red with weeping and filled with a pain that was almost too terrible to witness.

An arm went around each of our waists and she held us so close to her that I could smell the warm scent of Wright's Coal Tar Soap, Pond's Face Cream and the Yardley's powder that she always used to take the shine off her nose. It was my mother's own special smell, the one that clung to her old green jumper that I took to bed with me most nights after that terrible night, and held close to my nose, so that I could get to sleep.

It was to be the first of many nights that we were awakened by the haunting sound of our mother's crying. Father had left us, all of us, and he was never to come back to live with us again.

PART TWO

Hard Knocks

7

The Family Brains

'How was school today?' Mother asked wearily, though I knew she wasn't really interested.

Father had only been gone a week, and we were still reeling from the shock.

Actually Mother had a pretty shrewd idea what my very first day at school had been like, because she was the one who had had the unenviable task of getting me there. What's more, I knew that my teacher had told her everything when she came to get me at going-home time. I really, really had not wanted to go to school that morning, despite her and Peter's efforts to make it sound like a jolly good thing to do.

'I don't want to go to school,' I had screamed, as she forced my reluctant arms into a blazer so big that I was certain it would go once round me and twice round the gasworks. I hated that blazer because it reached down to my knees, and I looked as if I had no hands at all. Worse, it was scruffy and buttoned up on the boy's side – it had been my brother's blazer before being handed down to me.

'I want my daddy!' I screamed even louder. 'I want to go out with Daddy. I want to go flying. I don't want to go to school.'

'Well you can't,' Mother snapped. I remember her face – so white and strained; she must have been close to breaking point. 'You can't go with Daddy, because he's not here, is he? Now get a move on, or I'll give you something to cry about.' It was the first day of the new school year, and lateness was not an option for either teachers or pupils, but particularly not for teachers.

For once, my terror and misery overcame my fear of upsetting my already deeply distressed mother. I dragged my heels at every step of the journey and once we were at school, I had hysterics. I screamed, I blubbed, I threw myself on the floor and refused to get up again.

All I would say – or, rather, scream – was, 'I want my daddy. I want my daddy. I want my daddy,' over and over and over again.

Miss Thomas, the teacher who taught the Infants' reception class, had an interesting, sing-song kind of a voice. I stopped screaming just long enough to listen to what she said to my poor, unhappy mother.

'Don't you worry, Joan.' Miss Thomas's voice was soothing. 'It's not unusual for them to be upset at being left on their first day. You cut along now, I'll look after her, I'm used to this kind of performance. You get yourself going, or you'll be in trouble with Miss Clayton, and that won't do at all.'

In the end, Miss Thomas persuaded Mother to leave me with her. It was, after all, true that Mother had her own duties to attend to over in the Juniors, where she taught one of the third-year classes.

Relieved to be getting away from her screaming child, Mother left me and hurried off to her own classroom. That wasn't the end of it, though, not by a long chalk. Sure enough, my tantrum stopped almost as soon as she was no longer there to witness it, but I wasn't finished with being a nuisance.

The first that Miss Thomas knew I had gone AWOL was when a policeman appeared in her classroom, with me at the end of one arm.

'I was passing on me bike when this little tyke shot out of the school gate and crashed straight into me,' he told her sternly, holding me firmly by the hand. 'Just as well I wasn't a car. As it is, I bent me wheel in the collision. I think she's all right; a bit shaken up, maybe the odd bruise, but nothing's broken and there's no blood anywhere but on her insides, where it belongs.'

Miss Thomas thanked the policeman profusely. Once he was gone, she turned to me. 'Where did you think you were going?' she asked me gently.

A tear rolled down my cheek. 'I want my daddy,' I told her. What I wasn't able to tell her, because I didn't have the words to explain, was that I had also wanted to make sure that my mother and my brother had not disappeared as my father had done.

We had been let out into a little yard to play under the supervision of a lady called Mrs Blundell. It had been very easy to give Mrs Blundell the slip – all I had to do was wait until her back was turned before I darted back into the building. My first thought had been to track Mother and Peter down. The trouble was, it was a new school year, so Peter was no longer in his old classroom, and neither was my mother in hers.

I wandered the long corridor for ages and ages, but I could not find either of them. The corridor was gloomy, and it stank of school dinners and something that I associated with having a tooth out at the dentist's. I hated going to the dentist's. It took me a while to realize that the awful pong came from chairs stored in stacks in the school hall. They had rubber feet to stop them slipping and scratching the glossy, parquet floor, and the gas mask at the dentist's was made of the same, stinky old rubber.

I was too short to peer through the windows in the closed classroom doors, and too afraid of being told off to open them. In the end, I gave it up and decided to make my way home to see if anyone was there. I knew in my heart that no one would be, but I needed to check just the same.

It was to be a feature of my first months at school that, at some point during the day, I would make a break for it and appear like a lost soul in the doorway of Peter's classroom, and then in the doorway of Mother's. I knew it was naughty; I knew it got on everyone's nerves – but I couldn't help it. Every school-day I would be overwhelmed by the terrible thought that they had gone away and left me behind. I simply had to check to make sure that they were still there.

In the end, Miss Thomas had the bright idea of making it official: I was escorted to Mother's and Peter's classrooms by Mrs Blundell and, reassured, would go back to where I belonged. This went on for some time – until the head-mistress got wind of it.

'If you let her get away with this,' Miss Clayton harrumphed, 'they'll all be wanting to see where their mothers are. She is the daughter of a member of staff, so all this special treatment smacks of favouritism. It must stop. The little madam can just get used to school, as everyone else has to do.'

After Miss Clayton's interference, Miss Thomas made a point of keeping me close to her desk, so that I couldn't leg it. However, kind Mrs Blundell would seek me out at play-time or lunchtime. 'Your mother and brother are still here, little one, so don't worry that curly little head of yours,' she'd whisper, and I could relax once again.

I tried, I really did, but I simply could not settle down at school. I was always staring up at the sky, hoping against hope that my daddy would swoop down in his Tiger Moth and whisk me away. I missed him so much that it hurt like a toothache. It nagged in the background a lot of the time, but would stab me with an agonizing pain when the sound of someone's laugh, or of uneven footsteps, reminded me that he was not there. For a while, his old Harris tweed jacket hung forgotten in the hall cupboard, and when I held it to my nose I could smell the mingled scents of peat-smoked tweed, his tobacco and his shaving soap, and it was as if he was holding me close once again. Then I opened my

eyes, and it was just his empty old jacket; misery and loneliness would fill me up until I thought that I must surely die
of it. After a time, even his smell faded from the jacket, and
then, one day, it disappeared altogether, in much the same
way that he had done.

Apart from his smell, I had the memory of our days
tramping around Soho together and our trips in the Tiger
Moth always in my mind. I missed Father's stories the
most, especially the bedtime serial that Peter and I had
shared, 'The Adventures of the Abominable Snowman'.

Story time always began the same way. 'Where were we
yesterday?' Father would ask.

'Snurg, the evil scientist was just about to clout
Abominable over the head with an ice-pick and spread his
icicle brains all over the place when Mrs Snowman, Pots
and the Pippin Sist [one of Father's nicknames for me; the
other was Porky Fat Belle], the intrepid Snowkids, rolled a
huge snowball down the mountain, starting an avalanche
that smothered Snurg, but was just like a nice cool, refresh-
ing shower for Abominable,' Peter and I would tell him,
eager to hear what happened next.

Father would nod, as if we'd just passed some sort of test
(now, of course, I realize that he was making it up as he
went along, and had no idea what he said the day before),
then launch into the next instalment. 'Snurg, the evil
scientist may have been buried beneath tons of sodden, soft
snow, but Abominable still had to find his secret laboratory
before it was too late. Snurg's malicious minions, the
Crepuscular twins, Cringe and Crud, were still working

hard on the plan to create a match the size of two Eiffel Towers, laid end to end, a match so mighty that it would burn for a dozen days and a dozen nights and melt the valley of the snowfolk clean away . . .'

Our magic half-hour in the world of snowpeople and malicious minions would always end with the same, ritual words. 'And what do you think happened then?' Father would ask.

As one, Peter and I would wail, 'Oh no, not tomorrow, Daddy.'

But 'I'll tell you tomorrow,' Father would inevitably say. Now that he had gone, though, there was no bedtime story 'tomorrow', or on any other day. Sadly, as I lay in my bed, I wondered if Peter and I would ever hear what happened to Abominable, his family and the Crepuscular twins in the end.

Of course, my inattention at school meant that I did not seem to learn much, the way the other children seemed to do. I was proving to be a serious disappointment to my mother. 'What a pity you didn't inherit the family brains,' she sighed when she had finished her meeting with Miss Thomas at the end of my first year. The news had been broken to her that I had made little progress in the three Rs; that I was unable to read, write or do arithmetic to any acceptable standard. It was official: I was the class dunce.

My apparent lack of brilliance was a great blow to my poor mother, because she came from a family that prided itself on its advanced intelligence. They were high-flyers –

or at least, most of them were. One of my great uncles was the editor of *The Times Literary Supplement* and the author of a well-respected English textbook, as well as several novels, and another was the Mayor of Bromley. Two of their sisters were headmistresses, and the rest of that side of the family were teachers. On Grandfather's side, they were all Methodist ministers.

'And what's this I hear about you not mixing with the other children?' Mother continued. 'You're not supposed to skulk in corners, keeping out of everyone's way. How in God's name are you ever going to make any friends if all you want to do is hide?' I don't know what my father thought of my failure to shine. Perhaps he didn't know what a clod I had turned out to be, or now that he had his new 'tramp', perhaps he simply didn't care. I was a bit confused about the 'tramp' bit. The tramps I saw sleeping in Soho's doorways, walking the country lanes, or begging for food or copper coins in Romford's market, were scruffy, unshaven men in tatty army (or sometimes navy or air force) greatcoats. Perhaps my father had turned into a tramp as well. It was an awful thought, because I hated the idea of him having to beg for food, or being cold and wet if he was forced to sleep rough on winter nights like the other tramps did.

Perhaps it was because of the embarrassment I was causing her by my academic failure, but Mother left that school at the end of my first year there and took up a post a good few miles away. It was then that Peter became my escort and we

became latch-key kids. I can
feeling the house always had ɩ
fires and made tea. I was always .
turn up, especially if she was late.

'Mummy, Mummy, look what I ɑ.
would yell, waving my painting at her ɑ
the door at the end of a long, hard day. 1
blue star for my picture and I was very prɩ   ɪe
first star I had ever got for anything, and 1   ɩoping
against hope that Mother would be pleased witɪɪ me. She
often mentioned my failure to inherit the family brains;
perhaps my modest success would change her opinion of
me, if only a little bit.

'How many times have I told you to go and play and to
leave me alone for at least an hour after school?' Mother
asked wearily, a warning edge creeping into her voice. A
great lump of desolation settled in my stomach. She wasn't
interested in any answers, or my picture, or my wonderful
blue star.

'I've been listening to kids' voices and looking at
pictures all bloody day, and what I'd like now is one whole
hour of peace and quiet to read my newspaper, do my cross-
word and drink my coffee in peace and quiet.' She paused
and drew a long breath, closing her eyes as if in supplication
to a deity that she didn't believɩ in. 'Is that too much to
ask?' I slunk away, still clutching my picture. My happy
triumph had evaporated.

It always felt as if it was my fault that Mother did not
have the solitude she so craved at times. It seemed to be my

somehow been bypassed by 'the family as if I'd wilfully been standing behind the door en they were handed out. I also thought it was my fault that Father had gone and left us so broken-hearted. I don't know why I felt like that, but I did, and the feeling grew and grew as the miserable months after his departure dragged on. I was convinced that absolutely everything that went wrong was my fault, and that my mother heartily disliked me for it.

I tried hard to be a good girl, so that she would be able to love me, but it was no use; I was stupid, I was whiney, I was always ill and I was a dreadful disappointment to her. As long day followed long day, I became certain that her dislike of me would eventually spill over into genuine hatred; that it would overwhelm her and that, in the end, she would be driven to kill me.

At first, I thought she would stab me with the wicked carving knife she had thrown at Father the night when he left us. The fear was so great that I could only sleep facing my door, in case she crept up on me in the night and plunged the knife deep into my back. The habit became so entrenched that it was several decades before I could either sleep or sit with my back to a door, and I'm not keen on it even now.

Then I thought that if she couldn't catch me all unaware with her knife, she might use poison. Mealtimes became a nightmare, as I expected to die in agony every time I ate. Looking back on those years now, my fear seems scarcely credible, but at the time I truly, truly believed that I was about to be murdered by my own mother. She had, after all, tried to kill my father more than once when booze, rage and jealousy had driven her to violence, and she had loved him deeply. What would she do to me, a child she couldn't seem to love, if I annoyed or disappointed her enough?

After a few months, Mother's pain and anger had subsided enough for her to decide to allow Peter and me to visit our father at his flat in Soho, his and my old stamping ground. This relaxation of the embargo was, I'm sure, partly due to the realization that she'd get the odd weekend to herself if she changed her mind, but was mainly due to the fact that, when she eventually calmed down, she appreciated that, for all his many faults, he *was* our father, and that we loved him dearly and, in his own peculiar fashion, he loved us dearly too.

'It's not your fault that your father's a swine and he left you when he left me, and that must have hurt you deeply,' she explained when she broke the news to us that we were going to visit him. 'But the old bugger does love you, you know, and he misses you dreadfully.' She grinned a wide grin before adding, 'And you never know, you may even find out what happened to Abominable, the snowkids and the evil Crepuscular twins. You'd like that, wouldn't you?' As one, we agreed that we would.

The first time we went to visit Father in Soho, it felt as if I was coming home at last. Although Peter was also excited, he didn't have quite the same relationship with Soho and its people as I did, because he hadn't spent anything like as much time there as I had. I loved being greeted by name by some of the shopkeepers, having my cheek pinched gently and being told, 'I 'ave missed you, *cara mia*, so good to see you once again. 'Ave some sugared almonds, do. And your 'andsome brother, 'e must 'ave some too.'

'Daddy, Daddy!' I screamed at the top of my lungs as I spotted him limping down the street to meet us. I let go of Mother's hand and tore along as if I was a low-flying, half-crown rocket on Guy Fawkes Night. I collided with him with such a thump, I almost knocked him off his feet, and clung to his legs so tightly that any movement was impossible for several moments. Peter and Mother had to bring up the rear and wait while Father laughingly disentangled my skinny arms and hoisted me up on his shoulders.

'Hello, Porky Fat Belle,' he chuckled. 'Hello Pots, and hello Joan.'

There were some awkward minutes while our parents negotiated when and where they would meet again, to hand Peter and me back into the care of our mother, and then Father said, 'Let's go, there's someone who is dying to meet you.'

'If only that were true,' Mother smiled sweetly; 'the "dying" bit, I mean. Right, you two, I'll see you tomorrow. Give us a kiss.'

It hadn't occurred to me that I was going to meet the woman who was to become my stepmother. I'll call her Gabrielle, or Gaby for short, although it wasn't her name. I hadn't really thought much beyond seeing my daddy again:

that had been enough for me. We met her in a café where she was sitting at a table in the window, looking as nervous as I felt. I was struck dumb by the exotic-looking woman before me. She was very thin, with dark skin and very long dark brown hair, plaited into a single, fat braid that snaked down her back and brushed her bum. When it was loose, I was to discover later, she could sit on it.

If I was rendered speechless by the sight of this strange woman, Peter was not. His large, blue eyes bored into Father's lover as he said, 'So, you're the one that stole our father.' He was nine, and so very grown-up, and what's more, I thought he was incredibly brave. 'When I grow up,' he went on, 'I will never leave my children.' And sure enough, he never did.

I can't remember much about that first meeting, except that Peter and I never did hear what became of Abominable, the snowkids and the evil Crepusculars. I did discover that Gaby barely spoke English, and that she had moved into Father's little attic flat in Old Compton Street, and worse, that she had no intention of doing the decent thing and moving out again. I also sensed, but didn't have the words to express it, that not only had she taken my daddy away from me, but that I was never really going to get him back, and that I would have to work hard at being a good girl if she was ever going to allow me to share him – even a little bit.

8

No Passport to Pimlico

It was a miserable, wet, cold Saturday morning, and we'd schlepped all the way into Romford on the bus. We'd shivered and queued for a month or so at the bus stop, and then again in the post office, and Mother was gnashing her teeth in frustration.

I expect I was whining; I often was, apparently. I was not a happy child. There wasn't much in the way of skipping and dancing about from me, not when my mother was already cross. Fidgeting only made her crosser, and I always would end up being directly in the line of her fire, even if it was Peter doing the fidgeting – or so it seemed to me.

Of course, I realize now just how hard this time must have been for all three main parties in the triangle, but at the time the only person I could see was my mother. She had lost her husband to a younger woman, with all the heartache and hardship that that entailed. She was frowned on by society for being different. And she was an alcoholic single parent in a day and age when women automatically earned less than men who were doing exactly the same job. The excuse was that men had families to keep, but as Mother said, 'What the hell do they think I'm doing?'

The unfairness of life made her feel intensely bitter and, looking back, I can understand why. The problem is that bitterness is corrosive and it is very hard to live with. Bitterness overflows on to innocent bystanders, who just happen to be in its way. And in our house, those innocent bystanders were invariably Peter and me.

That Saturday sort of summed it up, really. The weather was awful, the waits were endless, Mother was probably dying for a drink, I was whingeing as usual and the post office clerk was being obstructive and officious – simply because he could. He had the power, and we had none. And nothing, but nothing, was more guaranteed to cheese off my mother than men with power over her. She had a low opinion of men generally, Father had seen to that, and officious swines who got between her and her money were the absolute dregs. We had been collecting our maintenance at Romford post office ever since Father had left us, and the payments were fairly regular, although they stuttered a bit on occasions and arrived either late or not at all. Most of the staff had come to know us quite well, but that Saturday there was a strange face behind the counter.

'Identification?' the new clerk asked.

Mother rummaged in her handbag and found an electricity bill and a rent book in her name and slapped them down on the counter.

'These won't do,' the clerk told her with enormous satisfaction as he pushed them back over the counter with one finger.

'They've got my name and address on them.'

'Yes, but they could be anybody's.'

'Why would I have someone else's rent book and electricity bill in my handbag?'

I could hear that the question was being forced through tight lips, and I felt the strange sensation run down my spine that I felt whenever I was around when either of my parents lost their temper. It was like a shiver running through water; it's the only way I can describe it. It came and went in a flash, but I always felt it and I was always afraid. The fact that I didn't know what I was afraid of made it worse, somehow. It was all too easy to imagine my brains, such as they were, spread out on the floor, or a knife sticking out of my bony chest.

Having spotted the look in Mother's eye, the clerk wavered. Just for an instant, he seemed a little uncertain of his ground. Then, stupidly in my opinion, he stiffened with a new resolve. 'You could have stolen the handbag. How do I know that it's yours?' he asked.

Mother's teeth were now clamped so tightly together that her words had to hiss through them. 'How do you suggest I go about proving that the handbag *is* mine?'

'How about a passport? Have you a passport?' The clerk's face was aglow with triumph.

That did it! The clerk had pushed the 'Blast off' button, and Mother promptly let rip.

'I came into Romford on a bloody double-decker bus in the pouring rain. Where did you think I was going that I would need a passport? Fucking *Pimlico*?'

Several people in the queue that had rapidly formed behind us and was now steaming gently tittered nervously, despite Mother's foul language. 'That's right, you tell 'im, love,' someone muttered in encouragement. Virtually every one of them would have seen and enjoyed *Passport to Pimlico* at their local Odeon not so very long before, and they quite enjoyed seeing the cocky little clerk turn a deep shade of beetroot. Besides, his red-hot face was just about the only heating to be had in the entire building. Luckily for the clerk, his superior, an old hand with awkward types like my mother, stepped in and dealt swiftly with the problem by hastily handing over our money. Next thing we knew, we had been hustled politely and safely out of the building and on to the grey, glistening wet pavement. Clutching my mother's hand, I heaved a sigh of qualified relief. I had avoided being the focus of her terrifying rage this time, but the clerk had lit Mother's blue touchpaper and she was still fizzing. I felt that she was just looking for a place to go off, and I was mortally afraid I'd be caught in the explosion.

The next stop was my ballet class. It was held in a freezing cold hall situated behind a sooty Victorian church; more of a chapel, really. It was a squat and ugly thing. If that church had been a person it would have had no neck, a great many warts and knuckles that dragged along the ground. To reach the hall, we had to walk down a narrow pathway bordered by an unkempt privet hedge on one side and untidy rows of graves on the other. In winter, the privet dripped rain or snow down the necks of many a budding ballerina and made the path treacherously slimy and slippery underfoot. The graves would look even more sombre and forlorn in the low, grey light. In summer, the privet flowered like fury, and its cloying smell choked the air and made me feel nauseous. But the graves looked less sad in the bright sunshine, which was something.

I wasn't a regular attender at ballet classes, but sometimes it was handy for Mother to have somewhere to park me while she zipped around and did some food shopping without me to slow her up. If she took me with her, I tended to drag a bit, either because I was interested in the hustle and bustle around me, or because I was grizzling for some wonderful thing that I had seen but could not have. I yearned for a yo-yo decorated in bright primary colours, just like the ones the big boys had at school. Or I fancied a lovely blue tin whistle, so that I could learn to play it like the scruffy, one-legged man who entertained the queues outside the Odeon on Saturday afternoons and evenings. Besides, if I was tagging along, there was no question of getting the shopping done fast enough for Mother to have time to enjoy a jar or five at the Red Lion before meeting up with me once again.

Peter was usually off doing his own thing with his friends, and was no problem on Saturdays. The trouble was, he wasn't even the tiniest bit interested in having his pesky little sister dragging along behind him: he had enough of that during the week when he had to take me to and from school. Therefore, if we had the three bob to spare, which wasn't always, I was dropped off at ballet and had to lump it.

The erratic nature of my attendance at classes meant that my progress in dancing was indiscernible to the naked eye. I went for quite a while, on and off, but acquired neither good posture, nor grace, nor a promising ballet career. It never seemed to occur to any of us to try me at tap, the usual alternative for girls who did not get on with ballet.

Once the path had been safely negotiated, we pitched up at the hall, although 'hall' is a bit grand for what was, in fact, a kind of giant shed. A very elderly benefactor had offered the necessary cash and the hall had been thrown up in some haste, before the old fellow died and his heirs withdrew his offer. It cowered there, damp, under-heated, in perpetual shade, unloved and bullied by the church, which hulked over it. A rather tatty notice pinned inside the porch informed us when the Boys' and Girls' Brigades met, and that the local Drama Club took the place for regular rehearsals and meetings, as did the Mothers' Union and a host of other societies, clubs and unions: the list went on and on. The Academy of Dance booked the hall for the whole of Saturday, with ballet in the morning and tap in the afternoon.

On Saturdays, come rain, less rain, smog, snow, sleet, or even shine, that old hall shook to its rafters every time twenty or thirty little feet landed, roughly in unison, on its battle-scarred floorboards. On the occasions when I was there, I always feared that it would collapse around our ears at every landing. But it didn't. Rattling the windows over in one corner, as she pounded an ancient upright piano, was a little old lady dressed from neck to ankle in grubby white lace, like an ancient bride. The only visible colour in her ensemble was provided by the previous week's menus, which wound up decorating her flat chest. A smear of egg here, a drop of mutton stew there, the odd dab of tomato ketchup, and perhaps a lick of bright yellow mustard, all added to the culinary picture splattered across her bosom. Sometimes, when I was very bored, I would try to work out from the evidence exactly what she'd eaten since last I had seen her.

'Oh well done, Penelope, I hardly saw that wobble at all,' our dance mistress called. 'Madame' was a tall, strong young woman, not fat at all, although her bones were sturdy and solid. At dance classes, she dressed in a variety of homemade, shapeless, knee-length creations, a bit like sacks, which she wore cinched in at the waist with a wide, black elasticated belt. For the morning sessions, she sported an ancient pair of well-used and rather tatty ballet shoes, and in the afternoons they were swapped for tap-dancing shoes in a similar condition.

'Oh, that's splendid, er, yes, you at the back in the nice red woolly. It would've been absolutely perfect if you hadn't kicked Carol.

'How are you, Carol dear? Do you think you'll be able to walk again? Eventually perhaps . . . ?

'Jennifer, love, perhaps you'd do better if you took your wellington boots off. You can't do a nice pirouette in wellies, now can you, dear? That would be silly, wouldn't it? No? Well, *I* still think that it would be silly, so take them off, there's a good girl.'

As I stepped out of my mac and sturdy winter lace-up shoes in the changing area of the hall, Mother handed me a paper bag with a pair of black leather, rather scuffed ballet slippers inside, gave me a hasty peck on the curls, thrust three shillings into Madame's ready mitt and headed for the door, eager for her freedom. There would be no kids cluttering up her landscape, but she still had the market to tackle. She would shop for fruit and veg while I pounded the boards. That done, she could settle down for a drink in peace until she picked me up again.

Sometimes we went straight home on the bus, but on red-letter days we would stop for something to eat at 'our' greasy spoon café, the Regent. When we were well-off, we went to 'better' establishments like a Joe Lyons or a Bewley's, but mostly, the Regent was our place. I loved eating at the Regent, because not only did I love their chips, but I was certain that Mother wouldn't get the chance to poison them.

There were two markets in Romford in those days, the open air one that was held on Wednesdays and Saturdays and had pens for stock as well as the usual stalls for produce, and the indoor, corridor-type one, which opened every day except Sunday. Both markets had their complement of cafés, but the Regent sheltered in the relative cosiness of the covered market.

I loved both markets for different reasons. If you arrived early enough at the outdoor market, the pens would be full of livestock waiting patiently to be taken to a new home, the slaughterhouse, or back to the old farm if they had not sold. Being new to school, I hadn't yet learned all about the little lambs, bullocks and piglets winding up in our bellies, via the dreaded slaughterhouse. My ignorance left me free to enjoy staring into a pair of liquid brown eyes fringed with lovely long lashes, or twiddling a set of warm, furry lugs and trying not to giggle when an animal dropped a huge heap of steaming manure on the cobbles. I'm not sure when they stopped selling livestock at Romford Market – some time in the mid-1950s, I think – but I do know that most of the joy went out of it for me once the animals had gone.

The lure of the covered market was very different. To begin with, you could browse in relative comfort if it was pouring with rain, or worse, sleet. Of course, it didn't have the lure of the lambs, but it did have a fascinating haberdashery stall that brought spots of colour to a very dull old post-war world, and it brought plenty of mystery, too. There were all sorts of weird and wonderful things to find on that stall if you had a good poke about. For instance, there was a whole selection of things called 'whalebones' for replacing broken ones in corsets. Whether, by the 1950s, whales actually donated their bones for these torturous undergarments, I really couldn't say, but I do hope not. There was a glass-fronted drawer full of suspenders in white, black, peach or a sort of tan colour, for replacing the business ends of your suspender belt, should you lose one.

If you just lost the button bit, that was OK, because a sixpence or a threepenny bit did just as well in an emergency, but if the metal 'eye' disappeared too, it was off to the haberdasher's to buy more.

Next to the suspenders was a drawer of crescent-shaped pads, which were sewn into garments under the armpits. That way, the pads soaked up any perspiration and could be washed separately from the clothes. It was easier to wash and dry the pads than the clothes. People stank in the 1950s, because antiperspirants had yet to be invented, and deodorants, if they existed at all, were hard to come by, as was perfume, while the washing of both bodies and clothing was not to be undertaken lightly. Sweat was murder on precious clothes; it left nasty salt stains, especially on dark fabrics or delicate ones like silk. Salt stains could not be got out, and anyway, no lady wanted to be spotted with sweaty armpits, with or without added salt deposits.

Huge needles, with big eyes, or strange bent ones – some so cruel-looking that they would have fitted nicely into any torture chamber – were meant for people who did their own upholstery, and were kept next to the studs, webbing and hessian also needed for the job.

I knew all these needles and studs were necessary because, along with 'Charlie's dead', 'Spud' was a common cry in the school playground. 'Charlie's dead' meant that your petticoat was hanging below the hem of your skirt, a terrible thing in those days, while a shout of 'Spud' meant you had a hole in the heel of your sock and the flesh was poking through. This phenomenon was supposed to look like a potato.

'Spuds' were a common sight, as were women busily darning socks with the aid of an implement that looked like a mushroom and wool unravelled from an old jumper. Rationing and austerity had made 'mending and making do' a way of life for us all, and nobody thought anything of wearing black socks with a red darn in one and a yellow darn in the other. Rumour had it that the Queen even darned the Duke of Edinburgh's socks, or at least had a maid to darn them for her. But that was probably only propaganda, to try to keep our spirits up. Even if it was true, I bet he had the right coloured darns in *his* socks.

I remember thinking this when I watched Mother trying to darn my socks, a chore that did not come naturally to her. Mother's lumpy darns made every step an agony, as the lumps pressed into tender heels and bruised them, but the pain had to be borne in silence, because Mother liked her efforts to be appreciated and harm could come to a girl who failed to grin and bear it. It was a massive relief when my mother finally gave up darning my socks.

Discreetly tucked away behind the haberdasher's counter was a set of glass-fronted drawers that held the items that were not for open display, like pairs of Directoire knickers with long legs that gripped the knees and came in pale yukky pink or white. White Aertex knickers, pants and vests, for men, women and children, took up six more drawers. Aertex underwear was made of cotton and had tiny holes all over, to allow, in theory, for the free flow of air in summer, which was supposed to make a person sweat less, always a boon and a blessing. What's more, a vest was easier to wash and iron than a shirt, blouse or jumper. In winter, the little holes were supposed to make you warmer, but I was never quite sure how that was meant to work.

Sanitary belts, in white or pink elastic, were kept out of sight, along with big, fat sanitary towels. Sanitary towels had a loop at each end and the belts had hooks to catch the loops and hold the whole thing in place. Menstruation was a shameful thing back in those days, and ladies would scuttle into the haberdasher's, looking furtive, and whisper their requests for towels, or a new sanitary belt, into the shopkeeper's ear. She, in turn, would look about her, making sure there were no men lurking about to witness this secret transaction. Once the coast was clear, she would hastily slip the offending articles into a paper bag and hand them over the counter. Mother always hid her sanitary towels and belt at the bottom of a deep drawer. Used towels were wrapped in newspaper and burned on the fire. In summer, they were still burned in the grate. Heaven forbid that one should end up in a dustbin, with the risk of the bin men finding it.

On wet days, everyone's coat would steam and add to the general fug in the Regent café. There's nothing quite like the smell of wet flannel, cheap fags, hot grease, strong tea and, overlying the whole thing, a whopping great dash of over-cooked cabbage. In the 1950s, cabbage came out of the pan so soggy it was almost liquid, and in some cases you were hard pushed to work out whether to eat it or drink it. It also stank so badly that the smell seemed to seep into your clothes and into the walls. The Regent was a big believer in cabbage as a valued (and cheap) part of their Saturday Special and, indeed, as part of any other day's Special – except Sunday's. On Sundays, the Regent took its obligatory day of rest and over-boiled its cabbage at home.

I remember listening to a conversation between 'Mrs Regent' – we never knew her name – and my mother.

'Fat lot of bleeding rest I get,' she complained. 'I'm washing for the family and all the tea towels from here, cooking for the family and the caff, changing the beds, washing that lot, running a mop round a bit, then nipping round to me mum's with her Sunday dinner and me *Woman's Own*, stopping there for a cuppa and a chat, poor old thing, then it's back home to make tea and whip an iron over his shirts for the week, my blouses, aprons and the kids' school uniforms. Then, if I'm lucky, I can put me plates up for half an hour before I toddle off to bed ready for another six o'clock start on the Monday. There are times when I feel like one of them furry little buggers that run round on a wheel all day. What're they called, Hampsteads?'

'I know the feeling,' Mother assured her, looking down at me. 'I never seem to stop either.'

If Mother was in a good mood, which she was sometimes, I really enjoyed our Saturday mornings together. The only problem with it was that I could never quite predict how her drink at the Red Lion would take her. Sometimes a swig or several made her jolly, which was great fun. Then we'd laugh until we cried at something silly, like a farting cart-horse dragging his load through the market or some daft joke I had heard at school.

But on other occasions, a drink – and just one could do it – would make her angry, bitter and blisteringly sarcastic. There would be no laughing then. Then I would try my best to be as quiet as a mouse with no squeak, not to fidget and to be as good as I could possibly manage.

I would always be tense on the way home on those bad days, terrified that Mother would finally crack and shove me under a passing bus.

9

Mother's Little Helpers

'Mummy, Mummy,' my voice rang out. 'You can get the custard creams a penny a pound cheaper at the Co-Op *and* you get the divvy as well.'

Several people in the queue turned and smiled down at me as I peered into the glass-topped boxes of broken biscuits. Each variety – Garibaldi or 'dead fly' biscuits, Rich Tea, coffee creams, shortbread, Bourbon and digestives – had its own large, silver, square tin, but they were often empty bar some stale old crumbs. Biscuits, even broken ones, were a luxury that was just creeping back into the grocers' shops as rationing began to relax its grip, but supplies were still limited.

'Do you rent her out?' asked a thin lady with surprised eyebrows and a smiling red mouth.

My mother smiled back, 'Yes, and our rates are very reasonable – she's worth every penny. Only last week she marched back to the greengrocer's with a pineapple that was rotten inside.'

The lady looked suitably surprised. 'Really? How *old* is she?'

'Not very – she started school last September – but she had an eye for shopping long before that,' Mother told her, 'and she not only took that pineapple back to the shop, but she demanded a full refund when they told her they'd run out of pineapples.'

The lady's already surprised eyebrows rose so high in astonishment, they almost disappeared into her hair. 'Did she get it?'

'Oh yes,' Mother grinned, 'she did indeed. And what's more, they gave her an apple for her efforts, free, gratis and for nothing.' I think that was the only time in my life when I heard my mother sound proud of me. My chest puffed out so far as I listened to the exchange going on above my head, that I almost popped the buttons on my pinafore dress. It was around that time that my mother first began to call me 'Madam', because, according to her, I could be a right little madam when I chose.

I had been so incensed when our precious, and extremely rare, pineapple had proved unfit to eat once we sliced it open, that I simply could not believe that my mother was going to let the matter slide. When it was obvious that she was, I took matters into my own hands. I was heartily fed up with hearing about exotic treats like pineapples and never getting to sink my teeth into one. Actually, I had hoped that the shop would replace it, so I'd finally get to know what pineapple tasted like.

We were all so fed up to the back teeth with rationing,

austerity and the government that, for me, the rotten pine-apple had been the last straw. We were aching to look forward, and if we couldn't pop a bit of Bourbon biscuit or fresh pineapple into our mouths every now and then, we were liable to get very grumpy indeed. Enough was a long way past being enough, and I, for one, longed for broken biscuits and fresh, exotic fruit to be on our menu on a more regular basis.

I often helped Mother with the shopping, and I kept my eagle eye on prices. I may not have been able to read, but I knew early in life that there was often no money to spare in our house, so I took on the twin roles of 'returner of defective goods' and 'penny-counter' when we were out shopping together. Not only did we not get stiffed with dud fruit when I was on the case, we saved money. Best of all, I knew that it pleased my mother no end.

Peter and I were dab hands at helping with the other chores too. We'd discovered that it was a good way of not getting on Mother's nerves, and getting on Mother's nerves was all too easy after Father left us. We would be like whirling dervishes as we rushed to smooth our profoundly distressed – and very angry – mother's path. We found it safer that way. Nobody could dish out a tongue-lashing like our mum when she was tetchy, and neither of us wanted that.

'Pots, fill the coal scuttle, will you, the fire's getting low?' Mother asked, a Kensitas tipped cigarette hanging from her bottom lip. A smelly wisp of smoke curled its way upwards towards her pretty hazel eyes, making her squint a little.

Peter shrugged on his coat without any ritual grumbling, ready to brave the elements, and headed out of the back door where the galvanized metal coal bunker lurked. Getting in the coal was such a filthy job, with coal dust having the ability to get in everywhere, that Mother always insisted on gloves and an old, cast-off coat. It saved hot water, a precious commodity, and it saved having a decent coat expensively dry-cleaned.

'Where *is* that damned boy?' Mother demanded about ten minutes later. 'What's keeping him? The fire's going to be out before he gets back here with the coal at this rate. Stick your head out of the back door and see what he's up to.'

I did as instructed, and heard a hoarse whisper from somewhere near the bunker. 'Is that you?' the voice asked.

'Yes. Who's that?' I answered.

'Me, you great dollop. Who did you think it was? Come and give me a hand, I'm stuck.'

I peered into the gloom and saw that Peter had forgotten to put on his gloves. On dark, frosty nights in deepest winter, an icy metal coal bunker could nip fingers something rotten, and naked fingertips could stick to metal. The trick was to blow hot breath on the spot where finger met metal, then wiggle the digit like fury to stop it sticking again when the breathy droplets cooled down and became ice in their turn. For some reason, the usual drill had not worked. Maybe Peter didn't have enough huff or something.

'OK, now blow,' Peter instructed once I was standing, shivering, beside him. I hadn't put my coat on, thinking that only my head was going to be outside in the cold.

'Say "Please".'

'*Don't be stupid, just blow.*'

'Why don't *you* blow?' I was indignant at being called 'stupid' and at being made to stand outside in the dark and cold, when all the world knew that was a job for big boys.

'I *have* been blowing, nitwit, but it's both hands and once I stop blowing on one and start on the other, the first one sticks harder. Right, you blow like billy-oh on that one, and I'll do this one.'

'Why should I?' I asked, more for form than anything.

'Because if you don't, when I get out of this, I'll clump you,' said Peter in a matter-of-fact voice. 'Or better still, I'll drown your teddy in the bog and pull the chain.'

Incensed at the tyranny of older brothers, I abandoned him to possible frostbite and rushed wailing into the house. 'Mummy, Mummy, Peter says he'll drown my teddy,' I blubbed, being the big baby that I was.

Mother was unmoved. 'Where's the coal?'

I shrugged. 'Peter's stuck to the coal bunker again.'

Mother rolled her eyes in exasperation and spat, 'Jesus wept! If you want anything done in this bloody house, do it yourself. As if I don't have enough to do.'

She heaved herself up off the floor. She had been sitting on her feet, playing patience on the hearthrug. That was the way she always sat at home, with her feet tucked under her bum. She was still sitting like that not long before she died, a few months before her seventieth birthday. I tried many times to emulate her, but all I got for my pains was pins and needles in my feet, promptly followed by complete numbness.

'How many times have I told you to wear your bloody gloves when you're getting the coal?' I heard Mother ask in that heavily patient tone that she used when she was trying hard not to be too cross. She got no reply beyond a sulky mumble. 'Here you are, I've got some warm water. Now, when I start pouring, move your fingers, and for God's sake, don't put your hands back on the bunker this time, you fool.'

She got him free in moments, filled the scuttle herself and returned to the living room to stoke up the fire. Peter trailed behind her, examining the fingers missing their top layer of skin. With luck, the frozen skin would still be stuck to the bunker in the morning, when we could go and examine it in daylight.

'Sneak!' Peter hissed. 'I'll get you later,' he promised. And I'm sure he did. He didn't drown my teddy, though.

I liked to play with water, so I would clean the bathroom basin, the big white bath and the deep, white kitchen sink. I had to stand on a chair to do that, because the sink was deep enough to wash a pair of double sheets or a chubby baby in it with room to spare, which is pretty deep when you're on the short side. There was no chance of being frozen to the taps, like the coal bunker, although I did get my thumb stuck up a tap once. But not for long, and nobody had to call the fire brigade – more's the pity.

Monday was washday for all the other households, but

because our mother was at work all day it was usually done on a Saturday or even a Sunday. Washing on a Sunday was still frowned upon by some people but, as Mother said, 'Needs must when the Devil drives.' Besides, she was a devout atheist.

Her view was, 'I have washing to do and a full-time job. If washing on a Sunday offends Him that much, let Him produce a bloody miracle so that my washing ends up washed, ironed and in the airing cupboard with no irreligious effort from me.'

Our washdays entirely depended on the weather and on Mother having a day off from teaching, and that was that. If it upset the holy, then so be it.

Peter and I had the job of sorting the washing into batches and, Sunday or not, God help us if we got it wrong and something shrinkable went in the hot wash or something runny went in with the whites. First to go into the big copper were the 'delicates' – dresses, shirts, that kind of thing; the water would not have boiled yet, and it was clean. Next, when the water was not far off boiling, the sheets and pillowcases went in. These were accompanied by a blue bag, to give them that prized, extra-clean, slightly blue look that was supposed to mimic fresh snow or ice. Lastly, when the heat was turned off under the boiler and the scummy water was cooling, Peter's flannel shorts would go in, followed by his and my smelly, much-darned socks.

Mother's stockings were washed by hand in the sink. They were far too precious to risk in the boiler. She had to wear nylons for work, even in hot, humid weather, and as they were both fragile and expensive, they were treated with extreme care. Woollens were also washed by hand, in soap flakes rather than washing powder, and so was anything made of silk, although there was precious little of that fabulous fabric in our house, not until rationing was over and we had some spare lolly, which wasn't often. I was often set to do the hand-washing in the sink, if all it needed was a quick rinse; serious staining was left to Mother to sort out.

Every summer, the blankets got their annual wash. There was no point in doing them in the winter, because they wouldn't dry, and anyway, while they were hanging about, they weren't keeping us warm in bed. We didn't have spares. They were also washed in the copper first, but the gas was turned off before the water could get too hot and thus turn our blankets into shrunken, felt doormats. Most of our blankets were thin, khaki, army jobs that Mother had bought for a song from a spiv flogging them from a suitcase in Romford market.

Mother's biceps would bunch like a boxer's in training when she gripped the wooden tongs to yank heavy, wet sheets – or even heavier wet blankets – into the deep wash-tub, and then into the butler's sink for rinsing. Washday wasn't for the weak and feeble: this was especially true on blanket days, but every washday was hard, physical work. As well as the heaving about of wet sheets, the plunging and turning of the dolly, and the endless rinses in the sink, there was all the hand-wringing to get some of the water out before each item was rinsed yet again, and then finally fed to the mangle. A 1950s woman, so used to all that wringing, had hands as strong as a navvy's and could strangle a rhino – should the need ever arise – with no trouble at all.

Our 'laundry', or scullery, was tacked on at the back of the house and had a gas-fired copper, a sink, a large wash-tub, a formidable mangle, a central drain in the floor, washing lines for wet days and all the paraphernalia of washday, including the wooden tongs, buckets and a galvanized bath for moving big items between copper, washtub, sink and mangle. There were also bars of Sunlight Soap, a box of Tide washing powder, a store of Reckitt's blue bags in an old jam jar, a box of Robin starch, a bottle of cloudy ammonia, some Vim scouring powder, a tin of Harpic, a tin of Brasso, some Penguin polishing cream and, for stubborn stains, a box of washing soda, all stored high up on shelves, out of reach of exploratory little fingers.

There was a large, walk-in cupboard with shelves on the back wall and some handy hooks arranged along each side. This cupboard was a treasure trove of useful things, like empty jam jars ready for the jam-making season, the Kilner jars that were used for preserving fruit, pickled onions, chutneys and piccalilli, and two preserving pans – one for chutneys, another for jams. A washboard hung from a hook, as did the dolly. A dolly was an implement with a long wooden shaft attached to a disc, which, in turn, had sort of arms sticking out of it. You plunged your dolly into the washtub and beat, stirred and generally agitated the wash-ing to get the dirt out. It worked like the paddles of an old-fashioned washing machine, but was powered by a pair of strong arms rather than electricity. The big wooden tongs, the peg bag and a spare washing line (they were always breaking) were also hung on their own hooks. On the floor, under the shelves, was an extra bowl, several galvanized buckets and a washing basket. The tin bath hung on a hook on the back of the door.

On sunny days, the mangle would be wheeled out into the yard, and the wet washing would follow in the bath and some buckets. Once each item had been fed through the big rubber-coated rollers of the mangle, sometimes several times, the flattened washing would be put into the washing basket and then pegged on the line to let the breeze and sunshine finish the job. Peter was chief mangler because he was taller and stronger, and could turn the mangle wheel more easily.

My main contribution was to dance about getting in the way, but I also did some of the pegging out, once the line was lowered for me, then hauled back up again when I was done. We had a wooden clothes prop with a fork at the business end. This raised the line even higher, to catch more wind and to keep large items from dragging on the ground. If something blew off the line, dragged in the dirt or was shat upon by birds, it was a disaster: it would have to be washed all over again. A broken washing line was an utter catastrophe.

I loved pegging out washing, I liked to be out in the air, listening to the birds, bees and the distant cries of children playing.

Winter washdays were even less fun than in the

summertime. Sometimes the wet clothes froze stiff, and chilly fingers had to crack sleeves and sheets into shape to get them into the basket for bringing in. There was an airer fixed to the kitchen ceiling, which was pulled up and down with a pulley arrangement. It was meant for airing, but was also useful for drying stuff in a hurry in the relative warmth of the kitchen. The problem was, the ceiling wasn't that high; once the airer was loaded, you could get slapped in the face by a cold, wet sheet, an errant shirt sleeve or a thick, woolly stocking as you moved around.

Sheets had to be arranged and rearranged on the airer, and dried in sections. This could be murder in the cold, damp depths of winter, especially if there were six sheets to be washed, dried, ironed and aired. Flannelette sheets were the worst, because they were so thick and heavy. They were bliss on one's bed on a cold winter's night, but hell in the tub on washday. That's why we 'topped and tailed 'em'. The bottom sheet would go into the wash, and the top sheet would take its place to last another week. That way, there were only three sheets for the wash each week.

Knickers, socks, stockings, woollens and vests were dried and aired on a clotheshorse that opened out into three sections to be placed in front of the fire. It worked fine, except that when it was loaded with washing, nobody got any heat from the fire. The combination of direct heat and damp washing also meant that the windows steamed up something awful and droplets of moisture even ran down the wallpaper. Hot, wet wool had a strong and distinctive smell that pervaded the atmosphere in our living room for a while even after it was dried and put away.

Our one labour-saving device was a vacuum cleaner, a sausage-shaped thing with a hose that plugged into one end of the sausage for suck, and the other end for blow. It was a Goblin, and it weighed a ton. Doing the stairs was the worst job, and much cursing and swearing ensued on stairs days. The hose, unlike the elephant's trunk that it resembled, was not very flexible. It fought back, and bucked and jerked whenever it was in a tight spot.

Later, when I was about seven, as we moved up a bit in the world, we rented a larger, detached house in Wincanton Avenue, right on the very edge of the estate and with wide open, rather flat, countryside stretching out beyond the Bear pub. Every Saturday, a man with very strange ears came to call. His lugs had perfectly round, dangling lobes, as if someone had slipped large marbles into them. They would swing in a light breeze like Christmas tree baubles, only not as pretty. Those gently swinging lobes could mesmerize the unwary. They certainly mesmerized me: I couldn't take my eyes off them.

When she heard him ringing his bell, my mother would nip out to hail the man with the lobes, and he'd stop his lorry and trundle a washing machine down a ramp, across the pavement, up our garden path and into our kitchen. Coins would change hands, and we'd be the proud possessors of a washing machine for a whole morning or an afternoon. The big old copper was ancient history. It was the beginning of the New Elizabethan Age, and time for mod cons.

*

Even though she worked full time, Mother was responsible for all the cooking, cleaning and most of the shopping, because, in the 1950s, real men did not sully their hands with such domestic stuff. I can never recall Father doing anything that could even remotely be described as housework. Occasionally, he did a little light shopping, but usually only if it was something *he* wanted. As he always had champagne tastes, he'd buy the odd spot of caviar for himself – we didn't eat it – at Fortnum and Mason, expensive cheeses and salamis from one of the many delicatessens in Soho, or some Cuban cigars if they were available, but he rarely schlepped boring stuff like potatoes, cabbages and carrots home from the shops.

I now know that Father, even before he finally left us, repaid Mother for providing our only steady income and seeing to all the domestic chores by regularly betraying her with other women and stealing her housekeeping money to spend on his bits of sly, as well as gambling and drinking it away. No wonder the poor woman was bitter and depressed.

Looking back, I wonder how much help, if any, she got from her parents. The trouble was, the convention was for the man of the house to see to money stuff and the woman to do the domestic things, so I suspect that our profoundly conventional grandfather took the hard line, and refused to give financial aid because he would see it as Father's job. And anyway, he saw Father as a wastrel who would simply 'throw good money after bad'.

Grandma did slip her daughter the odd few pounds as and when she could, and tried to offer sanctuary when she realized it was necessary, but, once again, I think Grandad made visits very difficult for all concerned: he didn't like young children much, and anyway, he believed that Mother had made her bed by marrying a ne'er-do-well like Father, so now she had just better lie in it. I suspect, too, that Mother was ashamed of her situation, and kept the knowledge of the vast majority of her misery away from her parents. After all, most women who feel trapped in abusive marriages keep the secret out of a sense of shame.

'I liked your father,' Grandma told me once when I was old enough to talk to in a 'woman to woman' way. 'He was a real charmer. He could be very kind, too, although he was an awful husband to your mother, I knew that. Your grandfather wasn't very sympathetic. He thought she'd brought it all on herself, you see. But as I told him when he grumbled at me giving her money from time to time, "It's not just Joan I worry about, Bob, it's those poor children. You can't tell me that they brought it all on themselves. They didn't ask to be born, after all." That's what I'd tell him, but he didn't like it, just the same. And he never liked you coming to stay, not until you'd grown up a bit. I think he was ashamed. You were such scruffy children; down at heel, if you know what I mean. At least Peter was a sturdy child, but you were such a skinny, tiny scrap of a thing that you looked half-starved.'

I probably was, indeed, half-starved, because eating at home had become so frightening that I often only pretended to eat, while in fact, I hid my food in my hanky. Later, I'd drop it in the dustbin. When Mother's back was turned, or she'd blacked out from too much booze, I'd sneak some bread and Marmite, some broken biscuits or fruit or any other grub I could be sure she hadn't poisoned. I didn't like to tell Grandma that, though; she would have been hurt that I could possibly have ever believed that her daughter was hell bent on murdering me. Like most unhappy families, we had our secrets, and I learned very early that I had to keep them.

10

Happy Families

'What the fuck is my son doing running wild in the streets with his arse hanging out of his trousers?' Father demanded, red in the face and with his eyes 'sticking out like dogs' bollocks', as my mother so graphically described them.

He had arrived at our house to be greeted by the sight of my brother playing in the streets and looking as if he'd been dragged through, not just the one hedge, but several acres of them.

'He's probably searching under rocks for his fucking father,' Mother yelled back, drink in one hand, fag in the other.

Neither realized that I was cowering on the grubby stairs, fingers in my ears, trying to blot out the sound of their argument. I had heard Father's uneven gait on the path and, after looking out the window to check that it was indeed his car that was parked at the kerb, had run out of my bedroom, where I had been reading, to greet him.

I had finally learned to read all in a rush, largely because I had been bored witless with the adventures – if they could be called that – of the dreary brother and sister team, *Janet and John*. I wanted to get on to the *Wide Range Readers*, which had proper adventure stories rather than the tedious daily doings of a pair of middle-class kids whose well-ordered lives bore absolutely no resemblance to my own.

'I want to read one of those,' I told my teacher and pointed at the *Wide Range Readers*.

'But you can't, your reading isn't good enough yet,' she replied, as she reached for the hated *Janet and John*.

'Yes it is,' I answered boldly.

'I don't think so.'

'I can read them,' I insisted.

This argument went on for some time, but I remained stubborn. I had made up my mind that I was not going to read about those ghastly children ever again. I wanted to read about Eskimos, Red Indians and Swiss maids who yodelled. I dug my toes in deep and refused point-blank to even glance at the book. After all, I was a Soho veteran, a seasoned smuggler and the daughter of an ace storyteller: I was used to much meatier stuff than the mealy-mouthed Janet and John, who would have bored *themselves* to death if they'd had to read their own books over and over again. In the end, my teacher relented with a sigh and told me to pick a book, any book, and to read it to her. I did as she asked and, to her utter astonishment, I read it pretty well. At first, she was convinced that I had memorized the story, having overheard other children reading it aloud. She picked out another, more difficult book, and I read a story from that too. We kept this up until I had read her the last story in the last, and hardest, of the series.

Mother was summoned to the school.

'Something peculiar has happened,' my teacher informed her.

'I know she's a funny little tyke,' my mother acknowledged cautiously, 'she always has been. But she's not normally naughty, as you know. What's she done?'

'Oh nothing bad, just something odd. I've never come across it before in all my teaching years.' The teacher paused. 'She's learned to read – apparently overnight. One day she was illiterate, and the next, she could read!'

'Are you sure?' Mother was as bewildered as my teacher.

'Certain. Watch.' My teacher plopped a reader in front of me and instructed me to read for my mother. I read. Mother was duly impressed. As I recall, she bought me the first book of my very own and enrolled me at the library, as rewards for my success. From that moment on, I never looked back when it came to reading. I read everything I could lay my hands on.

It was as if I had had the tools for the task, but had not been using them until sheer boredom and frustration had made me open the toolbox.

So, there I was on that weekend morning, sitting among the dust bunnies on the stairs, and torn between wanting to see my father and resentment at being dragged away from *Black Beauty* just to listen to my parents yelling at each other. I knew that I wouldn't be able to relax with my book while they were at it, and the fear that I would be discovered if I moved kept me rooted to the spot. I wasn't sure whether Mother had started drinking early, or simply hadn't stopped from the night before. Either way, her temper was uncertain. This was why I was holed up in my room out of sight and, I hoped, out of mind. It never did to catch the attention of a well-oiled Mother. So, when I heard the sound of the limping cavalry coming up the path, I rushed to meet him, but stopped dead at the top of the stairs as hostilities broke out.

I longed to make a run for it, and head for the peace and safety of Dog Rose Camp, but they were standing toe to toe in the hallway and blocking any possible way out through the front door or the back. I finally had the nerve to shuffle backwards on my bum along the landing a bit, so that I couldn't see them, nor they me – but I could still hear them.

By this time, we were seeing a fair bit of him and his lover, Gaby. Peter and I were often at their Soho flat during weekends and the school holidays. When Father was in funds, we would decamp to the South of France for a chunk of the long summer break. Between times, he would occasionally visit us, usually bearing expensive toys, despite the fact that sometimes he had not paid our maintenance for weeks. Gaby also sent things for us. She was a gifted needlewoman and once she knitted me a gorgeous dress, with knitted scarlet dots around the neck, hem and cuffs. I loved that dress.

I heard Mother go to the door to see who, if anyone, was waiting for Father in the car, but there was no one. He had come alone. Mother told me, when I was grown up, that for a few years after he left, Father had been unable to make up his mind between his two women. There was also the suggestion that, at one point, he had three on the go: Gaby, herself and a well-known popular singer of the day. As he had arrived unannounced and alone on this particular visit, Mother was pretty sure what he was after.

'The swine could *not* make up his mind, until in the end, in a fit of sanity, I made it up for him,' she explained to me much later. 'I realized that I couldn't put up with his womanizing, his endless toing and froing, and his lying any more.' Mother spoke with a faraway look in her lovely eyes, and deep sadness etched on her face. She could never have been called a pretty woman, because prettiness suggests a rather saccharine lack of character. Mother's face never lacked character. Pictures of her taken when she was young remind me of Ingrid Bergman with a Roman nose. She could be described as handsome, striking and, indeed, beautiful, but never pretty.

'God! Your father was such a liar,' she went on. 'Still is, as far as I know, but that's Gaby's lookout – I'm delighted to say.' She did not look even remotely delighted as she said it, though, just sad. 'When we were together, if he told me it was raining, I learned that it was always in my best interests to stick my head out of the window to check.' She laughed bitterly. 'When I found out about the singer, I was livid. All that cobblers he'd been telling me, about how I was really the only woman for him, that all he had to do was get shot of Gaby, and we'd be a happy family once again.' She paused, her eyes glittering with unshed tears. 'The thing is, we were *never* a happy family, not really. We had our moments, especially at the beginning, but that's all they were, moments. So, I finally crossed my legs firmly, and for good, and began divorce proceedings. Even then, the bastard begged me not to divorce him, said that if I did, he'd be forced to marry Gaby and he really didn't want to. I honestly don't know why he did marry her. He always regretted it, or so he said. But then, your father wasn't really the marrying kind. He would have been happy to have his very own harem – the man had stamina, I'll give him that.'

I learned, over the years, that my mother was right about my father being a compulsive liar. On the other hand, Mother always told the truth as she saw it: at least, I never caught her out in a deliberate lie. If Mother did not want you to know the truth about something, she simply kept her mouth shut, or dodged the issue, or stated baldly that she didn't wish to discuss it, but she did not lie. Therefore, I believe she was telling the truth about Father's indecisiveness over his women. I think he did to and fro between them, and that a swift knee-trembler was probably what he had in mind on the day that he saw Peter running wild around the neighbourhood. But on that occasion he didn't get very far, because the telephone rang into the ominous silence that always followed their angry words, and often preceded violence.

'Hello,' Mother said into the mouthpiece, then listened for a while. 'Yes he is. Hang on, I'll get him.' She put the receiver down on the hall table with a clatter and yelled loudly, happy in the knowledge that the caller could hear every word, 'Douglas, get your trousers on. It's one of your tramps on the line.' She picked up the receiver again. 'He'll be here in a minute. He's just got to find his underpants and pull his trousers up.'

'What'd you say that for?' Father demanded as he reappeared in the hallway to take his call.

'Because you did have to find your pants and pull your trousers up,' Mother answered, all sweet reason.

'But I was in the khazi! God, you're a bitch, do you know that?' Father picked up the receiver, then had to wait for the operator to reconnect him, because his caller had hung up.

Mother didn't bother to answer the charge. 'She's crying, says that you two have had a row. I suppose that's why you're here.' Her voice sounded so desolate and weary that I almost rushed down the stairs to comfort her, but caution made me stay put, out of sight.

'You'd better piss off back to her now, Doug, because you'll get nothing here. And watch what you say on my telephone. It's a party line, remember. I don't want the whole neighbourhood to know about you and your trollops.' It seems she had forgotten that she had just told any would-be eavesdroppers that he was busy betraying his mistress with his wife.

Father gave the number and waited to be connected. It didn't take long. His voice was cold as he spoke into the mouthpiece. 'Didn't I tell you not to ring me here? What do you want?' He listened for what felt like a long time. I was getting cramp huddled up in the shadows of the upstairs landing.

'For Christ's sake, you fucking idiot, she's getting you at it. Of course I have my trousers on. We were arguing about Pots. She's letting him run wild. She's getting her own back – that's all.' There was another silence, then he laughed bitterly. 'That's all we need.' He sighed heavily. 'All right, I'll set out now.'

I heard the receiver go down. 'I've got to go,' he said to my mother. 'The silly cow's got her knickers in some sort of twist, no thanks to you. Sorry I won't have time to see the kids. Better not tell them that I was here. What they don't know, won't hurt them.'

'Oh, I think you hurt them a long time ago, Doug. What's the matter with Gaby? Apart from you, that is.'

He sighed. 'She says she's been to see the doctor; she says she thinks she's gone and got herself pregnant.'

'Wishful thinking, I expect,' Mother observed. 'If she can produce a kid, she probably thinks she stands more chance of keeping you out of your singer's drawers and out of mine. Fat chance. Having two kids didn't stop you from scraping her up out of the gutter, did it?'

'God, you never let anything go, do you?'

'On the contrary, I am letting you go. Go on, back to your slut and leave me in peace. I hope you're right about her condition. What'll become of the kids you already have if you start a family with that baggage?' I could tell by the sound of Mother's voice that the idea worried her a lot. 'And perhaps it's time you knew where babies come from,

Doug. It takes two to make 'em, and I don't suppose for one second that Gaby "got herself pregnant" without any assistance from you' – Mother paused for a heartbeat – 'or some other man who doesn't mind shagging stick insects.'

'Yes, well . . .' Father began, then thought better of it. 'I'd better get going. Here, take this and buy the kids something from me.'

I heard the crackle of money changing hands. After another minute or two, the front door opened and closed, and then there was silence again for two or three minutes. Something heavy hit the wall and shattered.

Then, suddenly, Mother screamed with rage. 'That fucking man!' she roared. In a way, never a truer word was spoken, although, I have to say, I did not understand that at the time. I didn't know that the word 'fucking' actually meant something. I just thought it was a word my parents used – a lot – to show that they were angry. They were allowed to use it, but Peter and I were not, because children were not allowed to be cross.

Mother made the first move towards divorce proceedings while she was still seething with rage. She called a solicitor and made an appointment for the following Monday, at 4.30, straight after school. According to what she told me later, the pending divorce did not stop Father trying to seduce her now and then. Divorces took years in those days, even if there was a guilty party living in blatant sin with the co-respondent, so he had plenty of time to try to wear down Mother's resistance, but she managed to keep her new-found resolve and she never allowed Father into her bed, or her underwear, again.

*

It was around this time that I became aware that Mother was taking lovers of her own. Whether it was a case of what was good for the cock was good for the hen, I really couldn't say. Mother was a lonely, highly sexed woman, and if Father was no longer servicing her, it was probably inevitable that she would look elsewhere for the attention that she needed. She usually found it in the pub. Mother's drinking was getting worse, and her self-respect took even more of a battering as she kept waking up to thumping hangovers and strange men in her bed. It was an awful period for us all – and one that I find deeply painful to write about, even now. Sadly, alcoholism can and does rob the sufferer of their self-esteem and their morality, so that they wind up doing things that, if they were sober, would shock and disgust them to the core. It is so hard for children to watch someone they love being diminished inch by painful inch, and it is even harder for them to understand why. Like any other child in that position, I blamed myself. If only I could have been a good enough daughter, I believed, Mother's disintegration would have stopped.

Gaby's pregnancy was a false alarm on that occasion, but it was not too long before she did indeed become pregnant. I know because she told me. I can't have been very old when she did, seven or eight maybe. It was on one of our first trips to the South of France. Father drove us there, and Gaby was in an ugly mood. It was hot and stuffy in the car, and the drive was long. As usual, it was difficult to get Father to stop for enough food and loo breaks, and we were all tired, thirsty and irritable by the time we arrived at Madame Belardinelli's, the pension in Nice where we usually stayed.

The curtains in the dining room were drawn closed to shut out the blistering afternoon sun and keep the room cool. We ate a hasty and, by Madame Belardinelli's standards, skimpy meal of omelettes and green salad dressed with vinaigrette, then headed for the Lido Plage, the beach we favoured on the Promenade des Anglaises.

Nice was such a different world from the housing estate in Essex, and even from Soho, which, although it had a much more continental air about it, was still grey, sooty and damp when we had left, even though it was August. Nice was basking beneath a hot sun, the Mediterranean was a tempting blue and a line of alien, but stately palm trees marched along the parched grass that ran along the centre of the Promenade des Anglaises. Some of the buildings that faced the sea looked frothy and edible, as if they had been spun out of the sugar icing that Soho's master bakers used to make their fancy birthday cakes. Others dripped rosy or purple bougainvillaea from sturdy trellises.

The sea front itself was divided up into private beaches that you had to pay to go on. There was no sand, but decking covered the stones and these decks, in turn, were covered in jauntily striped parasols and loungers, which had thick, colourful mattresses that made them so comfortable, it was almost like being on your own bed. Elegant ladies, clad in brilliantly coloured beach wear and large sunglasses, draped themselves like exotic butterflies on the loungers and smoothed fragrant unguents on to their bronzed limbs.

Every café and restaurant had tables outside on the wide pavements. Each had its own colour scheme, with ruby red, navy blue, bottle green or amber yellow tablecloths, and parasols and awnings fluttering like flags in the light breeze. The poshest places had thick, white, starched tablecloths with discreet dark blue or dark green piping at the edges. Glittering glassware and cutlery rivalled the blue-green sea for sparkle. Waiters, smartly dressed in black trousers and waistcoats, with brilliant white shirts and aprons, weaved gracefully between the tables, laden trays held high above their heads, beautifully balanced on one well-practised hand. In England, service was nearly always grudging, but in the South of France it was elevated to an art form. I always loved to watch the waiters. I never, not once, saw one drop anything, even if an unsteady customer barged into them, or inadvertently shoved their chair back into a waiter's passing knees.

The smell of the place was distinctive, too, made up as it was of rich French cooking laden with fish, garlic and wine, freshly ground coffee, Ambre Solaire sun cream, myriad French perfumes and sun-baked stones and pavements. In the backround were the scents of the thyme, rosemary and oregano that sprouted from terracotta pots, wooden window-boxes and old tin cans that stood on doorsteps, balconies and windowsills, whence they could be plucked to be popped into a steaming pot or a spluttering pan. Sometimes, if the wind was in the north, the heady perfume of lavender and the scent of cloves given off by acres and acres of pinks and carnations would waft in from Grasse. If I was blindfolded, I would know Nice again if I sniffed the air on a hot day, even after forty years and more.

Father disappeared off somewhere, leaving Gaby to look after Peter and me. Peter was much more independent, and soon found some French boys to play with.

'Why can't *you* find someone to play with?' Gaby asked me. I could not find the words to explain that I was too shy to approach strangers, especially strangers who did not even speak the same language as me. 'I want to lie down in the sun, I'm tired and I don't feel well. Go somewhere and play,' said Gaby imperiously.

With frightened tears threatening, I beat a hasty retreat into the shaded arches that formed the bar, dressing rooms and showers of the Lido Plage, to play as instructed. This subterranean area beneath the pavement of the Promenade is where the kindly Madame Albert, the beautifully dressed, coiffured, perfumed and dignified owner of the Lido usually sat, guarding her till. She soon noticed that I was lonely and in need of a little comfort.

'Look what I 'ave.' Madame Albert smiled widely. 'Someone left these. They are English, non?' With a flourish, like a magician whipping a rabbit out of his hat, she produced a familiar pack of cards from beneath her counter. She ordered Frances, the waiter, to join us and the three of us quietly played Happy Families while Gaby took her nap in the sun.

'Avez-vous Monsieur Bun, le boulanger?' Frances asked Madame Albert.

'Non, I do not.' Madame laughed, delighted, as she turned to me. 'Do you, my little cabbage, 'ave Monsieur Bun the baker?'

I never understood why Madame Albert thought that being called a cabbage was a term of endearment, but I answered to it anyway, and reluctantly handed over Mr Bun. Madame asked Frances for a card, then crowed with triumph and laid down the entire Bun family.

Later, Madame Albert was called away to the telephone, and Frances went to man the bar, leaving me alone again to watch a real life family playing together in the sea. Gaby came to find me. She smiled wanly as she sat down beside me. 'Perhaps it is best if you do not tell your father that I was cross with you,' she suggested. 'He will be very angry with you as well, if you do.' Gaby knew that I would do virtually anything not to make Father angry.

'I am very upset. I am not myself. Your father has forced me to have an operation and now I feel ill and tired.' I didn't know what to say, so I said nothing and continued to stare at the French family tossing a large, orange, inflatable beachball to one another, and shrieking when one of them missed their catch and had to swim after it.

And so I listened to my father's unhappy lover and watched the Beachball Family, as I'd decided to call them, splashing each other, the droplets of water glittering like diamonds in the sunlight. I tried to shut out Gaby's voice, and wondered what it would be like to belong to a family like that. Try as I might, I could not imagine it. As I watched them, I waited tensely for their laughter to dissolve into ugly shouting and their playful splashing to turn to slaps, but they played on happily, until finally, when the game was over, they all climbed out of the sea and chatted together as they took turns to dry each other's backs.

Meanwhile, Gaby's voice carried on and on, telling me things that I didn't want to hear: that my father had 'forced' her to have an abortion, and how very deeply she regretted it. That day, under the arches at the Lido Plage, was the first time I heard about this, but it wasn't to be the last. Gaby told me it many times over the years. Somehow, young as I was, I had become her reluctant confidante.

It was only when I was grown up that I began to wonder how a man could force a fully grown woman to lie still long enough to be given an anaesthetic and then to have an operation performed on her against her will. And whether any doctor, even an abortionist, would allow such a thing to happen. I was told that the doctor that they used was not a sleazy, backstreet type, but a Harley Street gynaecologist who would have had far too much to lose ever to consider performing operations on unwilling women. I hardly think the Harley Street man would have allowed Father to talk him into 'forcing' Gaby on to his operating table. 'Forced' was the wrong word; coerced, pressurized or persuaded were probably nearer the mark.

Being an unwed mother in 1950s England was a fate Gaby simply could not, would not face. She would have been left with only two other options: go through the pregnancy and have the baby adopted, or go for the operation. She must have chosen the operation, but in my opinion she spent the rest of her life blaming Father, Peter and me for it.

It is only as I write about it that I realize how both of Father's wives had their abortion stories, and how very different they were, with Gaby's the best that money could buy, while my poor mother was driven to perform a do-it-yourself job with a size eight knitting needle.

I have often wondered, as I've grown older, if Gaby was aware how the continuous drip-feed of her confidences was systematically destroying my relationship with my father. I still don't know. I now think how unhappy she must have been, and how lonely and isolated she must have felt. I see more clearly now that we were both victims of my father's alcoholism. We both loved him, no matter how unreasonable his demands or how miserable he made us feel. In the forty-odd years that I knew her, I only saw her with just one close female friend, and that poor woman died of breast cancer, when Gaby was in her late thirties.

At other times, I believe that Gaby knew exactly what she was doing. I think she saw me as a rival, and was determined to put me out of the running for Father's affection. Keeping Father all to herself must have felt like a priority, and if his relationship with his children was a casualty, then hard luck. Her need was greater than ours – if she recognized that we had needs at all.

It seems to me now that Gaby was not able to empathize with me easily. Peter always loathed Gaby too, from the moment he first got to know her, right up until the day that he died. Sadly, as I was only five when she came into our lives, I was more impressionable, and spent decades trying in vain to please her by listening to her stories of Father's wickedness and cruelty. It never seemed to occur to me, when I was very young, to wonder why she simply did not leave him and find herself a single man, unencumbered with an unwanted wife and children.

And so I listened, and I have wished many times since that I had not. I was too young. It was inappropriate and, ultimately, it was very destructive, because it drove a wedge between my father and me that neither of us was ever able to talk about or get rid of.

11

Goodbye, Pots

'I've decided to send Pots to boarding-school,' Father announced. 'He failed that damned eleven-plus thing, and now, according to his reports, he's failing in that shit-hole of a secondary school. All it's fit for is churning out gutter-snipes and factory fodder, and no son of mine is going to wind up working in a fucking factory.'

The thing about alcoholism is that it gets worse as time goes on, although the rate at which it progresses varies quite considerably from person to person. Some boozers take decades to graduate from the odd drink to dedicated old soak, while others seem to dive in head first and rarely, if ever, come up for air and a nice cup of tea again.

In Mother's case, losing her drinking companion/ husband was a devastating blow, and the resulting depression and bitterness helped to accelerate her drinking to the point where she was becoming increasingly difficult to live with. Her temper became more and more uncertain as her benders became more frequent, lasted for longer and involved shifting even more booze from glass to gullet. What's more, she was beginning to lose her moral judgement, and was bringing all sorts of deadbeats home from the pub to puke on our carpets, pee in our pot plants, share her bed and, on occasions, to scare Peter and me half to death during their midnight ramblings. It got so bad that we demanded – and got – bolts to put on the inside of our bedroom doors.

We developed an elaborate system of knocks on the wall to let each other know how we were doing. Two taps meant, 'Are you OK?' This enquiry would be answered with one for 'no' and three for 'yes'. Two taps followed by a pause and then another two taps indicated that the tapper was going to attempt to reach the other for company and comfort. The 'I'm on my way' signal became an increasingly rare one, because it meant that the one who was moving had to leave their bedroom door unbolted, and there was no telling what we'd come back to. A stranger snoring on your bed was the least of it; we discovered the hard way that they often stole things, broke things, peed themselves when they were asleep, threw up all over the place or set fire to the blankets when a lighted fag dropped from their fingers as they fell into a sodden stupor.

So it was hardly a surprise that Peter was ecstatic to hear that he was going away to school. He had read his fair share of Billy Bunter and Molesworth books, and he thought that life at a boarding-school would be 'whizzo', 'wizard' and downright wonderful.

'We'll have pillow fights in the dorm,' he told me dreamily. 'We'll have midnight feasts and tuck-boxes full of chocolate and biscuits and crisps and everything,' he added, enjoying the sight of his skin and blister (sister) going green with envy.

I thought there were times when a body could positively dislike her brother, and talk of tuck-boxes was more than enough to do it.

Mother was also keen on the idea of Peter going away to school, but she did not let on immediately. 'Do I have any say in the matter?' she asked Father when he made his announcement. Her tone was deceptively mild, but Father was not fooled for a moment.

'Of course, he's your son as well. But I can't see how you could object if you want what's best for him. You can't deny the boy's failing.'

It was true, Mother could not deny it. To her huge disappointment, neither of her children was a conspicuous success in the classroom. If he was in a smaller class, Peter might have learned something. Classes in state schools were huge in those days, sometimes there were as many as forty-nine children in one form, when the maximum allowed, I believe, was fifty. Throughout my school career, I was generally in a class of forty-eight. Needless to say, only the most determined and the most disruptive pupils managed to attract their teacher's attention in the scrum. Peter's public school, on the other hand, would have classes of just twelve pupils. Besides, the plan would get one of her kids out of Mother's hair.

Shortly after the announcement was made, Peter and

Gaby embarked on an orgy of shopping in the West End. The list of things that he needed seemed to have no end to it. There was summer uniform, winter uniform, a trunk, a tuck-box, pens, pencils, sports equipment and sports kit, including something called a jock-strap which I did not understand until Peter patiently explained.

'You know that boys have dangling bits that girls don't have?' he asked, and I nodded, having seen them many times. 'Well, a jock-strap is meant to keep all those bits tucked out of the way, so that when you're high-jumping or something like that, your balls don't hit the bar and make you sick, like that time you kicked me in the goolies.'

I remembered the occasion well. 'Come on, try to kick the ball,' Peter had instructed for the umpteenth time. I had caught on, though, and shook my head defiantly. The problem was, he was holding the ball, and every time I tried to kick it, he moved it away at the last second, so I came a cropper and landed on my bum. I wasn't going to fall for it again. 'I won't move it this time, I promise,' he said.

'Cross your heart and hope to die?'

'Yep, cross my heart and hope to . . .' He never got to finish the oath, because I took a hefty swing at the ball with my navy blue Clark's sandal. Unfortunately, Peter wasn't ready: I somehow managed to miss the big leather ball altogether, and my foot hit the far more delicate set that, being a boy, he kept about his person. The poor chap had doubled over in agony and promptly chucked his socks up all over the lawn. I, needless to say, had been mesmerized by the spectacle. It was the first time ever that I had managed to come out on top in one of our games.

Peter, being so much older, had always been able to beat me at everything. Like the time he had got me to swap my sixpence for his penny, on the grounds that his penny was so much bigger in size. He never mentioned value, the ratbag. More recently, he had put a very realistic plastic dog's turd, bought at the Romford Joke Shop with his pocket money, right in the middle of the hallway. When Mother had discovered it and, believing it to be real, had let out a roar of fury and demanded to know which 'dirty little bastard' had made such a disgusting mess, Peter had solemnly pointed at me. I received such a thorough tongue-lashing that Mother didn't pause for breath long enough for me to explain, so I bent down to pick it up, to show her that it was a fake.

'You filthy little cow!' she screamed. 'Leave that shit alone. Don't you dare touch it with your bare hands, you idiot. I'll clear it up.'

Of course, when she tried, she realized she had been had by one of Peter's practical jokes. That set them both off and they were so busy laughing at me that neither of them ever thought to apologize for the trouble I'd got into, or for calling me a 'filthy little cow' when I wasn't.

When all Peter's shopping was done, his trunk packed and re-packed, and the long summer holiday had come and gone, it was time to leave for his new school. All the new boys were supposed to meet at Waterloo station, with their trunks and much-envied tuck-boxes. As always, Father wanted to march to a different drummer, and had offered to fly Peter to school in a Tiger Moth. However, Mother put her foot down and declared that he would go by train, just like all the other new boys. 'That way, we can all wave goodbye, he can get to know some of the other new boys on the journey and, what's more, he won't arrive covered in vomit – with any luck. You know he's always sick in air-craft. Besides, how would you transport that bloody great trunk?'

Common sense prevailed, and when the great day came, Father arrived in the car to take us, along with Peter's luggage, to the railway station.

When we arrived at sooty old Waterloo, pigeons were perched high in the ornamental iron girders that held the roof up, and cooed their sympathy before loosing their smelly droppings on to the heads and shoulders of the unwary. There were many boys dressed in greyish herring-bone suits milling about, along with their parents. We joined the crowd around the luggage van and added Peter's trunk to the ones waiting to be loaded on the train. We watched in edgy silence as two porters heaved trunk after trunk effort-lessly into the mouth of the van and two more porters stowed them neatly away. Once we had seen Peter's lug-gage safely into the van, we all stood about, not knowing quite what to do or to say. Peter was itching to start his adventure, I was struck dumb with misery and Mother, Father and Gaby tried to make small talk that did not degenerate into a screaming row and embarrass us all.

Eventually, a little man with a Hitler moustache and patent leather hair appeared and coughed loudly before asking for our attention. Boys and parents waited obediently for the little man to embark on his speech.

'Good morning, everyone. My name is Watkins, and I am here, with my two colleagues, Mr Soames and Miss Langley, our Matron, to see the boys safely on board and to accompany them all the way to the school. Parents and relatives may, of course, stay for the formalities before our departure. I shall now read out the names of the boys who will be coming with us. Please listen carefully and indicate that you are here by raising your hand and answering "Yes sir," when your name is called.

'Andrews, M. Anstruther, P.' The list went on and on. When his name came, Peter's hand shot up and he answered 'Yes sir' in a loud, clear, ringing and joyful tone that seemed to bounce off the roof. There was no trace of the wobble that had afflicted the voices of some of the other, less keen, boys.

When Mr Watkins was done, he went on to instruct the boys to say their farewells to their families, then to form a crocodile, in pairs, and to proceed to board the train where they would be met by Matron and Mr Soames.

Peter wasn't even remotely sad. He kissed Mother, shook hands with Father, told Gaby goodbye and finally turned to me. 'Keep your powder dry, Midget, and stay out of my bedroom,' he instructed, with a private wink of one of his large, blue-grey eyes. He leaned closer and whispered, 'And make sure you stay well out of Uncle Will's way. Whatever you do, don't get left alone with him.' Then he ruffled my hair and joined the crocodile of boys climbing on to the train.

I felt desolate as I watched my brother moving slowly towards the carriage door, ready to be swallowed up whole by the long, snake-like train. Blinking back the tears, I watched some of the other families making their farewells. I was touched by the way these mothers flicked away imaginary dust from their sons' collars, straightened their school ties, tugged at blazer hems, in fact anything that would prolong physical contact with their boys without making their sons feel embarrassed because they were being 'soppy'. In contrast, our mother was perfunctory: I could tell that her thoughts were already straying to the pub. I had come to recognize the faraway look that came to her face whenever the siren call of gin was sounding in her inner ear. That look always preceded a dash to the boozer, or the cupboard under the sink where she hid some of her supplies.

Gaby and Father weren't even remotely sad, either, but then, that wasn't too surprising. Gaby and Peter didn't like one another, and the atmosphere between them had rubbed off on Father. He'd become much keener on nagging about Peter's supposed failings since Gaby had taken to pointing them out to him. She had felt compelled to let her own son go in the most permanent way possible, and every time she saw Peter it must have brought the memory of her lost boy closer. I also wonder, now I'm older, if she took pleasure in seeing Mother losing Peter, if only temporarily.

I looked at my three grown-ups waiting, with varying degrees of patience, to leave, then looked again at the other families who, in contrast, appeared so reluctant to tear themselves away until the train finally chugged out of sight. Some mothers were snivelling into their hankies, while their stolid husbands patted them gently, offering what comfort they could, manfully trying not to blub themselves. More tears welled up in my own eyes. Like a fool, I had forgotten to bring my hanky, so I wiped my nose on my sleeve. 'Don't do that, you grubby little tyke,' Mother snapped. 'I've got to wash that. Here, take my handkerchief, I don't need it.'

I heard the hiss of the brakes being released, saw and smelt the steam belch from the engine, and slowly, slowly the train began to inch its way out of the station. Peter's blond, tousled head poked out of a window and he beckoned to me. I galloped along the platform until I was alongside and he said, 'Look after yourself, little 'un, look after Mummy if you can, and look under my bed – you can have my skates.' He smiled at my stricken face. 'I'll be back for the Christmas holiday before you know it.'

The train sped up, and I couldn't keep up with it any longer. I sank to the ground and howled.

I was inconsolable. My brother had gone away. I had been left behind and I thought my heart would break. I was alone with Mother, and even before we arrived back home, I was lonely and afraid. There was no one to jolly me along. There was no one who understood without being told. I had lost my ally, my protector and my friend as well as my brother. And even though everyone told me that he would be back, I had a sneaking feeling that they were lying; that, like my father before him, he was gone for good. And in a way, he was. The person who returned to us was a posh stranger, one who was embarrassed by his humble home and his skin and blister with her cockney accent, littered with the nasal vowels and missing initial hs and final ts, that used to drive our mother mad.

Peter was thirteen years old and I was nine when he was sent away. From then on, I effectively became an only child, with all the aggravation associated with the job, but, sadly for me, virtually none of the perks. It was around this time that my wanderings began in earnest. Up until then, I had contented myself with holing up in one of my various camps when the going got tough at home, but after Peter left I became more adventurous. I loved to go to railway stations and the rapidly developing Heathrow airport. I was used to travelling about London, as Peter and I often got ourselves to Soho by bus, train and tube, for our visits to the Old Compton Street flat.

We also travelled to Nice by ourselves on several occasions, so I knew the route to Heathrow as well. The form was that Mother would see us off at the airport, complete with baggage tags around our necks, and Father and Gaby would meet us at Nice. In between Heathrow and Nice, the air hostesses and the pilots of the Comet aircraft we flew on spoilt us something rotten, with loads of special attention. As Comets did not have pressurized cabins, passengers were given boiled sweets, usually barley sugar, to suck to help to equalize the pressure in our ears. Peter and I always got more than our fair share of barley sugar and, if the flight was smooth, we spent quite a bit of it in the cockpit with the pilot and his co-pilot. In those days, airline pilots were always men.

The only problem we ever had on those flights was Peter being copiously sick at some point in the journey, which earned him enormous sympathy from the stewardesses, who clucked around him like so many well-groomed mother hens. The barfing into a bag took some of the gilt off the gingerbread for poor Peter, but not for me. Father used to love to tell the story of the time when we arrived in Nice and I skipped down the gangway and across the tarmac way ahead of my green-to-the-gills brother, yelling, 'Daddy, Daddy, Peter was sick, but it's all right, I ate his dinner.'

Once Peter was away at school, I spent more and more of my time and pocket money hanging around railway buffets and the airport. Looking back at it now, I wonder that nobody – not least my mother – seemed to worry about where I had gone. I loved to watch the people going about their lives. I noticed very quickly that people in transit are less guarded in their behaviour if they believe they are unobserved by anyone they may have to see again. What is more, I felt anonymous and safe among the crowds who were taking absolutely no notice of me. It was such a relief to be away from my mother, her drinking and her moods.

I was in my element in a railway station buffet, tucked away in my corner. There was something about the belching urn, the steamed-up windows, the clatter of thick, white cups on thick, white saucers, the chatter of a dozen voices and the constant opening and closing of the door that allowed a little whoosh of cold air into the room, that I found comforting. I loved watching the people come and go, and tuning in to snatches of conversation.

'I told her it weren't natural. But would she listen? No she would not. She went ahead, not a care in the world, and we all know what that led to . . .'

I wanted to tell the plump lady in the worn, grey flannel coat and the moth-eaten, tartan headscarf that I didn't know what it had led to, or indeed, what hadn't been natural about it in the first place. But of course, I kept schtum. I couldn't draw attention to myself, because that would lead to awkward questions, like Where was my mummy? and Was I all by myself? Stuff like that. The truth was, I don't think my mother cared much where I was, as long as I wasn't under her feet or in her way.

'I turned around and told him, "You talk to Dick about it," I said. "He'll tell you what's what and all about it. I'm a chiropodist, feet are my line," I told him. "I don't know anything about lead flashing or leaky roofs."'

'I didn't like her right from the very start.' The younger woman's lips thinned, her eyes narrowed and her pretty youthful face, with yellow hair, was transformed for an instant into that of her mother, who sat across the table from her. 'And how right I was.'

'What do you mean?' the older woman asked, leaning forward a little so that her chair creaked loudly in a sudden silence. We all waited. Yes, what did she mean? The girl with the yellow hair blushed at being thrust into unwelcome limelight.

'I'll tell you later.' You could almost feel the gale as twenty sets of lungs let the air out. That was typical, that was: a story would start well, only to fizzle out, or be brought to an abrupt end by the arrival of a third party, an untimely attack of discretion or the announcement that the 2.39 from Southend was approaching platform three.

I always took particular notice of families. I liked to watch how they got along together and compare it to the way my lot carried on. As I grew older, the oddness of our set-up became more and more apparent to me. If a man was with a party that included mother and children, I found that I tensed, waiting for an argument to break out, and was always amazed when one didn't. I was incredulous – and more than a little envious – when families laughed together at shared jokes, teased one another in a good-natured way, and then rose from their table, leaving all the china intact. Such families actually appeared to enjoy one another's company! This was a huge revelation to me, because I had never realized that such a thing was possible. I always noticed when young children grew strident with excitement, or shrieked with merriment, and nobody said, 'Shut up, for Christ's sake, can't you see I've got a headache?' To this day, I am genuinely surprised if I see parents, particularly fathers, playing with their children and looking as if they are enjoying it.

I remember the 1950s as a Golden Age of gloves. There

were summer gloves, winter gloves, and spring and autumn gloves, too. Spring and summer gloves were made of cloth or lace, or were crocheted, and were white or cream for the most part, although other colours could be worn with formal wear, to match a gown. Autumn and winter gloves were leather, and in winter, fur was a popular choice, too. Colour usually hinted at the season. Dark green, russet tones or light tan were autumn colours, definitely. Dark brown or black were for winter. A very pale tan pair of gloves on a man suggested 'spiv' straight away, or 'cad' at the very least. Red gloves, like red shoes, screamed 'tart' or, just possibly, 'arty', depending on what was worn with them.

Some people coming into a room in the 1950s could make a whole business out of fiddling their way out of a pair of gloves. Gloves are very handy for appearing to take a lot of attention, while leaving the eyes free to take in the room.

While some made removing their gloves into a performance, an art form even – stroking each finger out of its sheath, peeling back the body of the glove and then, with a flourish, whisking the whole thing off with a nifty final twirl – others simply took their gloves off and made no bones about it.

Once you were in a station buffet, there was a limited range of options. You could bag a table by leaving a shopping bag on one of the seats, or approach the counter to order first, then worry about a seat. In the 1950s, self-service was still a very newfangled thing, and hadn't yet taken off. So there was no necessity to juggle gloves, handbag, shopping bag and umbrella with a tray that held a scalding hot pot of tea, a jug of milk, a bowl of sugar, a cup, a saucer and a spoon. All you had to do was sail from the counter to a seat, and your order would follow along in due course.

Selecting a seat was fraught with difficulty for the naturally reserved English person. A lone woman would not sit at a table with a lone male if she could help it. It was far better to sit with another single woman or, better still, a woman with a child. That way, both women could concentrate on the kid, and it gave them a topic of conversation that allowed them to overcome the awkwardness of strangers sitting together at a table.

'What an adorable little boy. How old is he?' the new arrival would ask.

'Thank you. John is just two and a half.' John's mother would answer proudly.

I'm not sure how I managed to melt into the background the way I did on these jaunts, but few people seemed to notice me, so I must have been quite good at it. I suppose I had honed my melting-into-the-background skills early in life when I tagged along after my father as he made his restless rounds of his favourite Soho haunts, negotiated with French booksellers in his fractured French or swapped tall stories with his drinking pals. While he chatted, wheeled, dealed, argued and philosophized above my head, I watched the world going on around me and listened intently.

I have never really understood what adults think children are doing while they wait for them to stop nattering; they seem to forget that children have ears and eyes and are busy taking everything in. Equally, as a child, I never understood those children who just stood there, eyes glazed with boredom, while their adults talked.

I was always interested in what other people were talking about or doing, and I still am. I can listen in fascination to gossip about the minutiae of the lives of people that I am never likely to meet, and if I am trapped with a load of strangers, say on a train that is stuck because of leaves or cows on the line, I am content to make up stories about my fellow passengers to amuse myself and pass the time. No wonder I eventually became a novelist. I have been observing human behaviour, practising storytelling and learning about dialogue through eavesdropping all my life. It is as if I knew that being a nosy little bugger would come in handy one day. And blow me, it did!

12

The Three o'Clock Tribunals

The divorce came through.

One day towards the end of 1955, I found my mother sitting at the bottom of the stairs with tears in her eyes and a large brown envelope clutched in her hand. 'Are you all right?' I asked as I slipped a tentative arm around her shoulders, uncertain as to whether I'd be told to 'Piss off and leave me alone' or not.

On this occasion, as it was a school-day morning in the middle of a week, Mother was not only sober, but not even remotely hungover either, and she was grateful for the comforting arm. She was going through a period when she reserved her drinking for weekends, as far as she was able. There were occasions when she failed in her efforts at control, but the night before had not been one of them.

'Not really, darling,' she answered gently. 'But I will be.' She squared her shoulders, stiffened her upper lip, got her coat on and handed me mine. It was time for us to head towards our respective schools.

I felt particularly lonely that morning on the way to school – and again in the afternoon on my way home. In the good old days, I would have had Peter for company. Mother had looked so sad when she got her letter and I knew that, had Peter still been at home, he would have made her laugh. I didn't have the knack somehow, and the house still felt so empty without him. I missed him most when Mother needed cheering up, because he was so good at that. It was also miserable getting in from school and having no one to talk to – or to squabble with, which was more usual.

That evening, I was anxious as I let myself into the house because it had been obvious that Mother had received a hefty blow. I was dreadfully worried that she would hit the bottle to cheer herself up, and I was racking my brains trying to think of something to take her mind off things. Try as I might, I could come up with nothing. In the end, all I could think of to do was to wash up our breakfast things, put a match to the fire and to get the sausage dish on for our tea. At least, if I did those things, all Mother would have to do when she got in was relax with a coffee, her fags and her newspaper. Personally, I always found the smell of cooking very comforting when I walked into the house, and I hoped like mad that Mother would feel the same.

Mother always insisted to her friends that she was thrilled to be free of Father at last. I knew better, because I saw her tears and heard her crying herself to sleep for quite some time after the official notification of the divorce came through. It was her second dead marriage, although I only discovered that when I was an adult. Apparently, the first had been a rebound job that she was terribly ashamed of and kept a secret from Peter and me throughout our childhood. We only discovered it by accident when we came across her first set of divorce papers when we were looking for something else. Two divorces must have felt dreadful to a woman who had such a low tolerance of any hint of failure.

'Do you mind?' I overheard Mother's friend Myrna ask, through a mouth full of chocolate biscuit, a few days later. 'About the divorce, I mean?'

'Not half as much as Doug does.' Mother laughed bitterly. 'It means Gaby will finally get him up the aisle. He's been trying to dodge that all along, and now he can't use me as the excuse any longer. The bloody man is footloose and fancy free. At least, he is for the time being, but I wouldn't put any money on that state of affairs lasting for very long.'

'So they'll definitely be getting married then?'

'Oh, yes. But I've no idea when they'll do the deed. The damned thing is so hush-hush, you'd think it was a military secret. It's just as well neither of them has access to a tank, is all I can say. Doug and I used to fight, God knows, but those two are really dedicated.' Mother paused for a moment. 'Why that idiot insists on marrying him, I really could not say. And why he's not heading for the hills at a rate of knots is another question, too. You would have thought that living together for a few years would have cured them both of that particular insanity, but it hasn't. So, there'll be a wedding all right, but when we'll get to hear about it is another matter altogether. Probably not until after the event.'

When I was younger, I often asked myself what kind of person marries a violent drunk. And my father *was* a violent drunk. I was told that on one occasion, he threw Gaby down most of the sixty-five stairs that descended from their flat to the street. And that was just once: I know there were more, because Gaby would insist on telling me all about them.

Time and more experience of life has supplied one answer to my question. That is, that a romantic will marry a violent drunk, happy in the knowledge that she can change him. I'm sure there are other answers too, but I have learned that romantics will believe what they want to believe, and nothing will shift them once their minds are made up. And Gaby's mind *was* made up. Despite four years of living with him, Gaby finally got her man to mutter 'I do' in the spring of 1956.

Still, like many a romantic before and since, Gaby had a handy get-out clause if reality failed to live up to the fantasy. She could simply blame Father for not responding to the ministrations of a good woman, as he was supposed to do. And she did. Never, in all the years that I listened to her blaming Father for their collective misery, did she ever address the issue of the part that she may have played in forming, and maintaining, their unhappy, dysfunctional and abusive union.

*

185

I caused quite a stir the first time I walked into the scruffy old room above a pub with my father one wet Sunday afternoon. I had been to many a peculiar place with Father in my time, including snooker halls, drinking clubs, spielers and dirty book shops, and all had been tucked away out of sight, down a dark alley or above a legitimate delicatessen, shoe shop or antiques emporium, but there was something particularly odd about the men and women I could glimpse through the dense haze of cigarette smoke. The air was so thick with it, it was making my eyes water. At first glance, it was difficult to see the individual members of the group.

'What ho, Douglas old chap. And who is this little lady? Isn't she just a tad young to be in trouble with the demon booze already, or did you feed it to her with her mother's milk?'

I realize now, of course, that, as a baby, I probably did get more than my fair share of booze in my milk, and even while still in the womb. Mother often said that, when she was pregnant with me, she survived largely on chalk stolen from the pub's dartboard (other chalk would not do, apparently) and the large jars of pickled onions that were kept on the bar. She didn't mention the endless fags and industrial quantities of alcohol, but I think we can take them as read.

'Very funny, Julian,' my father answered. 'This is my daughter, and I'm meeting her mother here later.' The man he was speaking to was vaguely familiar. He had a cut-glass accent and incredibly shabby clothes. His pinstripe trousers were shiny at the knees, and his turn-ups frayed and tatty;

his black jacket had a light sprinkling of dandruff on the collar, and was also frayed, this time at the cuffs, as was his grimy shirt. His tightly knotted old school tie – or perhaps it was a regimental job – was almost clean, with just the odd spot of soup here and there. The upper of one of his battered black brogues was trying to part company with the sole, so that it made a soft, slapping noise as he walked towards us.

His face was coarse-skinned and red, as if he spent most of his time out of doors in all weathers, while the wrath of grapes showed up clearly in the twisted, thread-like veins that scurried frantically across his nose and cheeks. He squinted slightly as the smoke from his Woodbine curled past his grey eyes on its journey to join the rest of the fag fug that hung just below the ceiling.

Greetings over, all three of us moved as one towards a table at the back of the room. It was stocked with an urn, a large metal teapot, several cups and saucers, a bag of Tate and Lyle sugar with a spoon sticking out of it, three bottles of milk, one opened, a plate of assorted broken biscuits and, next to that, another plate of slightly curled fish-paste sandwiches.

It was when I clapped eyes on the sandwiches that I remembered where I had seen Julian before. He was one of the small army of sandwich-board men who paraded up and down the streets of the West End, advertising patent remedies such as Friar's Balsam and Doctor Collis Browne's mixture. They also advertised restaurants, clubs, shoe shops, dress shops, gents' outfitters and various food emporia on their boards. One even told us that THE END OF

THE WORLD IS NIGH, which scared me half to death until Father assured me that 'it was a load of Christian cobblers' and that I was not to take any notice of 'all that bollocks'.

I hung tightly on to my father's hand as I tried to take in what I was seeing. I was a shy nine-year-old, and I was overawed by this peculiar bunch of people. The tea lady behind the table was a heavily made-up woman who wore a lopsided hat with feathers and a dead fox draped over her shoulders. She twinkled at us as we approached.

'Don't tell me, Doug, dear, you like yours weak with a gallon of milk and four sugars – you greedy sod. And for young missy here? Can I interest you in a cup of milk and a nice Bourbon biscuit?' When she smiled at me, I noticed that she had bright orange lipstick smeared on her teeth, but I was too polite to tell her. I was not about to upset anyone who was offering me a Bourbon biscuit, and anyway, I liked her twinkly eyes. They looked kind.

I nodded silently. 'What do you say?' Father prompted.

'Yes, please,' I answered quickly, too afraid to say that she could forget about the warm milk. I got enough of that at school. I hated milk. For some reason, the little bottles of school milk were usually plonked right next to the radiator and it was always lukewarm, in the winter as well as in the hot days of summer. It was disgusting.

'Thanks, Hazel.' Father smiled back. 'This is my daughter,' he told her, with a touch of pride – or so I like to think. He turned to me. 'Take your milk and biscuit over there, and sit quietly while I say hello to a few people.'

'Oh, don't send the poor little mite off on her own,

leave her with me. I like kids,' Hazel told him. She winked at me. 'I always wanted a little girl like you, so I can pretend for a little while that you're mine – that's if you don't mind?'

I shook my head, still too shy to speak without serious prompting. I sat on the chair that she indicated and placed the hated milk on an empty seat beside me. While she got on with serving the men and women around us, I was free to give them all the once-over. I liked people-watching, but even I had never seen quite such an unusual selection of people socializing together before. In the 1950s, the posh usually stuck with the posh, working people usually stuck with working people, tramps with tramps, the middle lot with the middle lot, and so on through the myriad levels of the English class system. If you saw a working man talking to a posh lady, it was usually because he was receiving instructions on what she wanted him to do first, clear the drains or paint the guttering; they did not stand around idly chatting, the way the motley crew in front of me were doing.

Another thing that struck me as most peculiar was that nobody seemed to have a surname. Normally, people would be introduced as 'Mrs This', 'Mr That' and 'Lord and Lady How's-Your-Father' and you only got to know their Christian names when you became friends. Nobody, but nobody, introduced an adult to a child by using the adult's first name. Children, in their turn, never used a grown-up person's given name, even if they knew it, unless the adult in question was a relative or a close family friend; then it was always preceded by an 'Auntie' or an 'Uncle', even if they were no such thing.

A short man with wildly bowed legs and few teeth was hailed by Julian as he sidled through the door. 'Arthur, old man, over here,' he bellowed jovially.

Arthur nodded and approached across the scuffed floor-boards like a crab scuttling along a beach. 'Wotcha, Julian. 'Ow're you doing? I'll just get a cup of splosh and I'll join yer. Strong with two sugars if you please, 'Azel.'

'Right you are, Arthur. How's your better half?'

'Vera's in the pink, ta, 'Azel, now that she's 'ad her feet done. Them corns of 'ers were pinching something cruel, they were. They made working down the caff a bleeding nightmare.'

'You found a job yet, Arthur?' Hazel asked as she poured his tea and popped a couple of Rich Tea biscuits in his saucer.

'Yerse, as it 'appens, I 'ave. I'm doing a bit of portering down Billingsgate for a mate, temporary like, while one of his blokes is on the panel. Poor sod had 'is Chalfonts done, and something went wrong and now 'e can't 'ardly walk, let alone sit down. So, if you fancy a drop of fish of a Friday, I'm yer man.' Arthur grinned, and his gums gleamed dully in the weak light that fought its way through the sooty grime on the window. 'I'll just nip over for a chinwag with old Julian there. Let my Vera know if yer fancy some fish on the cheap.'

'I'll do that Arthur, ta.'

I looked around for my father and spotted him in the

middle of a small huddle of men on the other side of the room. I whispered 'Excuse me' to the ladies and went over to him and gave his sleeve a tug, which he ignored. He was too busy listening to an Irishman with a beautiful soft lilt to his voice.

'People tell me that they used to piss in the bed when they were in drink' – he paused just long enough to make us all wonder what was coming next – 'but I never pissed in the bed in my life – I pissed in the wardrobe.' Father threw back his head and let out a bellow of laughter, and I laughed too, although I couldn't quite see what was so funny, having mopped up more than my fair share of other people's smelly old wee in my time. I tugged again.

'What is it?' he asked irritably. He'd been enjoying the laugh.

'When's Mummy coming to get me?' I asked.

'When she gets here.' Father looked at his watch. 'Any time now, I should think.'

Sure enough, Mother walked nervously through the door a few minutes later, and I galloped over to meet her.

'Hello, Mummy. Can we go soon? *Robin Hood*'s on later.'

But before we could get out of the room, everyone started praying, except my mother and father, who none the less bowed their heads politely and didn't utter a single word about anyone being a God-bothering cretin, which was what usually happened if anyone got holy on them.

'May God grant me the serenity to accept the things I cannot change, the courage to change the things that I can, and the wisdom to know the difference.' The oddly assorted group intoned the words solemnly, and I noticed that neither parent even rolled their eyes, which was a miracle in itself.

Father had found Alcoholics Anonymous, and I was at the Sunday Club with him in the very early days of his membership. AA was an American idea that had made its way across the Atlantic and Father became one of its first, and most enthusiastic, members in this country. It is tempting to believe that Gaby's romantic notion that she could change her new husband had come to fruition, but Father always disputed this. He used to say that an alcoholic may attend a few meetings to keep his spouse quiet, but that no one ever got sober for anyone but themselves. Certainly, over the years that I listened to countless alcoholics talking when they visited him, it did seem that he was right. Family pressure may get a man or a woman into AA meetings, but it couldn't keep them there. The only thing that seemed to work was that the booze-hound in question got so sick of themselves that they simply could not carry on.

'And if their wives, children and dear old mums benefit, so much the better. But if a drunk is determined to carry on drinking, then wives, children, and even their dear old mums can just fuck off and leave him with his bottle,' Father said more than once.

By his own testimony, Father had finally got sick of being drunk. He called his epiphany 'the three o'clock tribunals'. In the early hours of one dark and dreary morning he lay awake, vomiting, shaking and sweating, and saw clearly, for the first time, the kind of man that he had become. And he hated himself. He was sick and tired of the way that alcohol had taken his money, his health and his self-esteem, and decided that he had to do something before he drank himself to death.

'The trouble with drinking yourself into the grave,' he'd say to whoever would listen, 'is that you don't just die; that would be easy. No, you have to go mad first, or worse, drink yourself into a wet brain.' I asked him once what a 'wet brain' was, and he kindly explained – although I rather wished he hadn't, because the pictures it conjured up were gruesome, to say the least.

'Booze, and a great deal of it, over a period of time, turns the brain from something that resembles a large, pinky-red walnut into a grey sort of sludge. Once you've drunk your way into a wet brain, there's no coming back. You have to spend what's left of your life shambling about, seeing things that aren't there and gibbering like an idiot, which of course you are by that time. It's tragic really.'

It was indeed, and it left me wondering why the grey sludge didn't ooze out of earholes and nostrils, but I didn't like to ask. I had bad dreams for some time after he told me the gory details, and saw my mother or father dripping wet brains all over the lino. It was no wonder that Father had decided to stop drinking. Wet brains and madness didn't bear thinking about.

Of course, having found AA and taken to sobriety like a convert takes to God, Father became imbued with a missionary zeal that made Christ and all of his Apostles look like slackers. He made it his business to encourage

Mother and, indeed, her much younger brother, Tony, to knock the booze on the head too.

To give Father his due, he never gave up trying. What's more, contrary to his nature, he was remarkably kind and patient about it as well. Handing me over to Mother at the Sunday Club, after my weekends in London, became a regular thing, and part of Father's devious conversion strategy. The Sunday Club was a special place. Many of the men and women who crawled through the doors of their first AA meeting had lost family and friends during their drinking career. They found that the loneliness of Sundays was a severe strain on their infant sobriety, and thus the Sunday Club was born. It was not a meeting as such, simply a meeting place, where the lonely and desperate could offer company and support for a few hours. I suspect that the club saved a good few lives in its time, because it gave a focus to an otherwise empty day. It was easier for the members not to pick up a drink first thing in the morning if there was understanding company to look forward to later in the day. All they had to do was hang on for a few hours.

My face became quite a familiar one in that shabby little room above that shabby old pub, and in a funny kind of way, I became quite fond of the people in it. The only worrying thing, for me, is that some of the faces would disappear, never to return, and the whisper would go around that they had returned to drinking, had died or, worse, had chucked themselves off one of London's many bridges or in front of a tube train, usually one that was travelling on the Northern Line. I have never understood why the Northern

Line appeared to be so popular with suicides, but apparently it was, and I sometimes wonder if it still is.

I never did know how Father found AA, but once he had found it, he was never to let go of it again. It, and the men and women in it, helped to sustain him for the rest of his life.

13

Uncle Tony

Father's patient nagging finally paid off. With great courage, Mother faced the grim reality of her drinking, joined AA and started her long, and often painful, journey towards recovery. It was an immense relief to everyone – except, perhaps, to the local publicans and some of their regulars.

Mother was at an AA meeting early in her recovery, and I was being baby-sat by one of her friends from school, when the telephone rang. I galloped into the hall to answer it. 'Hello,' I said into the receiver and waited for the caller to identify himself.

'Hello, Porky, is your mother there?' Father often called me 'Porky'; it was short for 'Porky Fat Belle'.

'Hello, Daddy. No, she's at a meeting.'

'Oh well, never mind.' Father put his hand over the mouthpiece, but I could still hear him say to someone who was with him – Gaby, I presumed – 'She says Joan's not there, she's at a meeting. Perhaps I should leave it till another time, when her mother's home.'

I heard a heavily accented female voice answer, but I couldn't make out what Gaby said.

'How are you?' I asked, wondering why he had bothered to phone us if he was only going to talk to Gaby, who was standing right next to him.

'What? Oh, I'm fine, and how are you? How's school?'

'I'm fine, too, and school's school,' I answered. The less said about school the better. My father tended to get a bit cross about school. Once again I heard Gaby's voice talking into his other ear.

'OK, I suppose so.' I could tell Father was reluctant to carry out whatever instructions he was being given.

'I just phoned to tell you that you are expecting a baby brother or sister around Easter. What do you think of that?'

I said nothing. Polite telephone conversations were grown-up stuff, and I had learned that, whenever I was in doubt what to say to my father, it was best to say nothing. It was often safer that way, and anyway, his usual response to my silence was to tell me what he expected me to say. He didn't disappoint.

'Aren't you excited?' Father wanted to know. He sounded deflated by my silence.

'I don't know,' I answered honestly. 'I've only just heard.'

The truth was that I wasn't at all sure how I felt about it, or how I was supposed to feel about it. I wished my mother was there to talk to.

'Goodbye, Daddy,' I said, and hung up.

*

When I got in from shopping at the local greengrocer's a few days later, Mother was on the phone to my grandma.

'We're going to visit him tomorrow, Mother. Any messages?' She listened for a moment. 'OK, I'll tell him. You'll post it on to him, will you?' There was another moment's silence, then, 'That's fine. No, I've got to take her with me, apparently. Gaby's not feeling too well, what with her bloody pregnancy, and they can't have her nearly as often as they used to.'

Grandma made a comment, and Mother answered her rather testily. 'No, a mental hospital is obviously not an ideal place to take a ten-year-old, but what do you suggest I do with her?' Another pause. 'I have no idea how the kids feel about the new brat, they're not saying.' Yet another pause, then, 'I'm sorry, Mother, I didn't mean to sound cross and yes, I'll try to say "baby", and not "brat", in future, but you must admit, the man has impeccable timing. He ups and leaves us just a week before the poor child starts school, doing untold damage there. And now he's going to drop another bra— er, baby, just as she has to move from cosy old primary school to secondary school. As always, how he feels is the only thing that really matters.'

Mother was quiet for a while. Grandma was obviously putting in her two penn'orth. 'As you say, she's been the baby of the family for ten years now, so of course it'll be a shock for her. Look, I'll have to go, she'll be in for lunch soon and I haven't even got it started yet. What? Oh, a nice lamb chop, she's just nipped to the shop to get us something to go with it. Bye for now. Give my love to Father.'

There was a clatter as she put the phone down, and I nipped out again through the back door and made a noisy entrance, so that it looked as if I had just returned with the spuds and greens. I was thoughtful throughout lunch. Going to visit a mental hospital seemed more scary to me than the prospect of a new brother or sister. The new baby was going to happen in the future, whereas we were off to the hospital the very next day.

'Are we there yet?' I asked for about the forty-seventh time. It was a gorgeous day, far too lovely to be stuck in a train carriage that reeked of old fag smoke and the burning coal from the engine. Little did I know then that there would come a day when I'd miss the whiff of a steam train, but at the time, the smell of coal, so redolent of winter, seemed out of place on that beautiful, clear, spring day.

'We'll be there soon. Settle down and read your book.' Despite Mother's instructions, my eyes kept straying from *Swallows and Amazons* to the world racing past the grubby train windows. I wanted to be out there, gulping in fresh air and charging across the grass.

We were on our way to visit my Uncle Tony, my mother's 'baby' brother, who was in hospital once again.

My unfortunate grandparents had had three children. First was my mother, then, a good few years later, Uncle John. Uncle John was severely Down's syndrome – or a Mongoloid, as they used to call them in those days. Then, eighteen years after Mother, Uncle Tony came along. John died at nineteen, never having got out of nappies or having learned to speak or to walk, while Tony, bless him, was an odd, solitary child from the start. 'Boys would knock on the door, asking Tony to come out to play, but he rarely went,' my grandmother told me sadly. 'He preferred to spend his time on his own. I don't know why he was like that, but he always was, even as a very little boy.' Which, no doubt, is why my solitary habits worried Mother so.

Tony was a thwarted musical genius – thwarted because Grandfather forbade him to play his piano once it became obvious that Tony was better at it than him – and a mathematical whiz-kid as well, but he also had a terrible drink problem. According to my mother, he'd line up a dozen or so shorts on a bar and down them methodically, one after another, with absolutely no attempt to be even remotely social about it. He was going for oblivion, with a capital O, and nothing else would do.

Tony had just finished his latest course of 'aversion therapy', and it appeared that he'd be banged up in the bin for a while yet. Whether he'd admitted himself for treatment, or had misbehaved so badly that someone had put him there, I have no way of knowing for sure, but my feeling is that Grandfather had lost patience with him and had had him committed. The only basis I have for that belief is that Mother was acting as a go-between between Grandma and Uncle Tony, which suggests that it was difficult for Grandma to get to see her youngest child. Besides, Grandfather had never been that keen on his younger son, and hints later dropped by Grandma suggest that he had washed his hands of Uncle Tony.

Grandfather was, after all, the son of a Methodist minister, so two alcoholic children must have been very embarrassing for him. He'd had a couple of alcoholic older brothers that he remembered being poured on to the doorstep night after night, until Great-Grandfather, in true Victorian style, had shipped them off to America to get them out of his way. Grandfather's sense of shame had been well honed when he was young, and it must have felt dreadful for him to realize that his children were staggering in the unsteady footsteps of his brothers. Worse, he was not in the position to ship them off to some unsuspecting place well out of his line of vision.

'Are we there yet?'

'Next stop. Now, collect up your stuff and be ready to gallop, because the bus we want to catch is supposed to leave two minutes after the train gets in. No dawdling, or we'll have to wait a couple of hours for the next one.'

I wonder why the big, institutional mental hospitals are nearly always out in the sticks somewhere? Is it because greenery, relieved by the twitter of birds and dotted with the odd herd of cows, and possibly some sheep or horses, is soothing for the troubled? Or was it a question of cheaper land prices in the days when most of them were built? Perhaps it was simply a way to get the 'lunatics' out of sight. It may have been cheaper than doing a Great-Grandfather, and sending them to far-flung countries that might eventually object to being a dumping ground for our unwanted. It may even have been a combination of all those factors, but, in my experience, the larger and most forbidding institutions are usually well away from regular and easy public transport.

Uncle Tony's new hospital was no exception. The main building itself was Victorian Gothic with a lot of small, mean windows, some of which, on the lower floors, were complete with bars. There was a collection of smaller, more modern buildings – huts, really – that huddled around the main edifice like ugly ducklings around an ugly duck. I hated them, and was much happier once we got away from the buildings and I could run around, flap my arms like a bird and whoop a bit before we settled down under a tree to eat our picnic in the beautiful grounds.

Mother and Tony talked about nothing much – the weather, mainly – leaving me free to concentrate on the food and our surroundings. We were sitting on a small hill, under a tree, and it was warm enough to wear just our cardigans and sit on our coats. Tony looked well enough; perhaps a little thinner and paler than usual, but not haggard, or wild-eyed, or anything. There was, though, a nervous, detached air about him. I remember that he kept putting his hand to the corner of his mouth as if he was picking a pimple, only he wasn't; he was rubbing part of his cheek between his thumb and forefinger as if he wanted to rub it away. His wary, wounded, clear blue eyes were focused on something a long way away, something that I couldn't see. I suspect that Mother couldn't either. She nattered on as if she hadn't noticed her brother's faraway mood, but I was sure that she had.

'Mother sends her love, and she says she's popping some of your summer underwear in the post for you, and one or two shirts.'

My mother took a sip of orange squash from the thick, white cup that a nurse had lent us, along with some small plates from the hospital's china cupboard. Then she fished about in an oilskin shopping bag and hauled out three scruffy, greaseproof paper packets. Mother's parcels were always scrappy; she was famous for it. Two of the packets held sandwiches, a different filling in each, and the third held three modest slabs of dark brown, left-over-from-Christmas, very fruity, fruit cake, thick with yellow marzipan and white icing like plaster. Mother always baked two Christmas cakes, one for the holiday and a spare to save in an airtight tin for later. Those were the last three pieces of the spare.

A brown paper bag held three rather tired, past the end of season Cox's apples and three spotty bananas. Finally, with a flourish, Mother produced a small tablecloth in white linen, embroidered with a crinolined lady surrounded by the obligatory hollyhocks, marigolds and cornflowers. It had been made by one of her and Tony's many aunts – or possibly by their own mother, who was no slouch in the handicrafts department, either. There were a lot of embroidered tablecloths, tray-cloths, doilies, runners, arm rests and antimacassars floating about Grandma's large family. Grandma had many handy sisters, who crocheted and tatted as well, then passed on their efforts to their sisters and sisters-in-law as Christmas and birthday presents.

Tony stopped rubbing his face and staring at nothing long enough to laugh gently as the sandwiches and cups of orange squash were laid out on the tablecloth.

'I like the final touch,' he told my mother with a smile.

'I thought you might.' She smiled back. 'Have a sandwich. Cheese or shrimp paste?'

'One of each.'

We all took our share and munched in silence for a while. Past the tall boundary wall, a flock of rather grubby sheep grazed and waited to be shorn of their winter fleeces. Patients wandered the grounds, some in the company of nurses, others alone. Nobody seemed to be making a great effort to talk with one another if their paths crossed, or even to make eye contact, save for the nurses, who chattered brightly to everyone they met, as well as to their charges. I noticed that Tony's eyes were focusing as they followed one particular couple, and his hand went back to its obsessive rubbing. Mother tried to distract his attention with a bit of idle gossip.

'You know Mrs Nichols? The thin-faced woman with the poodles? Turns out she has a previous husband – not Mr Nichols – living just around the corner. And two older children.'

Tony seemed not to hear as he continued to watch the couple – a small, dark-haired nurse and a tall, thin man in a check dressing gown – as they paused at the second hut in the row of four. The nurse knocked on the door, opened it after a very brief pause and guided her charge through it. A moment later, the nurse came out alone. She stood for a moment, scanning the grounds. Tony stopped rubbing his cheek, abruptly got to his feet and waved to the nurse. She waved back and began the trek across the lawn to our picnic site beneath the tree on the grassy knoll.

'Hello, Tony,' the nurse puffed as she reached us.

'Hello, Anne,' Tony replied, all vagueness gone as he smiled widely. 'May I introduce my sister, Joan, and her daughter.' He turned to my mother. 'Joan, this is Anne. I wrote to you about her.'

'So you did.' Mother smiled at Anne and stuck out her hand to shake her small, neat mitt. Formalities over, she asked if she'd like a sandwich and a little cake.

'I'd love to. It'll be half an hour at least before Miles finishes his session with Dr Armstrong.' There was a small, rather awkward pause. 'Isn't it the most splendid day? It's so warm for spring.'

Mother and Tony agreed that it was, and I kept my mouth shut. Nobody was talking to me, anyway, not really, so I was free to watch and listen. I could tell that Uncle Tony was smitten with Anne, so I concentrated on her at first. She was petite, short and slender, which made Tony's six foot seem enormous beside her. Her dark hair curled a little under her crisp, white nurse's cap and she had soft, brown eyes the colour of melted dark chocolate. Her skin was very pale, almost translucent, and she had a few freckles scattered across her nose. As the three grown-ups chatted, it became obvious to me that Anne was equally smitten with Uncle Tony. Their eyes lingered on each other just a little too long and each agreed with everything the other said.

Mother, in her turn, was being very polite, and she wasn't sarcastic once. She obviously knew something that I didn't: that Anne was special to my Uncle Tony, and we all had to try hard to impress her.

I made sure that I ate daintily, didn't speak with my mouth full of shrimp paste sandwich, didn't slurp my orange squash and only spoke when I was spoken to – which wasn't very often. Once we'd dispensed with how pretty my name was and how I was doing at school, I was more or less done with.

'Have you been nursing long?' my mother asked. 'And do you enjoy your work?'

'I've been fully qualified for a year and, yes, I do enjoy my work. I understand that you are a teacher, Mrs . . . er . . . Joan? Well, nursing's like that, a vocation.'

'Anne's father is a vicar,' Tony volunteered. There was a bit of a glint in his eye, which he directed towards his sister. I wondered if he was warning my mother to keep her views on vicars and vocations to herself.

'Is that so?' Mother asked mildly and made no further comment on the subject. I heaved a sigh of relief. I didn't want anything to embarrass the nice nurse, or my nervous uncle.

'I wonder how long this lovely weather will last?' Mother continued. 'It is so difficult to know what to wear, jumpers or blouses.'

Anne agreed. 'Having a uniform helps. At least I don't

have to think about it while I'm working. Which reminds me, I had better go and be ready to retrieve Miles. His session will be over at any moment. Thank you so much for the sandwich, Joan. It was lovely to meet you. Tony talks about you a lot.'

'It's been a pleasure, Anne,' Mother, the perfect hostess, assured Tony's lady friend, for I was sure that that was what she was, as well as being one of his nurses.

Tony's eyes followed Anne back across the turf to the door of the hut and again as she escorted Miles back to the main building. 'What do you think of her?' he asked his sister anxiously. His hand rose to his cheek once again.

'She seems very nice. It's hard to tell much more than that after such a little time. But she does seem very nice.'

'She is,' was all Uncle Tony said. But he managed to make it sound really deep and meaningful.

After another hour or so, the afternoon sun lost some of its heat and we decided it was time for us to take our leave of Uncle Tony and brave the long trek home. We collected up our picnic gear and stowed it away in the oilskin bag. Back in the main building, the air was heavy with the institutional smell of disinfectant, floor polish and boiled cabbage, and our footsteps sounded loud on the shabby, but highly polished, dark green lino. I could hear someone crying in the distance, and we passed a few people who shuffled aimlessly in and out of rooms, their expressions blank.

No one spoke to us as we made our way through the seemingly endless institutional corridors. We had to see

Uncle Tony safely signed in again, and then get to the main door and the bus stop just outside. As we were negotiating a long corridor, I noticed that one of the many doors that lined each side was ajar. I wondered if it was a door to one of the barred rooms I had noticed on our way in, so I peeked in as we walked past. The barred window was high up and mean. Very little light penetrated the small room, but there was enough for me to see that it was completely lined with mattresses, the walls as well as the floor.

'That's a padded cell,' Tony informed me. 'That's where we wind up when we have aversion treatment.'

His tone was bleak, and I shivered so violently, my teeth clattered together.

14

Milking Almonds

Father's new baby was very quiet, so quiet that I had to watch her for some moments to make sure that she was still breathing. It was a relief to see her little chest rise and fall and her blue-veined eyelids flutter with her dreams. Do newborn babies dream? I wondered. If so, what do they dream about? It occurred to me, as I stared at the scrap in the cot, that they might pick up fragments of feelings and memories from their mothers during the long, boring months that they had to spend banged up in what is, effectively, a prison.

I knew where babies came from: they came from wombs, and wombs were dark places inside women. Everyone knew that. At least, that's what Peter had told me after he'd received his sex education lesson from Mother before he went off to boarding-school. As babies are in the dark for nine whole months, surely, I thought, they have to have something to amuse them – otherwise they'd go potty. The blokes in the war films were always expected to go a bit funny in the head when they got thrown into 'the hole' in a POW camp. That's what it was for, and that's how you knew that they were heroes, that they did their stint in solitary without going mad. But their stint was usually only days, sometimes weeks; rarely, if ever, nine whole months!

I don't remember much about the birth of my half-sister, Valerie. She was born in May, by Caesarean section, and Gaby had a great deal of trouble recovering from the operation. Valerie was born with a thick thatch of dark hair and she was a pretty baby in a very slightly Oriental way. I was fascinated by her hands and feet, which were sweet and, of course, minute. Her finger- and toenails were particularly fascinating. During the months of waiting, I had been asked to think of some names for both sexes, but all the ones I came up with were vetoed for one reason or another. I seem to remember that I rather fancied Alicia for a girl, but nobody else did. Apart from that, the big event is a bit of a blank as far as I am concerned.

To be fair, I did have pressing concerns of my own at that point, namely puberty, which was playing havoc with my hormones and my complexion. I found the whole business perplexing, frightening and, frankly, unhygienic. Mother had done her best to prepare me for periods, but in those distant days, when only a very few married women used the newfangled tampons, they involved sanitary towels and sanitary belts, and I don't think anything can prepare a person for those particular instruments of torture. Besides, up until I started my periods, bleeding had been a sign that something was dreadfully wrong, and I could not quite rid myself of that idea. Especially as the bleeding came from a place that girls were brought up to keep very private indeed, and to be thoroughly ashamed of while they were about it.

Then there was the furtive business of actually purchasing sanitary towels. A man might try and serve you at the chemist's, which was too dreadful to be borne, so I simply would not do it. In the end, my long-suffering mother had to do it for me. It was a big red-letter day, a proper rite of passage, when I finally bought my own sanitary towels, and an even bigger one when I lost my embarrassment about it. I also became convinced that I smelt bad, and became obsessed with bathing and changing my clothes with greater frequency than Mother, in her role as washer-in-chief, thought was strictly necessary. My main memory of puberty is one of deep, deep shame and enormous embarrassment.

It was around this time that Mother felt it necessary to point out sorrowfully that it was a pity that I hadn't inherited 'the family skin'. Instead of the peaches and cream complexion that she had been blessed with, mine owed more to lemons. It was, and still is, of a rather sallow hue and, worse, Mount Vesuvius had taken to erupting on my chin with monotonous regularity. I had what my great-aunt Dora, who was a fur buyer for Bourne and Hollingsworth, would have described as 'cheap skin, dear. Cheap skin'. Naturally, being a cripplingly self-conscious eleven-year-old, who had reached puberty long before most of her peers, I was just aching to hear that my skin, along with everything else, was not living up to the exacting standards of my mother.

Education was my second pressing concern. I was preparing for the transition from primary school to secondary education, and there was the whole business of the very important eleven-plus examination. Pass, and a body went to grammar school: fail, and it was the vastly inferior secondary modern. Mother was convinced that I'd fail the mathematics part of the exam, and she was almost certainly right about that. In my opinion, God, or Nature, had been mean when it came to digits, and ten (twenty if you count toes, and I did – sometimes) were nowhere near enough to help with long division or complex multiplication problems. Despite Mother's increasingly fractious attempts to help, algebra, fractions and percentages remained mysteries that all the fingers and toes in the world could not help to illuminate for me.

In the end, my mother decided that, rather than run the risk of failure, she wouldn't enter me for the eleven-plus exam at all. I wasn't to know it then, but this was a very bad decision. It taught me that it is better not to try at all, than to try and be seen to fail. It took me decades to get past this notion, and to realize that by not attempting frightening or difficult things, one failed anyway. Not taking my eleven-plus also branded me as an abject educational failure in my family circle, and was yet another reason to feel deeply ashamed of myself. Somehow Mother always managed to make me feel personally responsible for failing to inherit the brains, skin and small backside – all highly desirable attributes – that she felt characterized her side of the family.

It is possible that these personal problems may explain the huge, dark hole where memories of Valerie's birth, and how I felt about it, should have been. What I do remember, though, is sitting in my tree in Grandma's garden, wrapped in scarves, gloves and a heavy winter coat, some time in the chilly months before Valerie was actually born, and thinking very solemn thoughts.

It seemed that everyone expected me, the current baby of the family, to be a little jealous of the new arrival, because he or she would take my place. What they all failed to realize was that the place that was about to be taken really wasn't up to much. It had always been made very clear to me that babies were simply a bloody nuisance that trapped mothers against their will and sent fathers running for the hills. What's more, I was in my last year at the junior school, and my periods meant that I was maturing into a young woman, so I didn't really *want* to be the baby any more. Frankly, I thought I'd grown out of it, and a jolly good job, too! My conclusion was that babies do not ask to be born, and are therefore not responsible for putting people's noses out of joint.

There was also one enormous compensation: it meant fewer visits to the Soho flat. This outcome was a great relief to me, despite my continuing love affair with Soho itself, because Gaby and Father's marriage was, to the onlooker, a match made in hell. I found their rows profoundly distressing and terrifying, and with Peter no longer there to share the misery, the visits became even more of an endurance test for me. I don't remember ever visiting the apparently unhappy couple because I wanted to; I was packed off mainly because Mother wanted shot of me for a while and, just possibly, because Father wanted to see me. For Gaby, I think the visits were a duty thing, something she enjoyed occasionally, put up with most of the time, but often resented.

I made up my mind to try really hard to confound expectations, and to make sure my hooter stayed straight and narrow by keeping the green-eyed monster at bay. After all, a disjointed nose would only be seen as yet another failure, to add to the brains, skin and arse.

'Doug and Gaby read about some connection between leukaemia and something radioactive, called strontium-90, I believe, in the milk supply. Seems as if this stuff gets into the grass, the cows eat it and the milk becomes radioactive in its turn. So now, cow's milk is off the child's menu and they're buggering about with almond milk instead,' Mother told her friend, also called Joan, a good few months after my half-sister was born.

'What about mother's milk?' Joan asked, as she sipped her cup of tea.

'I don't think that idea lasted long with Gaby. It's not fashionable to breast-feed nowadays,' Mother replied tartly. 'The kid was on that formula stuff from the start, I believe, and now she's already moving on to solids.'

'Funny how there are fashions in everything, even baby

food. Lots of babies are being fed formula these days, you know.' Joan was quite a bit younger than my mother, and had just become engaged to be married, so she was keenly interested in all things to do with weddings, marriage and motherhood.

'I've really got no idea what goes on with babies now – thank God,' my truly grateful mother intoned. 'It's a whole lot of palaver if you ask me, sterilizing bottles and all that nonsense, when in the normal run of things, all you have to do is clamp the brat to your nipple, with no soaking in sterilizing liquid required. What I do know is that Gaby's got this bee in her bonnet about cow's milk being dangerous.'

That was the first I had heard about Valerie being at risk from something as ordinary as milk. It also amazed me that any milk at all could be got from something as solid as almonds. I tried to imagine milking almonds, but couldn't get past the lack of udders.

'Isn't this almond milk stuff terribly expensive?' Joan asked.

'Of course it is! Breast milk is free, cow's milk is cheap, so naturally, they've got to scour the bloody neighbourhood looking for the most costly option available. They'll get her mink nappies next, and a diamond-encrusted silver potty. Heaven forfend that any child of theirs has to place its arse on humble plastic.'

'Should we all be drinking this special milk? Or is it just for babies?' I was feeling worried, but also quite relieved. I'd never been keen on milk, and always made an absolute point of pouring it out of the window at school whenever I could. This was helped by the fact that I sat at the back of the class with the rest of the dunces and, as luck would have it, I was right next to a window. But that didn't help my worry for my parents, both of whom drank their tea with plenty of the dodgy white, wet and radioactive stuff.

'Oh for God's sake, don't you start!' Mother snapped testily. 'It's bad enough that they're hysterics, without you joining in. Why don't you go away and play or something and leave Joan and me to chat in peace?'

Your a snotty cow. wear going to get you at home time.
YOU STINK

The scrappy, ragged and faintly grubby piece of lined paper confirmed my worst fears about being smelly. It was a month after the beginning of the new educational year, and I had not settled well at my new school. Choosing to send me to the secondary modern school that shared a name and a playground with the primary where Mother was deputy headmistress had seemed like an elegant solution to coordinating our school holidays. It was always difficult for my mother to find something to do with me when our school timetables did not mesh. Childcare had become much more of a problem since Peter had gone away to school, and Gaby was preoccupied with her new baby.

As usual, my face didn't fit. Part of the problem was that the other girls had been brought up together and had played knock down ginger, He, skipping, two balls, jacks, five stones and hopscotch together in the streets clustering around the school. They had been classmates since the very beginning, at the age of five, and worse, almost all of them had, at some point, been through Mother's hands, either because they had been in her class or had been sent to her by their own teachers for a spot of discipline.

I, on the other hand, had never lived, played or attended school in Dagenham before. I was on my fifth school, and my mother, as a teacher, was classed as 'the enemy' at worst, and 'one of them' at best, by the other children. Naturally, I was tarred with the same brushes and automatically 'sent to Coventry', which meant that I was completely ignored most of the time. If I spoke, it was as if I wasn't there. If I tried to join in any game in the playground, the deafening silence that greeted me was broken just long enough for someone to tell me to 'piss off'. As usual, I got the message fairly quickly and kept pretty much to myself at playtimes. I was, after all, quite a solitary person by nature, or possibly by nurture – or the lack of it.

When it became obvious that ignoring me failed to achieve much response, apart from my relief at being left alone, my life at that school rapidly descended into another kind of hell. On a cold, but sunny lunchtime, it began with an almighty shove in the back that sent me sprawling on to the tarmac behind one of the bike sheds. I struggled to my hands and knees but was shoved over again, this time by a foot clad in a scuffed white winkle-picker with a pointed toe several inches long. I kept my eyes on the half-dozen sets of feet that surrounded me as I tried, once again, to get up. This time I saw the kick coming. The foot wore a dark blue

217

plimsoll and I remember thinking that at least it would be softer than the winkle-picker.

I was wrong. The plimsoll had far more weight and considerable venom behind it. It caught me in the ribs, knocked me over yet again and winded me so badly I could not move for several moments. It was the sight of another winkle-picker, this time a black job, pulling back to kick me in the face that galvanized me into action. I rolled to one side, felt the wicked point brush past my cheek and heard it crash into the wall of the bike shed. There was a loud scream of pain and anguish. The lengthy, black pointed toe had been reduced to a mangled stub by the force of the collision. Inside the shoe, the flesh and blood toe obviously hurt like crazy, because its owner was hopping about clutching her foot with a hand that boasted a set of well-chewed fingernails. I just had time to roll into a tight ball with my arms over my head to protect it as best I could, before the kicks came thick and fast from all directions.

My brains seemed to leave my body and note the proceedings, in a detached sort of way, from the safety of the leafless horse chestnut that towered over the shed. Some kicks seemed loaded with hatred, while others were more timid, as if the owner of the foot in question didn't really want to be there at all but had tagged along for want of something better to do with her feet.

I was just beginning to think that the booting I was taking would never end when I heard a voice shouting, 'Miss, Miss, over here, they're kicking the shit out of someone over here!'

The assault stopped as suddenly as it had started, and although I didn't see my assailants scatter, I heard them leave. One hissed at the whistle-blower as she passed, 'Bloody sneak. We'll get you an' all next time.'

To my relief, I heard Miss Roberts, my form teacher, say, 'Angela, *please* do not use foul language.' Then, after a brief pause, 'Oh I say!' A gentle hand rested on my hunched shoulder. I still had my head clutched in my arms and I appeared to be incapable of unclutching it for several long seconds. 'Can you move, dear? Is anything broken? Who did this to you? Angela, hurry and get Mrs Hampton. Perhaps you'd better bring the first aid kit while you are about it.'

I was lucky, I suppose. I had several nasty bruises in places that didn't show, but no broken teeth or bones.

'Are you sure you didn't see who did this to you?' Mrs Hampton asked as she poked about in my hair, like Nitty Nora looking for head lice, only she was looking for lumps and bumps. 'How many fingers am I holding up?' I told her three.

'Good. What day is it today?'

'Tuesday,' I answered.

'What's my name?'

'Mrs Hampton.'

'Good. Well, it looks as if they missed your head but you'll be sore everywhere else for a few days. There's no broken ribs, either. You'd be in a lot of pain if they'd broken your ribs. Now, once again, who did this to you?'

To be honest, I really wasn't sure, because I was initially

attacked from behind and, once I was down, I was too busy watching the feet or protecting my head to look up into any faces. But I did have a shrewd idea. The white winkle-pickers one attacker wore and the hardbitten nails of another gave me a clue, though I knew better than to say so.

There was one particular gang led by a popular girl called Cathy, who I remember bit her nails so far down to the quick that they often bled. Apart from this, she was a pretty girl who always seemed to be able to afford all the latest fashions, including the winkle-pickers that were all the rage at the time. I never did know why Cathy had it in for me – but then, I suspect, neither did she. She had a bosom pal, Trish, who owned the scruffy pair of white winkles and seemed to be ready, willing and able to do anything that Cathy told her to do. They were usually joined by an assort-ment of other girls, but these hangers-on changed all the time, depending who was in favour and who was not: it was Cathy who made those decisions. That said, the core group usually consisted of Cathy, Trish, Viv, Patsy, Ann and Beryl. Poor old Beryl was regularly dumped in favour of someone else, but she clung on, knowing that if she didn't, she'd wind up being picked on just like me. Or so she told me once, when she was on the outs with Cathy's gang.

I felt rather sorry for Beryl, a sad, lost soul whose dad had left her to the mercy of a foolish mother and her mother's abusive boyfriend, who would take Beryl out in his van and do things to her. Beryl would whisper these secrets to me one day, then help to knock me about the next. I often wonder what happened to her, and whether she ever got out of the clutches of that ghastly man. I also feel a bit guilty, even now, because I realize that I should have told someone about the boyfriend. At the time, though, I didn't really understand what she was trying to tell me, especially as she always seemed willing to climb into that little white van. Of course, maturity has taught me that she probably felt she had no choice in the matter, and she may have been so desperate for affection that she mistook his attentions for love. But I still wish I'd told someone, despite having been sworn to secrecy.

Most nights I'd try to hang around so that I could leave school with Mother and travel home with her, but this wasn't always possible. I was often dispatched to get our dinner on the go, to do some shopping or to render some other domestic assistance, while Mother stayed at school for meetings with colleagues or parents, open evenings, net-ball matches, rounders matches, or marking and displaying children's work – all of which took place after school chucking-out time. This gave the bullies plenty of oppor-tunities to pounce on me somewhere between the gates and the tube station. As I never knew exactly where the ambush would take place, it made dodging it even more difficult.

Then there were playtimes. There was ample opportunity to administer a few punches, kicks, scratches and wounding insults, hidden from the prying eyes of the authorities in the nooks and crannies that abounded in the playground.

There were more subtle tortures, too. I found the notes difficult to deal with, because they usually managed to touch a raw spot and they always promised future misery, which meant I spent an awful lot of time waiting for it to happen. The waiting was worse, in many ways, than the actual thrashing. Then there was the interference with the contents of my desk. This usually involved tearing up my exercise books, scribbling all over my work with crayons or pen, so it couldn't be rubbed out, and stealing or damaging equipment, such as rulers, pens and pencils. All of these things were at a premium at the school, and an exercise book had to be examined minutely, and any free space filled, before a new one would be issued. Pencil stubs had to be presented for inspection to prove that they were indeed too small to be held, and an enquiry was launched into every bent nib, broken nib-holder and missing ruler. This made telling the teacher that I had lost yet another book or pencil a real trial, and I was often sent to Mrs Blackmore, the headmistress, to account for missing or broken items. As I knew better than to grass anyone up, I had no plausible excuses and was usually put on detention for blatant profligacy or 'criminal carelessness', depending on Mrs Blackmore's mood.

Thinking back to those days, I am utterly amazed that I didn't tell anyone what was going on. But, as every bullied child knows, snitching only makes things worse, and I suppose I was already in the habit of not burdening my mother with yet more trouble. I was terrified of rocking our boat and giving her an excuse to hit the sauce again, so I kept schtum and suffered badly, as did my school-work. Much to my parents' disgust, I wound up languishing in the E stream.

15

The Red Mist

'What have you been up to?' Father asked out of the blue.

I was visiting the Soho flat for the last time: sixty-five stairs with a pram and bags of shopping had proved too much, and they were moving to a house in Twickenham.

I hated it when Father shot questions at me. He did it a lot. He liked to quote someone like Shakespeare, Oscar Wilde or some obscure Elizabethan poet, then demand to know who he was quoting. I always got the answer wrong, even when I knew it. It was the same every Friday, when our teacher tested us on our multiplication tables or spelling – but mostly the tables; I was better at spelling. My mind would go completely blank with terror, then, when I mastered it for a moment, she'd be several questions further on and I'd be in a sweaty panic. Sometimes I was actually sick. If I was in luck, I'd be sick *before* the test, then I'd be excused. The verbal tests were the worst. I didn't find writing the answers on paper anywhere near as hard.

'Are you deaf?' said Father. 'I asked you, what have you been up to? Your mother says the school wants you to see a psychologist. So, I ask again, what the fu—' Father stopped, sighed and tried again. 'What have you been up to, that they want you to see a trick cyclist?'

'They want to know why I'm not doing better with my school-work,' I whispered. How I hated talking about school. I was so sick of it and the misery it seemed to bring me, wherever I went.

Father thought about that for a moment. 'I suppose it's a fair question,' he concluded. 'You're obviously not an idiot, so you ought to be doing better than you are.'

I was surprised that this was all he said. I'd been expecting an explosion. He sometimes expressed the exact opposite view of my intelligence when I couldn't answer his literary and general knowledge questions. Just when I thought I knew which way my old man would jump, he'd jump the other way. There was no telling with Father. He was like the English weather, changeable: except that he was much, much stormier.

A few weeks later I was taken out of class, right in the middle of Religious Instruction, to the headmistress's office to talk to the 'trick cyclist'.

She stood up and smiled as I came into the room and introduced herself as Miss Dangerfield. She wasn't very old, perhaps in her late twenties, but of course, that was fairly ancient to me at the time. I was struck by how slender she was, almost weedy, and by her masses of frizzy ginger hair. It was so thick, a blackbird could have brought up a dozen chicks in it with no bother at all. Behind the thick lenses of her glasses, her eyes were a very pale, watery blue, and set in red-rimmed sockets that looked as if they were really sore. They were the kind of eyes that went all squinty in strong sunlight, and itched like mad in the pollen season.

I gave her clothes the once-over while I was at it. I liked clothes. Hers, however, were worthy and dull. I remember thinking that she would have looked good in lovely autumnal greens, russets and golds, but she had chosen a pale grey twin-set and a charcoal grey skirt instead. Her large, narrow feet were shod in sturdy brown shoes. If she had to wear grey, I thought to myself, then she should have worn black shoes, at the very least, but something a bit more exciting, like bottle green, would have been better. As she was a ginger-nut, red shoes were out of the question: they'd clash.

'What are you reading?' she asked me, breaking into my thoughts.

I showed her the book that had attracted her attention.

'*I'll Cry Tomorrow*,' the lady read out loud. 'What's it about?'

'It's about this actress,' I answered.

'What about her?'

'It's about when she was a little girl. Her dad was a famous actor and it's about how her mum and him didn't get on.'

'I see,' the lady said. 'Your mummy and daddy didn't get on very well either, did they?'

225

I didn't think it was any of her business. The silence between us grew as she waited for the answer I wouldn't give.

I decided to start again. 'So anyway, this actress's dad drank like a fish, and her mum was very cross about it.'

'I see,' the lady said again.

'And he took mistresses too, and she was very cross about that as well,' I elaborated.

'I expect she was. Do you know what a mistress is?' she asked. I wasn't the only one who could change tack.

'Like another wife, only it's not legal, like a proper wife is,' I answered promptly, proud that there were some questions I *could* answer. 'Or,' I added, being a smartarse, 'they are lady teachers.'

'I see.' She looked at me with slightly narrowed eyes. 'So,' she continued, 'this actor, he "drank like a fish", I believe you said. Surely fish drink water?'

I gave her an old-fashioned look. 'It's a saying,' I explained patiently. The poor woman was obviously not very worldly or, indeed, that bright. 'It means he was an alcoholic.'

'Indeed. And what is an alcoholic?'

I took pity on her and told her, at some length, what an alcoholic was. At the end of it she asked, 'And how do you know all this?'

I hadn't seen it coming. I should have done, but I didn't. There was a silence so long that I grew frightened, and the fear galvanized my brain for once, instead of paralysing it. 'It tells you,' I held the book up slightly, 'in here.'

'I see,' she said, looking at me searchingly over her glasses.

I didn't mention the bullying to her. It was no good involving grown-ups. It was better by far to manage these things alone. In my experience, grown-ups only seemed to make things worse.

I subsequently learned that Miss Dangerfield had recommended that I be taken from the substantial bosom of my mother and placed in a boarding-school. Lists of suitable schools were sought, and an inventory of items that I would need to take with me – such as a tuck-box, netball knickers, geometry equipment, towels, two complete sets of uniform (winter and summer), footwear (ditto, plus games shoes), and so on and on – was acquired from somewhere, so I presume a school had been chosen by somebody – but not by me.

I'm not sure why the plan, having got that far, foundered, although I think it may have depended on who was supposed to be paying for my new school. If it was the local authority, then all well and good, it might have gone ahead. But if Father was supposed to be coughing up, perhaps not. Things were looking decidedly sticky on his financial front at that time, and school fees would have been far too much of a stretch for Mother, as her salary was nowhere near as generous as a man's would have been for doing the same job.

I don't remember being upset that the boarding-school idea came to nothing, because I was afraid to go for all sorts of reasons. I was being badly bullied as it was, but it occurred to me that in a boarding-school there would be no getting away from it. At least at a day school, once I was inside my own front door there was some respite. There would be none at all if I had to live, eat and sleep with the girls who were bullying me.

I was also scared of what might happen if I left Mother on her own. What would I do if she wasn't there when I got home again? It was entirely possible that she could have legged it, or dived head first back into a bottle. I spent a lot of time, when I was young, being afraid that people would disappear in one way or another.

So, with no boarding-school and no more interviews with the trick cyclist, life went back to being pretty much as it was before, but with one big difference: something happened that stopped the bullying abruptly.

I had often read in stories that the hero or heroine 'saw red' when they became really angry, but I was utterly unprepared for it when it happened to me. I had had a note warning me:

Watch your back – were going to get you

I'd been afraid for days, waiting for the ambush that I knew was coming. When it came, in the form of being shoved and kicked, just once, around the corner from the school gates, I finally saw the fabled red mist descend before my eyes, blinding me to everything except my tormentors.

Instinct told me to get the ringleader, Cathy. Rather than backing away, I charged, much like an enraged bull, and knocked her clean off of her feet. I was astride her in a flash and had her head gripped firmly between my hands as I pinned her to the ground. Almost two years of pent-up fear and fury came roaring to the surface, and I believe I must have been going for the kill. According to witnesses, I was about to batter her brains out on the kerb when a voice boomed, 'WHAT'S GOING ON HERE?' and I was hauled off my enemy by the scruff of my neck. It was the local beat bobby, Constable Jenkins.

Cathy and I were marched back into school and into Mrs Hampton's room. Mrs Hampton was the deputy head, and also the history teacher. I liked history the way Mrs Hampton taught it.

'Mrs Blackmore about? Only I thought I saw her car leave a while back . . .' Constable Jenkins asked.

'You'll have to make do with me, Mr Jenkins. And what have these two been up to?'

The policeman hauled me up a little straighter and said, 'I caught this one, with this one's bonce' – he hauled Cathy upright to indicate her ownership of the bonce in question – 'in her mitts, looking as if she was about to kill her if she could.'

Mrs Hampton did not look pleased to hear this news. 'Oh indeed!' She glared at me. 'And what brought on this un- precedented fit of violence, may I ask?'

I hung my head in shame. I didn't like to upset Mrs Hampton. She was all right, and very interesting to listen to when she was teaching us, a fact I appreciated immensely. Most teachers I had come across could bore for England – or, indeed, the world.

'Well, in my opinion, it's been coming on for quite a while,' Constable Jenkins told Mrs Hampton. 'This one' – he waggled Cathy as if she was a puppet – 'has been bullying the other one for a long time now. I'd say this one' – and he waggled me in his massive paw – 'finally lost her rag.' He put us both down in front of Mrs Hampton's desk.

'I see,' Mrs Hampton said, looking at me again. 'Well, thank you for your help, constable. I believe you can leave them to me now.'

'Right you are, Mrs H. I just wanted you to know the extenuating circumstances.'

Mrs Hampton was hard but fair, I suppose. We both got a right old bollocking, Cathy for being a 'vindictive bully' who would surely 'be better occupied using her energies trying to learn something useful', while I was held responsible for 'resorting to violence, no matter what the provocation', when I should have 'used the option of seeking the help of your teachers'. As if I would! I rolled my eyes at Cathy, who rolled hers back at me. Grown-ups, even teachers, couldn't half be stupid, our eyes silently agreed.

We were sent on our way with a week of detention. The following week, Mrs Hampton, Cathy and I were kept together in one classroom while the other girls on detention were incarcerated elsewhere. Cathy and I were told to get on with our homework while Mrs Hampton did some marking.

It was peaceful in the warm classroom. All that could be heard was the wall clock ticking and our pens scratching as we laboured over our work. That week marked the end of the bullying. It was agreed between Cathy and me that the head-bashing incident would never be mentioned to my mother or, indeed, the headmistress. The whole incident, and the many months of bullying that led up to it, was kept between Constable Jenkins, Mrs Hampton, Cathy, her gang and me.

Not so very long after that, I changed schools, to one that was some distance away from Dagenham and which encouraged its pupils to think about taking a few GCEs. Everyone said it was because the psychologist had suggested that I needed the challenge of exams in order to pull my educational socks up, but looking back, I wonder if Mrs Hampton had had a quiet word somewhere, in order to get me away from that hell-hole of a school. I know she had a bit of a soft spot for me, because she told me so when I went to say goodbye to her on the day that I left.

'Goodbye, my dear,' she had said, her eyes twinkling at me. 'I hope you do better at your new school. I *know* you are far more intelligent than you let on, so work hard and you could go a lot further than you ever dreamed you could.'

'Are you sure?' I asked dubiously. After all, I knew that the family brains had passed me by.

'Oh yes.' Mrs Hampton smiled. 'I knew you had it in you when you took exception to the rule concerning long socks and stockings,' she told me.

I blushed. The socks versus stockings incident had been

my first act of rebellion at school, and I was still a little shocked at myself. Coloured long socks and stockings had become all the rage, and of course every girl in the school was soon sporting green, blue, red, yellow, maroon or purple legs. Yet, for some idiotic reason, Mrs Blackmore decided that she would allow long socks that stopped below the knee, but ban stockings that stopped a few inches above the knobblies. This meant that in cold, wet weather our knees would turn blue, and if you were a bit knock-kneed – which I was – they would chap so badly where they rubbed together that the skin would crack and bleed. However, if stockings were worn, there was no bare skin below the hem of our skirts. This kept our knees nice and toasty warm, and they also stopped the chapping. So I continued to wear stockings, despite the ban, and soon landed myself on the carpet in front of an angry Mrs Blackmore. Mrs Hampton had just happened to be present, to witness the scene.

'I see you are wearing stockings. Are you unaware of the school rule that forbids the wearing of stockings?' the head-mistress asked, as she sat behind her desk looking stern.

'No, miss,' I whispered, shaken rigid to find myself in trouble. I usually managed to pass relatively unnoticed in the great scheme of things.

'What on earth does "No, miss" mean? Are you aware of the rule or not?' Mrs Blackmore asked testily.

'I do know about it, miss.'

'Then why, may I ask, are you flouting it?'

I didn't know what to say, so I tried saying nothing, but Mrs Blackmore was not content with that.

'I asked you a question, and I demand an answer. Why are you defying the school rule concerning stockings?'

'Because it's silly,' I whispered.

Mrs Blackmore could not believe that she had heard me right, but Mrs Hampton, who was standing behind her, obviously had. I could tell by the way her mouth kept twitching. I was heartened by the apparent support of the deputy headmistress.

'Did I hear you correctly, young lady? Did you just tell me that school rules were silly?'

'No, Mrs Blackmore, that's not what I said,' I protested a little more boldly, reading Mrs Hampton's twitching mouth as encouragement to stand my ground, which was probably not what she meant at all. 'I said that the rule about the stockings was silly, not all of them. Some of them are very sensible, like the one about not climbing on the bike shed roof because it's not safe.'

'And why, pray, is the stocking rule "silly" in your expert opinion?'

I saw no reason for sarcasm and objected to being spoken to as if I was a raving half-wit – even if, on paper, I so obviously was. Nettled, I grew a lot bolder. 'Because those few inches between stockings and socks means that our knees get cold and chapped, and chapped knees are really sore. Sometimes they even bleed.'

'The fact remains that, despite your opinion on the matter, I have made a rule that I insist is kept by everyone. If I allow you to wear stockings, every girl in the school will want to wear them. Then where would we be?'

It was at that point that some devil in me decided to make its presence felt, and before I could clamp my gob shut I replied, 'We'd all be in school, only with warm knees and no chapping. You don't have bare knees, none of the teachers do, so why should we all suffer for some stupid rule that makes no sense at all?' Judging by the way Mrs Blackmore's mouth opened and closed like she was a landed guppy, she had no answer to hand. Meanwhile, Mrs Hampton had the whole of her bottom lip clamped between her pearlies, her eyes were twinkling brightly enough to light the Albert Hall and her shoulders were bobbing up and down with suppressed laughter.

In the end Mrs Blackmore found her voice. 'How dare you speak to me like that? I am very angry with you and think it is best if you get out of my sight for the present, to allow me time to collect myself. I will deal with you later, when Mrs Hampton is not waiting to speak with me about more important matters.' She pointed at the door. 'OUT,' she roared, 'NOW!'

I didn't need telling twice. Funnily enough, I never was recalled for punishment, and carried on wearing my nice, thick stockings. What's more, many of the other girls followed suit. We never heard another word about the stocking rule either. Perhaps Mrs Hampton had pointed out that it was hard work enforcing rules that made no sense.

I was really looking forward to a fresh start at my new school as I said goodbye to the old one. The only bug in the butter as far as I was concerned was that I would miss the only friend I had managed to make in the two years I had spent there. Joyce had, in my opinion, been very brave to befriend me in the face of so much hostility from her schoolmates, but I needn't have worried, we kept in touch. In fact, we are still good friends to this day. My husband always knows when I am speaking to Joyce on the phone because we giggle uncontrollably in much the same way as we did when we were girls together.

16

Raz and Rita

'As you're about to become a teenager, I've decided to throw you one last birthday party,' my mother informed me one day a few weeks before the end of my final term at that awful school in Dagenham. She managed to make it sound as if she had thrown dozens of muffin worries in my honour when, in fact, I'd had just the one, when I was a year old. I had no memory of that party, of course, and suspected it had been a bit of an excuse for yet another boozy do for her and Father and their friends, because by then my parents knew, or suspected strongly, that we were about to be evicted.

'You can combine it with saying your goodbyes to all your friends at your old school.' Mother's smile as she announced this plan was so happy, I didn't have the heart to tell her that if I invited all my friends from school she'd have to make just two fish paste sandwiches and one extra fairy cake.

I tried to look grateful. 'I'd rather have a day on Rita,' I suggested tentatively.

I had fallen in love with horsekind when I was much younger, but had only started riding when parental sobriety ensured that I received pocket money on a regular basis. I saved it up diligently in order to pay for my riding lessons. Rita was a huge pinto with a back as wide as a two-seater settee – almost – and rather fetching, shaggy white hoofs. Somewhere in her chequered ancestry there was a cart-horse, no doubt about it. And like many a cart-horse before her, she had the easygoing temperament of a gentle giant – unlike her feisty stable mate, Sadie, who took delight in standing heavily on at least one of my feet while grabbing chunks of my clothing in her tombstone teeth.

Rita and Sadie, along with several other ponies, belonged to Raz, a proper Romany horse trader who had parked his colourful varda, or traditional horse-drawn caravan, on a disused airfield one day and had decided to stay. The airfield was left over from the war, and over time, he stocked it with ponies and made a makeshift stable block by converting one of the redundant hangars. Raz was a big man of about forty, I suppose. He had masses of dark, unkempt hair streaked with grey, and he always seemed to be in need of a shave. His tanned face was heavily lined, having spent the majority of its life out and about in all weathers. He was the first man I ever saw who wore an earring – just the one – but that was his only finery. His clothes were well worn, dark and suitable for hard, often dirty work. He wore a waistcoat in summer and winter alike, and the only touch of colour was the knotted scarf he wore instead of a collar and tie during the winter months. Back in the 1950s and '60s, most men wore collars and ties, but Raz never did. I don't suppose he'd ever even owned such things.

Raz rarely smiled, and was a man of very few words. He preferred the company of horses and dogs to people, and the few words that he did speak were mostly directed at them. This might explain why he had stopped travelling with his fellow Romanies and had settled down in relative isolation on the airfield. Some said that he drank, but I saw no evidence of it, and others said that he had been thrown out of the Romany fraternity for taking another man's wife. If that particular rumour was true, then he had lost her somewhere along the way, because I saw no sign of her, either. I think he was just a solitary type with a tendency towards taciturn melancholy, who simply found animals less trouble than human beings. And on that subject, I was inclined to agree with him.

In return for mucking out stables, grooming ponies and hay-making in the long summer months, me and a few other girls and boys were allowed to exercise the ponies at a reduced rate, or sometimes for free, which helped me stretch my precious half-crown a week just a tad further. Looking back, I think Raz got a really good deal, frankly, but at the time it felt like an honour to be allowed to nuzzle a soft muzzle, inhale the whiff of warm horse and fondle all those sets of lovely lugs. I even loved the irascible Sadie – but not as much as the gentle Rita.

Every Saturday morning that was free from Father-visiting duty, I would cycle out to the airfield with a packed lunch and a bottle of pop in my saddlebag to commune with

Rita and her pals. The ride to the airfield was always fraught, because it involved some very lonely country lanes. One of them was the haunt of a man who would leap out of the hedgerow into the narrow road, coat and flies wide open so that he could flash his pride and joy at me as I passed. There was no alternative route, unless I wanted to push my bike across ploughed fields, through thorny hedges and across muddy ditches – which I didn't, largely because the farmers would not have liked it one little bit. Besides, that would have been the long way round, and I didn't want to waste a second of my precious horse time.

That grubby old devil had learned my routine off pat, and lay in wait for me, week in and week out. A little thing like foul weather didn't put him off his stroke. I would pedal like fury as I approached Flasher's Lane, as I called it, so that he couldn't grab hold of me as I flew by. I didn't tell my mother about him, because she might have stopped me going to the airfield, but I always approached his particular stretch of hedgerow in fear and trepidation.

Finally, I told one of the older girls about him, and she, in turn, must have told Raz. The next week, the flasher leapt out of the hedge, filthy coat flapping and flies gaping as usual, but before either of us knew what was happening there was a furious bellow and Raz crashed through the hedge opposite, brandishing a riding crop.

'You filthy buggerrrrr!' he yelled as he bore down on my tormentor, crop raised high. He brought it down with a resounding thwack on the offending member, which promptly shrivelled to a shadow of its former self. 'I'm telling your missus on you, Ernie, and all the fellas down the Hare and Hounds. And if I ever hear of you troubling any other young girl with your dirty ways, I'll bloody well geld you once and for all.'

Ernie looked as if he was about to collapse with shock and pain, but Raz wasn't finished with him. He hauled out and socked him so hard with his fist that Ernie landed on his back in the road, blood pouring from his nose. He began to whine and snivel for mercy, but Raz, a disgusted sneer on his face, pulled him to his feet and slapped him hard around the chops.

'I'll be taking you home now, Ernie, and we'll explain to your missus all about what you've been up to. Happen she'll castrate you herself and save me the trouble.'

Raz then turned to me, because, naturally, I'd stopped to watch. 'Time you cut on along now. P'raps you'll muck out Rita and give her a good groom and some exercise. I'll be back later, as soon as I've finished with this here.'

He shoved Ernie with his huge right hand so that he stumbled forward a few paces, then he shoved him again. Raz gave me one of his rare smiles and an even rarer wink and continued to push his captive in front of him. I did as I was told. I never saw Ernie again. When I tried to thank Raz for his help, he said that we would not speak of it again – and we never did.

The other girls and boys who helped out at the airfield became my weekend friends, and for the first time ever, I felt that I belonged. Nobody sent me to Coventry, nobody beat me up and there were no nasty notes to worry about. How I loved the times I spent ankle deep in horse manure and the long hot days in summer that I spent pitchforking hay into the back of a horse-drawn cart, along with the rest of Raz's willing helpers. Each time the cart was full, one of us would drive it back to the barn while the rest lolled in the heap of warm hay and stared up at the sky, listening to the slap of the reins on Rita's ample back, the steady clip-clop of her hoofs on the concrete runway and the comforting creak of the ancient cart.

Back at the old hangar that served as a barn, we'd empty the cart, then sit in the shade to have a swig or two from our pop bottles while Rita had a long, very noisy slurp from the cast-iron bath that had been recycled as a water trough. This done, we'd all amble back to collect more hay. When lunchtime came around, we'd picnic on the grass. Then, full of pop, sandwiches, fruit and the odd sucky sweet or two, and drowsy from the sun, I'd lie back and listen to the gentle hum of the insects collecting nectar and pollen from the purple clover, yellow buttercups, blood-red poppies and mauvy-pink corn cockle, and the idle chatter of my friends.

Three of the older girls, Anne, Carol and Sue, were in their mid-teens and thus deeply fascinated with the male of the species. Personally, I couldn't see what they saw in boys. Horses, dogs and cats were much more interesting, in my opinion. They often squabbled about who was more gorgeous: Elvis Presley, Cliff Richard or Tommy Steele in the pop star category, and James Dean, Montgomery Clift or Marlon Brando in the film star section. They never did reach a definite conclusion.

While we younger girls yawned with boredom, the boys discussed the relative merits of various motorbikes. The Norton Dominator invariably came out top of their list, which begged the question as to why they bothered to discuss it at all. But they seemed to find the subject endlessly fascinating, and as one of the youngest of the group, and a girl at that, I knew better than to argue.

Anne and Carol both had a crush on one of the boys – Chester was his name – and when he wasn't there, they ditched the Elvis versus Cliff argument and talked about him instead.

'I wonder why he's called Chester?' Anne mused one day when the lad in question hadn't yet arrived at the airfield.

'It's not what you might call a proper English name, is it? Sounds more of a Yank name to me; but he doesn't sound like a Yank at all.' Carol was right. His accent was mostly Essex boy, with a large dollop of East End thrown in for good measure.

I opened an eye and noticed the lad in question pedalling his bike up the runway even as they spoke. 'There he is now,' I warned them. 'Why don't you ask him?'

'We can't do that! He'll know we've been talking about him!' Anne sounded appalled at the idea. 'Why don't you ask him yourself if you're so interested?'

'I'm not really interested. I thought you two were!' I was indignant at the mere suggestion that I'd worry my head about something as boring as boys.

'Well, we are – sort of. Go on, ask him. I dare you,' Anne muttered hastily as Chester drew to a halt nearby, dropped his bike on the grass and whipped a greaseproof packet of sandwiches from his saddlebag, ready to join us for lunch.

'Ask me what?' Chester enquired as he plonked himself down among the daisies.

Anne nudged me hard in the ribs. 'We were wondering,' I said, 'why you're called Chester? None of us know any other Chesters,' I said lamely. 'It sounds American, but you don't. You're not American, are you?'

'Nah,' he answered, around a bite of cheese sarnie, 'but me dad was, according to me nan.'

'Don't you know?' I asked, much to the relief of the others, who didn't like to ask such a personal question.

'Not really. He pissed off before I was born.'

'So *his* name was Chester, was it?' Anne asked, forgetting that she was supposed to act uninterested.

'Nah, his name was Eugene, Gene for short, like that dancer bloke in the films. The one who ain't Fred Astaire.'

'You mean Gene Kelly,' I informed him.

'Yeah, him.'

'So how come your name's Chester, then? Why ain't you Gene?'

Chester rolled his eyes. ' 'Cause Gene's a girlie sort of name, ain't it? I don't s'pose me mum thought much of it neither.' Chester took another bite of his sandwich. 'If I tell you, you're not to laugh, and I don't want anyone taking the piss. Is that a deal?'

Fascinated now, we all crossed our hearts and hoped to die.

'Well, according to me nan, the Yanks who came over in the war loosened the local girls' knicker elastic by bribing them with stockings, bars of chocolate and packets of fags,' Chester explained, 'because everything was really scarce on account of the rationing. According to me nan, some girls would do almost anything for a pair of nylons, a chunk of chocolate or a packet of ciggies by the end of the war, and it seems like my mum was one of 'em.'

'We *know* about rationing and the shortages,' Carol complained.

'Well, me mum's favourite fags was Chesterfields, so when me dad buggered off back to America, not knowing he'd left a bun in me mum's oven, she decided to call me Chesterfield, in his memory, like, seeing as she didn't have a clue where he lived, or have the heart to call me Gene. So I'm named after a bleeding packet of fags. Bloody marvellous, that is.'

'Don't you like it?' Carol asked.

'Would you want to be called after a lousy packet of fags?'

'You should think yourself lucky she didn't smoke Camels. If she'd called you after them, you'd've had the right hump!' I giggled at my own joke.

'Oh very funny, very droll.' Chester grinned good-naturedly, while the others tried hard not to laugh. 'You promised not to take the piss. Just for that, I'll have to turn you upside-down.' And he did. Luckily, I was wearing my shorts, so he didn't get an embarrassing glimpse of my knickers.

To this day, the gentle hum of insects, the scent of hay and pong of warm horse are some of my favourite things, and they instantly remind me of the days I spent with Raz's ponies, when every second was utter bliss. Those days were, without any doubt, the very happiest times of my young life.

Mother was not to be deflected from her party idea. 'Why not do both?' she suggested magnanimously. 'Have your party *and* a day on Rita. You're in charge of the invitations, and I'll do the rest.'

I am ashamed to say that I shoved the problem of who to invite to my party so far to the back of my mind that I blanked the whole thing almost completely. When it did flit across my mind, I told myself that I had plenty of time and pushed the thought back into the darker recesses. Sadly, the time ran out and I still hadn't had the confidence to draw up a list of possible guests. I was so agonizingly shy, and so certain that no one would want to come to any party held in my honour, that I failed to invite a single, solitary soul, not even my best friend Joyce, or my friends at the airfield.

The great day dawned, and I still hadn't had the nerve to tell my mother that I'd failed so dismally on the invitations front. As I climbed on to Rita's back I told myself that I'd ride around and invite any likely candidates during the day. But I didn't. Once again, I shelved the problem and gave myself up to the joy of Rita's quiet company and steady amble. I had a lovely day's riding around the fields and lanes near the airfield, and discovered several nooks and crannies that I had never known were there, including a large, ornately carved stone horse trough parked on a little green in the middle of a small collection of farm cottages. The trough was far too fancy for its setting and I wondered how it had got there, but there was no one around to ask, so I never did find out. However, Rita was duly grateful for a drink and, as a special birthday treat, I gave her an apple from my picnic.

Eventually, the moment came to go home and face my mother, the music and the mountain of Marmite sandwiches, individual jellies and birthday cake that awaited me and my non-existent guests.

'What do you mean, no one is coming?' Mother demanded in exasperation. 'I've spent all bloody day churning this lot out. We'll never eat it all between us.' She sighed heavily, and glared at me. 'Why in God's name did you leave it so late?'

I couldn't answer, because I didn't have the nerve to tell her that I simply hadn't had the confidence to ask anyone. The silence from me dragged on and on, until in the end Mother roared up the stairs, 'Pots, come down here.'

Peter was home for the long summer holiday and was skulking in his bedroom, knocking up yet another model aircraft from balsa wood, tissue paper, glue and smelly old enamel paints. Heavy feet thundered down the stairs.

'Yes, Mater, what can I do for you?' Peter had taken to calling our parents 'Mater' and 'Pater': it was a public school thing, as was leaping to his feet whenever a woman entered a room, pulling chairs out for ladies to sit upon, and always walking nearest the kerb when in female company.

However, little sisters did not count as females in his view, and I was never on the receiving end of these good-mannered niceties – unless he was showing off to some girl he was hoping to impress.

'You can haul your carcass around the neighbourhood and drag any likely looking type in to help to eat all this grub, that's what you can do. Your half-witted sister seems to have "forgotten" to ask anyone to her birthday party. How she managed that, I shall never know, but manage it she has!'

Peter laughed. 'Typical! OK, I'll see what I can do.'

Anyone with a heartbeat was dragged to our table, despite vigorous objections from some of Peter's friends, who really didn't want to be caught eating jellies and party-ing with a bunch of thirteen-year-old girls. Luckily for them, there was little fear of that, because there were no thirteen-year-old girls, apart from me and Christina, who lived up the road and really wasn't supposed to be in our house at all. Her mother was a pillar of the local Baptist church, and deeply disapproved of her daughter fraternizing with the daughter of a divorced woman. Christina had to sneak in the back door just in case she was seen, and every-one present was sworn to secrecy.

In the end, we did manage to eat all the food, the reluctant guests appeared to have a good enough time and, as a punish-ment for my dereliction of duty, I was made to clear up the mess while Mother and Peter enjoyed a well-earned rest.

It was to be a decade or two before I attempted to throw another party, and even then I wasn't happy. It would seem that I'm just not a party animal, although I would have loved to have been. When faced with a large group of people, I still go straight into blind panic mode and either freeze up so no one can get a word out of me, or hog the limelight and talk nine thousand to the dozen, all with a slight edge of hysteria in my voice. I can hear it, I can will myself to shut the hell up, but I can't seem to do it. There is no middle way for me.

I am at my happiest when tucked into a corner with a good view of everyone else being sociable. Then I play games with myself, like 'Spot the alpha male' or 'Who's with who?' or 'Who is the boss in their household?' It passes the time, it keeps me happy and, best of all, it stops me from making a bloody fool of myself by running off at the gob.

Nowadays, I can, in all honesty, say that I am working when I'm watching my fellow humans from the sidelines. Their body language speaks volumes and helps me to develop the characters in my novels. What's more, calling it work stops me from thinking about what a useless social animal I've turned out to be.

17

Never the Bridesmaid

'You self-centred little cow, don't you ever think of anyone but yourself?' Mother demanded as I stood there, my head hung in shame.

Mother had just told me that she was going to marry again, and the first thing I thought of was to ask if I could be her bridesmaid. I had never been a bridesmaid, having so little family to do the deed for. Father's surviving half-brother, Will, remained a bachelor to his dying day, as did Mother's only surviving sibling. There were no cousins, no aunts, no nobody. I had seen so many photographs of other girls being bridesmaids and getting all dolled up in pretty frocks like little princesses and had longed and longed to be one of their number for as long as I could remember.

Sadly for me, my mother was not a frills and frou-frou kind of a gal. She was more your tweedy sort, and had decided long before that I was to be the same. There were all sorts of practical reasons for this decision, of course.

Sensible, sturdy clothes and stout shoes lasted longer, for one thing, which was always a consideration in a household where money was perennially tight and where the rigours of rationing, austerity and poverty had left an indelible mark. Mother had never forgotten the Rest Centre, and the abject misery and shame of being destitute still clung to us like a bad smell. Therefore, she took a very hard line on such frivolities as pretty dresses, silly shoes, jewellery and posh scent. For Mother, the height of girlie fun was to have a really good soap as a special treat, and, if absolutely necessary, a dab of powder on her nose and the merest smear of lipstick on her full and sensuous lips.

'If you're angling to get one of those ridiculous brides-maid dresses, you can think again. We can't afford clothes that you only wear once and then stuff into the wardrobe. *If* I decide to have you as my bridesmaid, and it's a bloody big *if*, you'll have a nice serviceable dress and sodding-well like it. It's *my* wedding, not some excuse for you to tart yourself up, and don't you forget it.'

Even as I blush at the memory of that one-sided conver-sation, I still think Mother was too harsh in her judgement of me. I was only a kid, and I'm pretty sure it's normal for young girls to long to be a bridesmaid, with all the fuss that it involves. That longing didn't make me selfish, it made me a fairly average sort of a girl – for once. I knew in my heart that Mother's wedding was to be my one possible shot at the prize, and I was right. I never did get the chance again.

Don, Mother's third and final husband, was much like Rita in a way: he was a gentle giant. He was not particularly tall, but he was particularly wide. His shirt collars fitted easily around my waist, and his barrel chest was huge, a fact that impressed Peter Pots mightily. Don had once been selected to play rugby for Scotland because, as Peter kindly explained to his ignoramus of a sister, once he got hold of the ball and started charging for the line, it took more than a handful of burly blokes hanging off him to slow him down.

'It's the momentum, you know,' Pots told me. I didn't know what momentum meant, but I nodded sagely, in case I was treated to an even longer discourse on the subject. I wasn't interested in rugby, or football, or cricket either, and I had grown just about old enough not to hang on to every single word uttered by my big brother. I still hung on to quite a lot of them, because Pots could be interesting when he chose, but the finer points of sport were tedious, frankly. Sport was boys' stuff, invented to bore the bums off girls, in my opinion. And that opinion hasn't changed a whole heap over the years.

Anyway, Pots was entranced by the notion of Don playing rugby for Scotland, but Don's father was not. Don was told that he had to be a civil servant instead, like his father and the rest of the family before him. Don gave up rugby, but, showing the defiance of youth, gave the Civil Service a miss and became a constable with the Metropolitan Police. The bonus of working in London was that it kept him well away from his stern, disapproving father, who lived in Edinburgh. Don worked as part of the section that was responsible for policing the Thames and enchanted Peter (but not me) with gruesome tales of fishing bodies out of the river, of grabbing a corpse by the arm only to find that it had come off in his hand. There was also a lot about bloating that I shut my ears to when Pots tried to relay these tales to me – which he did, with typical brotherly relish and a total disregard for his sister's delicate sensibilities and queasy stomach.

During the war, Don had been a flying instructor in the RAF, and was stationed out in what was then Rhodesia. He was thus spared the incredibly dangerous business of flying in combat. Don's flying Spitfires and other aircraft was, of course, a huge plus as far as my brother was concerned, as he had ambitions to be a pilot himself. Then, just to complete Don's hero status, when the war was over he worked in a motorbike shop. When Mother met him, he owned and drove a Norton Dominator. For Peter, the man was a god!

I liked Don for other reasons. He was a gentle man, a calm person and he made our mother happier than I had ever seen her. That's not to say that she lost her sharp tongue or her sarcastic wit, because she didn't, but he was solid and dependable and Mother needed that more than anything. Don was not the kind of man to betray or to batter his wife, or, indeed, his stepchildren, and for Mother that must have come as an enormous relief – even if she did, later on, find him just a touch boring on occasions. I never heard Don raise his voice, not once, and in a crisis his size and calm manner made him a rock-like presence and a great comfort to our mother and to me.

The whole family liked Don, even Father, who envied his even-tempered nature. For me, there was an added bonus.

Don became enormously fond of me. He'd once had a curly-haired little girl of his own, Diana. She was a brunette and I was a blonde, but my curls reminded him of the little girl he'd lost, and he loved me for it. Diana had had a brain tumour that had rendered her blind, partially paralysed and, eventually, deaf as well. She had died when she was about five, and Don's marriage to her mother had foundered shortly afterwards. It seems that his wife had been having a long-term affair and, once their daughter was gone, she saw no reason to remain with her husband.

Because of all this, Don was happy to become part of our funny-peculiar little family and to relinquish his lonely bed-sitter, bachelor life once and for all. He even flogged his beloved motorbike on the eve of the wedding, in favour of a family saloon that would take all four of us.

'Let her be a bridesmaid, Joan,' he told my mother when she relayed my request to him. 'She's just a wee girl, and it will make her happy. I have a few pounds tucked away. Buy her a dress with that.'

And so Mother and I went shopping, and I tried to hide my disappointment at the plain, pale blue dress and bolero jacket that she chose for me. There wasn't a frill or a bit of lace to be seen. 'You'll be able to wear that anywhere,' Mother informed me stoutly.

I was, however, allowed to wear a pair of sheer stockings instead of ankle socks and, on the day, I carried a pretty bouquet that Don had ordered for me when he had ordered flowers for Mother. I think the dear man had seen my crush-ing disappointment with my dress and had done his best to put matters right without getting on my mother's hair-trigger nerves. Don had caught on quickly that Mother could be a tetchy type and spent the rest of his married life, which I believe was happy for the most part, trying very hard not to get too far up Mother's roomy Roman nose.

Not long after the wedding, Don joined the Civil Service at last and worked at the Criminal Records Office at Scotland Yard. The increase in income that this change brought about enabled us to move to what was to become my favourite childhood home, a split-level Edwardian house in nearby Harold Wood. This move proved fortuitous, because it was relatively handy for my new school. I was, at last, free from the stigma of being a teacher's child, as nobody at my new school knew or cared about the history of my parents. Not a soul had even been taught by my mother, which was something of a miracle, considering just how many teaching posts she had held in Essex over the years. I was simply viewed as the new girl, and was accepted at last.

It was such a joy to go to school every day and to know that no one would be lying in wait for me in the playground or on the way home. I could go to the cloakroom each evening and know for a fact that my coat would still be in one piece and that there would be no notes lurking in my pockets. Each time I opened my desk, my school-books and pen case would be just as I had left them, and there would be no threats scrawled on grotty bits of paper there either.

I *was* called names, but then so were most people. It was more good-natured teasing than anything, and mine was the kind of name that lent itself to some unfortunate abbreviations that proved just too tempting for the boys. But compared to what I had come from, that was nothing. It was as if a huge and crushing weight had been lifted off me, and I was so very grateful and relieved that I even made some academic progress. True, anything to do with numbers was still a big struggle and almost a complete mystery, but those lessons that involved language skills, such as history and English, became my modest strengths. I even got the odd A- or B+ for my essays, which did not seem to impress my mother much, but impressed the hell out of me! I wasn't used to it and I was thrilled. I managed to stagger up a few grades during my time at the school, and wound up, eventually, at the bottom of the A stream instead of at the bottom of the E. I was also the only person in my year to pass both English Language and English Literature at O level, and I was so proud of myself, I thought I'd burst. It was only when I realized that I would have to move to yet another school in order to take A levels that my happiness deflated a little. But that came later. To begin with, I was simply delighted to come and go through the school gates with no fear and no bruises to my body or to my fragile ego.

Three months after my arrival at the new school, Father and Gaby had their second daughter, Nicci. Once again, the baby was born by Caesarean section, and once again, Gaby took quite a while to recover. Nicci, on the other hand, was a robust little thing from the start and, unlike her sister, was fair and blue-eyed like the rest of Father's brood. As she grew older, nobody seemed at all worried that she might drink radioactive milk.

Father had other worries to contend with. He was skint, boracic, tapped-out and stony broke, with an expensive wife and four children to keep. Something had to go. His first move was to stop paying Peter's school fees and the maintenance payments for me.

'Dear God, you really are a spineless bastard, Doug,' Mother told my father down the phone. 'Well, I'm not doing it. You can break it to him yourself. I hope that useless wife of yours is hocking her bloody jewellery, that's all. If I see her with genuine sparklers dripping off her, I'll personally tear her bloody eyes out. That should stop her shopping.'

Mother listened briefly, then exploded, 'I *know* you've had another baby. We could hardly miss it, could we? The fuss that woman makes, you'd think no other woman had ever been pregnant.'

The pause was briefer this time but her reply was even louder. 'I think you should keep that information for someone who *cares*! You had no trouble sending me out to work, did you, pregnancy or no bloody pregnancy? Meanwhile, I've got a son who is going to be heartbroken and humiliated when he hears that he's going to be dragged away from school just a couple of terms before his friends leave, and it won't be you or your bloody useless wife who'll have to bear it, will it?'

Mother slammed the receiver down so hard, I heard the brittle black plastic shatter. 'Bloody hell!' she roared. 'What next?'

Don and I looked at one another and decided to make ourselves scarce for a bit. I darted out to the kitchen, through the back door and down the path to my shed on winged feet. I have no idea where Don went, but I do know that the man could get up a surprising turn of speed when he chose.

We could never rely on Father hanging on to any money he made. All my young life, he seemed to yo-yo between rags and riches and back again. It was a very stressful way of life for his wives and his children, because we were dependent on him. There were no constants in our lives: one minute we'd be supping from silver spoons and the next, the spoons would be flogged to the nearest pawnbroker and if we had any food at all we had to eat it with our fingers.

These constant changes in fortune meant that we were always moving, either because we were evicted for non-payment of rent or because Father could afford to go up market. Mother had perennially itchy feet, and was always 'doing geographicals', so that I had to change schools as well as neighbourhoods. Over the years I attended eight schools in all. Weekends and school holidays were often spent at my father's various homes, which, in turn, meant that I wasn't available to play with neighbourhood children or schoolmates during my free time. This endless moving around allowed me very little opportunity to make friends, and when I did, I was fairly certain I'd be dragged away from them again.

In the end, I more or less stopped trying to form any

lasting relationships and developed interests that didn't require anyone else to join in. I read a lot, and the only sports I was ever even remotely good at, swimming and horse-riding, could be done on my own: the end result was that I never developed into a team player. The up-side of this character trait, though, is that it has come in very handy in my life as a writer, because writing is an even more solitary occupation than lighthouse-keeping used to be. Lighthouses were manned by at least three keepers, one per eight-hour shift, whereas the shifts I put in at the keyboard are always done alone.

After this particular low in his fortunes, Father set himself up in a mail order business, and in comparatively short order he was able to afford to buy an expensive house in Surrey's stockbroker belt, take long holidays in the South of France, drive an expensive Italian sports car, zoom around on a speedboat and deck Gaby out in mink and jewellery. I remember Gaby instigating the rule that whenever she and Father had a particularly bad row, he had to buy her diamonds before she would make it up. Perhaps this was a canny hedge against future bouts of poverty, for she could always hock them or flog them, should the need arise. There seemed to be a great many rows, and I recall that it didn't take long for her to sparkle like the Christmas lights in Regent Street. Once, she apologized for being late with the immortal line that she had 'Just had to pop into Garrard's to pick up a few things.' Then she'd had to explain, because I didn't know, that Garrard was the Queen's jewellers.

However, for all the trappings of wealth that surrounded

the unhappy couple, all was not well. I dreaded the long summer holidays in France that I shared with them, because Valerie, Nicci and I spent many miserable hours huddled together, trying desperately to shut out the screaming, shouting and awful abuse that they hurled at each other. Funnily enough, Nicci, the youngest, took these fights much more in her stride than Valerie or I were able to do. Somehow, Peter managed to escape most of these awful holidays, but I was always dragged along because I was a useful, very cheap nanny. Not that they put it that way: it was tarted up as a great big treat for me, but it wasn't. Those endless holidays were more of an endurance test than anything. I hated them, and anyway, I longed to make friends and there were horses to enjoy, if only I'd been allowed to. But once again, Mother colluded with the plan to get shot of me, so that she and Don could enjoy some time alone together.

In the end, in desperation, I developed such a violent allergy to French sand that, on the days that Father and Co. trekked off to sandy Juan les Pins, instead of the stony Lido Plage in Nice, I was able to enjoy a day by myself. The relief was so enormous, I can still feel it all these years later. I also think it is highly significant that only French sand brought me out in enormous, red and itchy hives. English sand never did.

When Father and Gaby were not involved in the latest round of their endless conflict, she treated me to tales of my Father's cruelty and, slowly but surely, my relationship with him was poisoned. It was easy for me to think of him as the villain of the piece, because he usually made the most noise.

It was Peter who later pointed out that Gaby usually started proceedings by winding him up and then watching him explode. If that was true, then she really must have wanted those diamonds, because their rows were horrendous.

When I was fifteen, and working towards my O levels, tragedy struck once again. I can't remember who told me – Mother, probably – that four-year-old Valerie was seriously ill. Her weight plummeted, and she developed a sore throat that would not go away. At first, the doctor entrusted with her care – the Queen's paediatrician, no less – thought she had a very severe case of tonsillitis, and recommended that she have her tonsils removed.

When Father and Gaby questioned his diagnosis, he said, according to Father, 'Nonsense, nonsense, take her home and, if she's naughty, smack her bottom. I'll see her again when we take her tonsils out.'

Valerie was actually on the operating table when the registrar discovered that they had failed to take a blood test to get a match for the blood transfusion that was usually required for a tonsillectomy. It was this man who finally broke the dreadful news with the awful sentence, 'We have noted a disquieting feature in Valerie's blood.'

The 'disquieting feature' turned out to be leukaemia. In those days, there was very little chance of a cure for any of its forms, and to this day, I believe, there is still no cure for the virulent form that Valerie had. Had the doctors gone ahead with the operation, she would have bled to death on the operating table, as even then she had very few platelets to help her blood to clot. As it was, even having dodged the operation, her future looked very bleak indeed.

Tragically, leukaemia was the very thing that Gaby and Father had feared when they had insisted that Valerie drank almond milk. Her sister, Nicci, having drunk cow's, milk for the greater part of her short life, remained robustly healthy. It seemed that God, Nature, or just plain Life, had a really ghastly sense of irony. The news that their daughter was almost certainly dying, short of some sort of miraculous intervention, left Gaby, Father and the rest of our little family reeling.

I'd love to be able to say that this terrible event pulled the family together, but it didn't. Father and Gaby could not seem to help one another, and they pulled in entirely different directions. Gaby became a Christian Scientist, and Father expressed his contempt for her flight back, not only into Christianity but, in his view, into a particularly weird version of it. Gaby, in turn, accused Father of killing his daughter by inches with his profane and atheist views.

While Valerie was indulged, Nicci sort of lurked about in the background. My heart bled for her, because I knew all too well what it felt like to be relegated to the sidelines. It seems to me that none of our parents was ever able to remember what it felt like to be a child, or was capable of putting the needs of their children first. What always mattered most, to all three of them, was how they felt, and what they wanted, and their children always seemed to come bottom of the emotional heap.

Nobody thought to even attempt to help the rest of us to come to terms with the dreadful events that were unfolding. Gaby and Father seemed to be wrapped up in their very real misery and their endless, endless war, and Mother was apparently unaware that her own children could be hurting at all. After all, we weren't the ones that were so very ill: what did we have to complain about?

I soon learned to keep my feelings on the matter bottled up. It was quite clear to me that, as a healthy sister of a profoundly ill child, I was not entitled to show any distress. It was my job, and the job of Peter and Nicci, to shut up, put up and get on with it.

18

Mother Said So

Father and I were at the Great Ormond Street Hospital for Sick Children on our way to visit Valerie, who had been admitted for tests and the first of what would be many blood transfusions. I'm not sure where Gaby and Nicci were; shopping for little treats for Valerie, probably. Gaby liked shopping, and having to watch Valerie suffering was incredibly painful for her. Father was seething. The bill from the paediatrician had arrived that morning and he was next to himself with barely repressed rage.

There was a polite 'ping' to let us know that the lift had finally arrived. Its doors opened with a hiss and a clang, and several people flowed out as we got in. We rode up a floor or two in silence. I knew better than to chatter when Father was having a seethe, in case he turned his fury on to me. Another 'ping', a hiss followed by a clang and, to Father's joy, the paediatrician in question was framed in the doorway. He stepped into the lift, the doors closed and the three of us were alone in the small metal box. The doctor had not recognized Father and was oblivious to the danger he was in.

Father drew the thick, creamy sheet of paper from his pocket, dangled it before the older man's startled eyes and asked, in a deceptively mild voice, 'What is this?'

It took a moment for the consultant to recognize the paper. 'I believe it is my bill, Mr er . . .' He didn't get any further.

'And just what are you asking me for payment for?' Father's voice was still quiet, but I could hear it wobbling slightly. The lift continued on its slow and steady journey upwards.

'My professional services, of course. Why else would I send a bill?' It was, I knew, a mistake to allow the little note of irritation to enter his voice, or the pompous air of self-importance to pervade the atmosphere of that small, metal box.

'What professional services, you brandy-soaked son of a syphilitic whore?' asked Father again in that mild tone. I began to quake.

'I beg your pardon, Mr er . . .'

'I said, what professional services, you brandy-soaked . . .'

'I'll have you know, sir, that I am a professional man and you cannot speak to me like that.' The doctor was spluttering. Indignation had turned his face the colour of plums – Victoria plums.

'What do you mean, I can't speak to you like that? I *am*

speaking to you like that, you cretin.' Spittle flew in all directions as Father finally gave full rein to the rage and misery that had made his red, tear-swollen eyes pop out like organ stops. I was pretty sure that he had been crying for his daughter for most of the night. We all had, except for Nicci, who was far too young to understand. 'You almost killed my daughter, you useless, puffed-up pile of dog's shit. Tonsillitis, you called it, tonsillitis, you useless bastard. She doesn't have tonsillitis, she has leukaemia!'

'Yes, well, it was most regrettable, of course, but it was a genuine oversight and I believe I apologized most sincerely at the time, Mr er . . .'

'So you did, so you did.' Father's anger appeared to abate for a second, but it soon came roaring back: 'What I don't understand is why the hell I should pay *you*, you useless prat, when it was the registrar who made the diagnosis. He stopped you from killing my daughter on the operating table. Explain to me why you deserve your fee when you fucked it all up so royally.' Father grabbed the paediatrician by his old school tie and glared into his face.

I think it was at this moment that both the doctor and I realized that his death was just moments away. I tried in vain to prise Father loose from the terrified man, but his grip was like a vice. Father forced his captive to his knees by the simple expedient of dragging down on the fat Windsor knot until the man was grovelling and fighting to breathe.

'Daddy, Daddy, you're going to kill him, let him go,' I begged, but for all the impression I made, I might not have been there at all. 'They'll hang you, Daddy, if you kill him, then what will poor Valerie do? She needs you, *please* don't kill him.' Mention of Valerie loosened Father's grip a trifle and the doctor took a long, rasping breath.

'Hell will freeze solid before I pay you for cocking up my daughter's treatment, you pox-ridden son of a five-bob whore,' Father informed the gasping man. 'Meanwhile, eat your fucking bill.'

To my amazement and the doctor's shock, he proceeded to stuff the thick sheet of paper into the doctor's gaping mouth, and then with two fingers to force it down and down, deep into his gullet. At that moment, when I thought the consultant must surely die, the lift doors wheezed open and a horrified ward sister took in the situation at a glance.

'Let go of him immediately,' she barked with natural authority. Father did as he was told. 'Now please leave the lift,' she requested with controlled politeness.

Father didn't even glance at her. 'Not until this prick has swallowed his bill. If you interfere, I'll give you such a smack, you'll be picking your teeth out of your arse for a week.' The ward sister shot a nervous glance at me, and although I was frozen to the spot, I was able to nod slightly to assure her that he would surely do it if she so much as blinked out of turn.

Father loomed over the distressed man, 'Now fucking *swallow*!' he bellowed, and the poor man swallowed. The whole incident must have taken a few minutes, but to me it had felt like hours.

Satisfied, Father strolled out of the lift and along the

corridor as if nothing had happened, while I unfroze and trotted fearfully, but silently, behind him. I looked back in time to see the ward sister help the shattered doctor to his feet and brush him down with her hand, while he tried to find his lost dignity as he straightened his severely mangled tie. I knew better than to speak as we completed our journey up to Valerie's room by the stairs. I was convinced that the police would turn up at any moment, as we visited my little sister, to march our father away.

They didn't, and Father never heard another word about the matter, despite the many times that he visited the hospital over the years of Valerie's treatment. We saw that ward sister often, but she never gave any sign that she had witnessed Father's assault on the eminent paediatrician or, indeed, that she had been threatened herself. Later, when he had calmed down a little, Father sent the surprised registrar the paediatrician's fee and, for the rest of his life, he gave annual donations to Great Ormond Street's funds.

Not that that excused his assault in any way, but it helped Father to show that he appreciated the hospital's unceasing efforts to save his darling.

Meanwhile, with Valerie's terrible illness as the ever-present backdrop, life, and indeed death, carried on as it tends to do.

When Father's half-brother, Uncle Will, died of a heart attack, Mother chose that moment to tell me that Father had shot his gun dog, Lady. Knowing that she couldn't keep

Uncle Will's demise quiet, she lobbed in the news about Lady while she was at it.

'I thought that if you were going to be miserable anyway, I might as well get it all over and done with in one fell swoop,' Mother explained. 'I hadn't the heart to tell you about Lady, and I was leaving it to your Father to explain why he killed her, but as I've got to tell you about Will anyway . . .' Mother's voice trailed off as my tears welled up, spilled over and dripped steadily off my chin on to my lap.

Lady was a yellow labrador with melting brown eyes and velvety ears, and I had loved her dearly. But, being young, she wasn't much of a gun dog, apparently, and in a rage one day Father had shot her. Uncle Will, on the other hand, was very creepy, and his loss was no great loss at all as far as Peter and I were concerned. Whether Father minded the death of his half-brother, I never knew. He just seemed to be furious with him for dying without leaving a will, which meant that all of his money went to an obscure missionary sister of his that none of us had ever met. Father thought that any money he had left ought to have gone to Will's three half-nieces and one half-nephew.

It was a maths lesson, so I was quite thrilled to be called out of class.

Then the school secretary murmured, 'Your mother is waiting for you in the headmaster's office' as I left the classroom, and panic rose in my throat. What was my mother doing at my school? Why had the headmaster asked to see her? What had I done wrong? I searched and searched for a reason for this rather scary turn of events as I made the short walk along the corridor and through the secretary's office before tapping on the door of the headmaster's inner sanctum.

'Come,' Mr Webster boomed.

I turned the handle and pushed the door ajar. Sure enough, there was Mother looking rather like an untidy tweedy bag of washing as she perched on the visitor's chair in front of the headmaster's desk. Both Peter and I had inherited from our mother our inability to keep anything tucked in where it was supposed to be. My school shirt was always coming adrift from my skirt, and my tie looked as if the dog had chewed it, except we didn't have a dog. True to the family form, Mother's scarf was half in and half out of the collar of her olive green tweed coat, and she was wearing one black leather glove while the other was hanging out of her coat pocket. Her thin, mousy hair had been blown into a scruffy halo by the wind. She sat with her feet neatly tucked together and her handbag clutched on her lap as if her life depended on it – which, given how much stuff she crammed into it, it probably did. I noticed that her glove-free hand was gripping the bag so tightly that her knuckles were white. Something was definitely very wrong, but I could not, for the life of me, think what I could have done that warranted her being summoned by the head. Her eyes glittered in the weak light from the window and, for one awful moment, I thought she was drunk. I took a surreptitious, but deep, sniff of the air as I approached her warily, but I could detect no fumes other than the smell of old ashtray that bore witness to the thirty or so Kensitas tipped that she smoked each day.

The headmaster rose, cleared his throat and avoided looking directly at me as he said, 'I'll leave you two to it, then. Take as long as you need, Mrs er,' – for a moment he forgot Mother's new name, then triumphantly remembered it – 'Stewart.'

'Right. Thank you, Mr Webster. You're most kind.' Mother's voice was husky, the way it sounded when she had been crying. I took a harder look at her. The glitter in her eyes was unshed tears, just waiting to be let loose. Pride, and a good old British stiff upper lip, made blubbing at the headmaster impossible – much to his relief, I'm sure.

We waited for Mr Webster to get out of his room and then Mother said quietly, 'I think you had better sit down, dear.'

I looked around for another chair and, finding none, I perched uncertainly in Mr Webster's. It was still warm, I remember.

Mother fumbled in her bag, drew out a letter and placed it with a shaking hand on the polished surface of the desk in front of her. She rested her hand firmly on it, indicating that I wasn't to take it from her. I noticed that the handwriting was Uncle Tony's, but I couldn't read the postmark. Uncle Tony was away working on the Tote, but he was based at our house, and shared a bedroom with Peter when he was at home.

'This arrived this morning.' She paused and took a deep, shuddery breath. 'I've spoken to Grandma and Grandad and they have received one too.' Mother's voice cracked, wobbled dangerously. A single tear escaped and slid down her face before she brushed the rest away with her impatient, gloved hand.

'Your Uncle Tony has committed suicide. In Doncaster, of all places. He likes –' Mother caught a harsh, strangled, painful breath, then corrected herself – 'liked Doncaster. It seems he's been planning it for some time, because he has been collecting sleeping tablets from doctors in every town he's ever been to with the Tote.' Mother paused again, longer this time, allowing me a moment to take in what she had just told me. 'And we thought it was such a nice job for him, working on the Tote. He loved it, he said, but all the time he was planning . . .' The last sentence came out in a heartbroken wail and I flew round the desk to gather my mother in my arms. We held each other as we cried together for what felt like a long, long time.

I remember thinking how funny it was that time could stretch and shrink depending on the circumstances. It seemed to me that terrible news always seemed to stretch time almost to breaking point, as if God or Nature was making sure that you felt every agonizing moment of it to the full. Mother's voice was a broken whisper as she went on to tell me that Uncle Tony had written his letters, posted them and then had embarked on one last monumental bender. According to the hotel receptionist, he had staggered back to his room at around midnight, clutching an almost full bottle of whisky. Apparently he swallowed enough pills to knock out half of the country, downed the last of his booze and had then lain down and died. He was just twenty-six years old.

There was a gentle tap on the door and the secretary popped her head in to say that Don had arrived to take Mother home. Mother nodded. 'I'm ready now,' she whispered, then turned back to me. 'You stay on at school and then see if you can go home with someone for a little while this evening. I've got to break it to your brother when he gets in from work.' At the time, Peter worked at Lloyds of London, but the world bored him rigid and he later became a laboratory technician at the local hospital.

I nodded, and after a swift, comforting hug from my stepfather, they left me alone in the headmaster's study. Nobody told me how I was supposed to go back to my classroom. So, after a while, I went to the cloakroom, washed my face in cold water then walked slowly back to the classroom door. I took a deep breath and marched in, head held high, and got on with my work for what remained of the double period of maths. The whole business had taken less than an hour, when I could have sworn it had taken most of the day.

'What did the head want with you?' my friend Frances asked at break time. 'What have you done?'

'Yeah. What have you been up to?' Johnny Rainbird asked. He always hung around the ring fence that divided up the playground, one side for the girls, the other for the boys. He had a big crush on Frances.

'My Uncle Tony topped himself in Doncaster,' I told

them in an unnaturally conversational tone, 'and I don't want to talk about it.'

The news spread around the school like wildfire. I could tell, because by lunchtime everyone was avoiding my eye, and my friends were clustered quietly in a protective circle around me, talking amongst themselves about the usual stuff – lessons, teachers and, of course, boys. Nobody mentioned my Uncle Tony.

Our little family all mourned Tony a great deal in our own ways, but we barely spoke of it. Poor Peter, possibly Tony's only close friend, was heartbroken, but misery was not encouraged in our family. When it was unavoidable, it was tacitly agreed that no one acknowledged it. I heard Peter crying to himself in the room he had shared with Tony, but he would not discuss it with anyone. I think Mother, in common with many who had lived through the war, thought that outward shows of grief were, in some way, self-indulgent. We all must have suffered dreadfully, especially Mother, Grandma and Peter, as families always do when a suicide takes place, but everyone kept it firmly to themselves. It was the done thing.

Not all that long after Uncle Tony died, I had a peculiar thing happen to me. It started with a short piece I'd read in the newspaper about some American schoolchildren slashing a new pupil with razor blades. The new girl suffered from cerebral palsy, and she had just started school for the first time. The other pupils had surrounded her, attacked her and, as they were slashing away, they screamed, 'We don't

273

want misfits here!' I was appalled and for days and days the article preyed on my mind. I couldn't get the images of the attack out of my head or get over the fact that children could be so cruel to one another. I was obsessed with just how unjust life could be. The girl in the article was disabled, through no fault of her own; my sister was dying, also through no fault of her own; Tony had found life so unbearable that he would rather die than carry on with it; my mother, brother and grandparents were suffering badly, and Lady had been shot, and the whole lot swirled around in my mind until I thought that I must scream and scream and scream – but I didn't. I couldn't, because I felt that I had no right to such strong feelings when the various parents' suffering was so great. And there was no one to talk to, to relieve the pressure that was building inside me.

It was a Friday night, folk club night in Brentwood. I had taken to going to the folk club on a regular basis, and that evening an American called Art Garfunkel was singing. He was a friend of my friend Kathy's boyfriend, another American called Paul Simon. They were later to become very famous indeed, but then they were unknown except to devoted folkies. I certainly hadn't heard of this Garfunkel fellow, and had no idea what to expect. He had a beautiful voice, pure and soaring, and it filled the small room above the pub with songs of protest and of sorrow. And, to my horror, suddenly, right in the middle of his performance, I went blind, deaf and dumb. It was as if I could not bear to see, hear or speak of any more misery, and everything simply shut down. I don't remember being taken home, but

I must have been. My mother was sufficiently alarmed to call a doctor.

'It's a touch of hysteria,' I heard the doctor pronounce from a long, long way away. My hearing was coming back, and I could see his bulk outlined against the light from the lamp in my bedroom, but I still could not speak. 'Has anything happened lately to bring it on?'

Mother shook her head. 'No, I don't think so.'

When the doctor had gone, Mother hissed, 'You can stop showing off now, madam. For Christ's sake pull yourself together. You're not the only one who is upset, you know. We all are, but you don't see the rest of us carrying on like this.'

So, after a while, I did pull myself together and carried on as if nothing had happened. It was the done thing: Mother said so.

19

Work, Work, Work for the Master

'Isn't it about time you got yourself a job and left home?' Mother asked on the morning that I received notification that I had passed my two A levels – just.

Well, actually, I hadn't done too badly on the english one, but I scraped through the history by the skin of my teeth. Both were something of a miracle, because in the English exam I had had to answer a question about a character in one of Virginia Woolf's novels without ever mentioning the character's name. I had completely forgotten it, and intense brain-flogging would not bring it back, so I had to keep writing 'the artist' this and 'the artist' that. Naturally, the minute I walked out of the examination room, the name came flooding back to me: such is the power of examination terror. The feeling that I was as dim as a Toc H lamp had dominated my educational life, and I simply could not shake it.

The history exam was even worse. I had to write about

England's Civil War and every firm fact, name and date I had ever learned about it had fled my brain as if the demons of hell were after them. In the end, I was forced to invent a Cromwellian officer whose oldest childhood friend was an officer on the Royalist side, and I explored, at some considerable length, the wicked way that civil wars divide families, friends, neighbours and communities at such appalling cost. No wonder it felt like miraculous intervention that I had passed those damned exams at all.

'I said, isn't it about time you thought of branching out on your own? After all, your brother's married and gone and it's high time you went as well. Don and I would like to spend some of our married life alone, without kids cluttering up the place, if that's all the same to you.' Mother was unable to keep the note of mild irritation out of her voice. I should, apparently, have thought of it for myself.

The message was clear: she felt she'd done her bit by her children, and it was time I showed proper appreciation by buggering off. All of my peers were having a really terrible time even broaching the subject of leaving home with *their* mothers, whereas my dear old mum was virtually hauling out my suitcase and redecorating my bedroom as she spoke. She had earmarked my room for her new study long before the ink was dry on my certificates and my sheets had lost the warm imprint of my body.

True, the new, South London flat we had moved to was very small compared to the house that we'd left in Essex, and space was at a premium. Mother had made sure of that. 'I've watched my friends. They no sooner get shot of their kids than they start moving back in again. Well, I'm not having that. If the place is small enough, my two will just have to stay away and lump it.'

I took the hint and moved into a flat in Finsbury Park, North London, with Reg, a friend of my brother. Again, unlike other mothers, mine had no problem with me flat-sharing with a young man. In fact, she had convinced herself that, as I was still a virgin at the ripe old age of seventeen, I must be a lesbian.

'There's nothing wrong with it, you know. People can screw dogs, as long as the dog is willing, and the same goes for homosexuals,' Mother informed me one day when she was probing to find out if I was engaged in any sexual activity.

'What? Are you saying that homosexuals sleep with dogs?' I asked, thoroughly confused.

'No, no, you idiot. What I'm saying is, it's OK to sleep with other girls as long as they're willing. The same goes for men with men, despite the stupid law. There's nothing wrong with any kind of sex as long as all parties concerned agree to it.' Mother paused for a second. 'So, are you a lesbian?'

'I don't think so. I mean, how would I know?' I asked.

'Oh, I think it becomes obvious over time,' was Mother's vague reply. She then lost interest in the subject, and I heaved a great sigh of relief. Other people's mothers didn't pry into their daughters' sex lives, or lack of them. In fact, I'd only ever had one boyfriend, and he'd dumped me for a girl who was far more willing than I.

I sincerely believed the problem pages of the women's magazines that I read in secret – Mother didn't approve of women's magazines because they were 'such utter rubbish' – and, on the sage advice of various agony aunts, I'd always held firm when it came to youthful fumblings. I honestly felt that sex was best left until after marriage, so as not to run the all too real risk of pregnancy. No 'nice girl' in the 1950s and early '60s became pregnant out of wedlock, and if she did, there was all hell to pay. In reaction to the enormous number of illegitimate births during the war years, attitudes to sex swiftly reverted to old-time values. I'm not exactly sure when the contraceptive pill was developed, but I do know that if it was available at all in the early '60s, it was not easy for girls on the threshold of womanhood to get hold of it. National Health doctors did not prescribe it to unmarried women and, although there were a few special clinics, like the Marie Stopes one in the West End, there were way too few of them to be of much use to the general population.

According to Mother, the mechanical methods of birth control were not to be trusted, either. 'French letters spring leaks, Dutch caps can slip, and the Holy Roman rhythm method is useless, which is why there are so many little Catholics running about. Those spermicidal creams are hit and miss at best – and anyway, they taste awful.' This latter statement confused me a great deal: how could a cream you stuck in your mouth stop babies? I didn't have the opportunity to ask for illumination on this point, because Mother was in full flow, and she hated to be interrupted.

'The only sure form of contraceptive is a glass of water. Not before or after, but instead,' she would opine. Alternatively, she would advise 'a sixpence – clenched between the knees', thus showing a double standard in her view of my sex life. On the one hand she seemed to be urging me to put myself about a bit, to prove that I wasn't a lesbian, and on the other hand, she was saying that the only certain way to avoid an unwanted pregnancy out of wedlock was to say 'no' and stick to it.

This was a bit rich, coming from a woman whose own son had attended her wedding to his father. But then, Mother was nothing if not unconventional. Unlike any other mother I had ever met, or discussed with my friends, mine was very frank about sex and made no bones about the fact that she thoroughly enjoyed it. I think this was probably a reaction to the tucked-up attitudes of her own mother's generation.

'Your grandmother never mentioned sex or contraception to me when I was growing up. As far as she knows, I still have no idea where babies come from,' Mother chuckled. 'But then, I don't suppose for a second that her own mother explained it to her. According to Dora' – the most worldly of my great-aunts – 'my father had to send for a doctor, a priest and a tin-opener on their wedding night. She refused to believe it, you see: the whole thing was a terrible shock to her, poor woman. No wonder there were such big age gaps between me and my brothers. I expect it took Father that long to prise her legs apart.' Mother laughed again, but without a trace of mirth. 'That's why I've always been so straight about the facts of life with you and your brother. I didn't want either of you to be ignorant on the subject – or ashamed either.' This time Mother's smile was genuine. 'Sex is just a fact of life, like eating, sleeping, bog-trotting and the rest, only much more fun. It should be enjoyed, not feared, or – worse – thought of as dirty.'

Having passed my A levels and duly moved away from home, as instructed, I was in urgent need of a job. As I had no particular skills, it was decided that I should work in Father's mail order astrology business as a general clerk and dogsbody until I found out what I wanted to do with my life. His offices were in London's West End and his printing works were in Brewer Street, in the heart of my beloved Soho.

Father had set himself up as a fortune teller, and he had three rooms on the sixth floor of a large building. There was a large one for 'the girls' who opened the mail, processed the requests for tarot readings, typed addresses on large, noisy manual typewriters, kept files so that established punters could receive 'shots' or offers of further products, stuffed envelopes with horoscopes, lucky charms and further offers, answered queries and dealt with complaints. Along one wall were two long trestle tables, where the mail openers sat and processed the hundreds of forms that arrived daily: there was one pile for new customers requesting horoscopes, and others for customers wanting charms to bring them good luck. In front of each person was a long, wooden receptacle divided into sections for cheques, postal orders, pound notes and ten-bob notes.

On the wall above the table were large sheets of card with the signs of the zodiac. Each one was allocated a number: Aries was 1, Taurus was 2 and so on until number 12, Pisces. Each horoscope request was boldly marked with one of these numbers, so that the next link in the chain could pop the right reading into the right envelope, along with flyers for further products and, of course, the all-important return envelope to make further orders easier.

I can't honestly say that I enjoyed the work much. I found it boring and monotonous and, being the boss's daughter, I was never quite accepted as a member of staff. Also, I felt that flogging horoscopes, lucky charms and assorted bits and pieces along the same lines was a dubious activity at best, and immoral at worst. Some of the letters we received were truly heartbreaking. It seemed to me that vulnerable and gullible people were being conned into buying a little bit of much-needed hope.

The thing I enjoyed most about working with Father was the opportunity to spend time with interesting people that, in the normal run of things, I would never have met. There was lovely Ron, an old friend of Father, who had suffered so mightily in a Japanese POW camp that his health had been ruined for good. Ron never spoke of his suffering, or of his days working on the notorious Burma railway, but I knew that he woke screaming some nights and shaking uncontrollably on others, because his wife told me so.

Ron was a gifted artist, but his large paintings were often so very disturbing that he rarely sold any: they were so difficult to live with. The poor man suffered bleak bouts of depression, but he relieved these with his own particular brand of humour. Each morning, when he arrived at work, he'd crack a whip he'd made from a broom handle and a bit of string and cry, 'Work, work, work for the master!' before settling down to the dreary business of stuffing envelopes or collating horoscopes.

He also enjoyed teasing perfect strangers to relieve the monotony. 'Form a queue, form a queue,' he'd hiss out of the side of his mouth as we walked across the grass of Regent's Park in our lunch break. Dutifully, we'd line up behind him right in the middle of a wide open space and, sure enough, if we waited for long enough, people would attach themselves to the end of our queue without even knowing what they were queuing for. The habit of queuing was still so engrained from those distant days of rationing and shortages in the 1940s and early '50s, that people simply joined any old queue, no questions asked. It was amazing. Once we had a good few newcomers, Ron would signal and we'd stroll off, leaving our fellow queuers stranded and looking just a tad foolish.

Another of Ron's ruses was to stick one of those knobbly, rubber-thimble-shaped things that you put on your fingers for counting money, in the middle of his forehead, or on the end of his nose, before contorting himself like the hunchback of Notre Dame and strolling down Brewer Street, where he would approach any likely-looking man or woman and say, 'If I give you a melon, would you roll in the hay with me, my dear?'

This startled his poor victims somewhat, but had the rest

of us laughing hysterically. What the people he approached thought, God only knew, but they mostly took it in good part. Ron was a truly gentle man and we all loved him for it.

Long before it was fashionable or legally required, Father was an equal opportunities employer, and made a point of paying women the same wages as men for doing the same jobs. He also actively sought out Africans and Asians to work for him, because he was so incensed by job advertisements of the time stating that 'no coloureds or Jews need apply'.

He also objected to age discrimination, and over the years employed several people who were way past retiring age, but who needed the money. His only proviso was that they could do the job for which they were hired. One such person was an aristocratic lady who had fallen on very hard times when her husband died. Beatrice had never had to work in her life before, but Father liked her because she was 'a game old bird', who never missed a day through illness. She even staggered in once when she'd badly sprained her ankle and broken her arm over a weekend when, as she said, she had 'too much gin taken'.

Waiting for a bus with Beatrice was always a bit fraught, because she'd never really understood the first come, first on the bus, principle of public transport. She'd sail to the front of the queue waving her brolly and yelling airily, 'Take no notice of this rabble, dahling', and climb aboard, oblivious to the outraged folk behind her. On one occasion, she was fumbling in her purse in order to pay the conductor when she dropped it, scattering coins everywhere. 'Oh shit, fuck, bugger,' she roared in her plummy tones, much to the shock of the conductor and the other passengers.

'Madam,' the conductor remonstrated, 'a lady does not swear.'

'On the contrary, young man,' she informed him, as arch as a duchess – which she was, almost – 'Only a lady can!'

Those were mostly happy days for me, despite the dullness and dubious morality of the work. It enabled me to spend time with my adored father without my stepmother's unsettling and unwelcome presence. I didn't have to share his attention with my half-sisters either. The fact that we saw one another virtually every day also meant that I could cut down my visits to the house in Surrey, where the family had moved when Father began to make some serious money.

Father always said that he was five foot eight, but I'm sure he was shorter than that. As a young man, he had been very slender indeed, but in middle age he was a little on the stocky side. I used to joke – but never in his hearing – that his height depended on which leg he was standing on: his left leg was somewhat shorter than the right, thanks to the polio he contracted in childhood.

He always dressed well and he had a knack, which I envied and wished I could emulate, of being able to combine colours and patterns. I cannot imagine him ever wearing anything drip-dry, and I never saw him in either a cardigan or a sweater. It was smart jackets and a shirt and tie, even at home. He was immaculate in his grooming: his hair was well cut, his face closely shaved and his fingernails were spotless and neatly trimmed. In the days when most people bathed once a week, he bathed daily. Because of the polio, Father had his shoes made for him in Bond Street as soon as he could afford it. I suppose Father was still attractive to women, but I always thought this quality owed more to his charisma than his actual looks. The person who reminded me most of my father to look at was the comedian Tony Hancock, another man who was apparently very attractive to the opposite sex.

The main problem with working with Father was his outbreaks of filthy temper, which once resulted in his slinging a five-drawer metal filing cabinet through his sixth-floor window. He managed, by an enormous dose of sheer luck, not to kill, or even maim, anyone in the crowded West End shopping street. Over the years he smashed so many recalcitrant telephones – his record was nine in one day – that the Post Office eventually refused point-blank to replace them. On another occasion, he tried to hurl me down the lift shaft because I'd organized the girls to demand an hour for a lunch break, instead of the piddling half-hour that they were allowed.

The strangest thing was the loyalty that Father inspired in his workforce, and in his friends, even though his rages terrified one and all. Mavis, one of his office supervisors, summed it up. 'We all know he's as mad as a bleedin' hatter, but when he ain't smashing the place up, your dad's the kindest bloke we know. And in his own peculiar fashion, he's fair – when he ain't ranting, that is.' She flashed her beautiful smile. 'And, of course, he pays well. But then he'd have to, with that temper of his.' Despite his many failings, Father had a real gift for inspiring loyalty and deep affection in all who worked for him.

The summer that I turned eighteen we went on the much-hated (by me) annual pilgrimage to the South of France, and we had reached the eve of our departure back to London. I'd flown there from Heathrow, Father had driven his sports car and Gaby had brought the girls down by train. The six weeks had, as usual, been punctuated by frequent furious fights between Father and Gaby, and I, for one, was heartily relieved to be returning to England and my relatively peaceful flat.

I awoke on the morning of departure so convinced that my plane was going to crash that I insisted on being seen off at the airport by Father, in case I never saw him again.

'Don't be ridiculous,' he snapped. 'You're not usually superstitious. What's got into you?'

'I just have this feeling there's going to be an accident,' I told him, unable to shake the doom and gloom that I felt so strongly. 'And as I'm the only one flying . . .' I didn't finish my sentence.

Father rolled his eyes in exasperation. 'Gaby was going to drive you to the airport before she set off for the station. I suppose it won't matter if I drive you, but you're a bloody nuisance, all the same.'

Just after breakfast, the weather broke. A huge electrical storm was still raging over the airport as we arrived, confirming my suspicion that I was about to cop it. My flight was delayed for so long that Father began to mutter and pace up and down, up and down, showing his habitual impatience in the face of adversity. He was itching to be gone, and off on his own journey back to England. In the end, he announced that if I didn't get airborne in the next half-hour, I would be travelling with him.

Twenty minutes later, the storm blew itself out, and five minutes after that, my flight was called. I kissed him good-bye and gave him a huge hug for good measure.

'Yes, yes, all right,' he harrumphed, secretly pleased at such an unusual display of affection. 'Off you go now. I've got to start driving, I want to get home too, you know.'

I arrived safely at Heathrow and travelled back to the flat in Finsbury Park to be met by a worried-looking Reg. 'You'd better phone your mum,' he told me, even before we'd said hello.

'What is it?'

'Just phone your mum.'

I did as I was told. Mother's voice was strained as she answered. 'Your father's had a terrible accident. They thought he was dead,' she told me. I could hear the tears in her voice. 'A gendarme threw his cape over him, but then someone saw him twitch. He's in hospital. He's cracked his neck in three places, and his typewriter flew forward from the back of the car and whacked him in the head. It's touch and go. Stay by the phone and I'll let you know what's going on. I was just about to call the hospital in France.'

Nobody ever knew for sure what had happened. No other

car was involved, and there was no mechanical failure of Father's Maserati, but for some reason he had skidded at well over a hundred miles an hour. The car had flipped over and over and Father had been thrown clear before it finally came to rest on the opposite verge of the autoroute. Father was found some distance from the wreck. Some people thought he'd blacked out, or had had some kind of seizure. Others thought he might have swerved to miss an animal that had long gone by the time he was found. Had I been with him, I would certainly have died, because the roof above the passenger seat of the car was crushed virtually flat.

Father did live, although he sustained an injury to the temporal lobe of his brain from the flying typewriter. For quite a while, he showed no real symptoms. Then he began to suffer from petit mal, or mild bouts of epilepsy without the fits. It manifested itself as brief 'absences'. They lasted seconds, maybe a minute or two, and they left him looking grey in the face and disorientated. His temper tantrums grew more irrational, more violent and more unpredictable as time went on, and in the end the doctors decided that his brain was very slowly atrophying. The prognosis was that his condition would progressively worsen over the years until, as Gaby put it, 'He will end up a vegetable.'

Father, who had been such a huge presence in my life, would slowly change over the last decade and a half of his life from a larger than life and frightening character, to a pitiful shadow of his former self. Sadly, his behaviour became weird, as well as tempestuous, and that was even more frightening in a way. The change from being in awe of him, to feeling profound pity for him, was one of the hardest transitions I have ever had to make. It was, I think now, the beginning of the real pain of my growing up into adulthood.

PART THREE

The World Outside

20

Valerie

A year had passed since Father's accident, and he hadn't yet begun to show any obvious signs of his brain injury, so we had all made the summer trek to the Côte d'Azure as usual. What was not usual was that Valerie, despite some gruelling treatment involving a drug made from the periwinkle plant, which made her face swell like a balloon and caused some of her hair to fall out, was still not at all well. She was listless and depressed, and every movement was an effort for her.

I looked over at her and noticed silent tears slipping steadily down her poor, pale, yellow-tinged, swollen little face, but I knew better than to try to comfort her. She had never liked to be cuddled much, and since her last treatment, she positively hated it. I think that physical contact had begun to hurt her.

I passed her a clean tissue and gave her a small smile, which, try as she might, she could not return. Her effort looked what it was: a sickly twitch of the lips that didn't reach her dull and mildly yellow eyes. I turned my gaze to her pink, plump, blond little sister. The contrast between them was startling – and frightening.

Father and Gaby were arguing again, but Nicci looked utterly unconcerned at the turn events were taking, and continued to munch on her banana in silence. The poor lamb was used to the storms, and had learned to switch off from them early in her young life. Neither of her older sisters ever learned that trick, sadly.

Eventually it was decided that Father and I would return to London with Valerie to have her checked out at the hospital, while Gaby and Nicci would continue with their holiday as planned. We would rejoin them as soon as Valerie felt better and the hospital gave the OK.

Gaby drove us to Nice airport in the hired car the next morning, still maintaining that as Valerie had been given treatment before we left, it was likely she would feel better in a few days.

Father clamped his jaws together and said nothing, but it was obviously a massive effort; a vein beat steadily in his forehead and his eyes bulged dangerously. I thought that he'd have a stroke if Gaby didn't simply shut up. At last we arrived, and after a flurry of goodbyes the three of us were safely in the departure lounge and there was no more opportunity for a last-minute fight in public. Once we were on board the aircraft, the pilot and cabin crew, who knew she was sick, made much of Valerie, and she was photographed in the cockpit wearing the pilot's cap. She tried to look thrilled, but it was such an effort for her. Everyone was so kind.

Father's Rolls-Royce Silver Cloud, the car he had bought to replace the destroyed Maserati, was waiting for us. After his accident, Father had briefly employed a chauffeur, Harry, but it hadn't taken him long to get fed up with being driven, so he'd let Harry go. However, the kindly chauffeur brought the Rolls to the airport and drove us straight to the hospital. Once there, he gave Valerie a small present and a sympathetic smile, and left us. Father would drive us back to the house in Surrey, once Valerie's tests were completed.

It was a long day. Throughout her years of hospital visits, treatment, remissions and relapses, Valerie had shown remarkable fortitude, patience and bravery, but she had had enough. She was tired of it all, and said so in no uncertain terms. It took Father and me ages to get her to agree to the tests, and when finally a sample of her blood was taken and whisked off to the lab, we were wrung out and emotionally exhausted. After another long wait, the test results came through. Valerie's blood cell count was dangerously low. She needed yet another transfusion, and quickly. When the news was broken to her, Valerie promptly had hysterics. She refused to undergo any more treatment; and frankly, we couldn't blame the poor child. Father was tender and oh, so gentle, as he persuaded her to allow this one last blood transfusion.

'I don't want to stay here,' Valerie begged. 'I want to go home.'

'How about you have the transfusion, and Daddy and I will promise you that we will take you home with us when it's all over? How about that?' I asked, as Father took a rest from his patient pleading.

'Cross your heart and hope to die?' Valerie demanded.

Father and I glanced at the doctor, who nodded slightly. 'Yes, the doctor says that will be OK.'

'Do it,' Valerie instructed. 'Cross your hearts and hope to die. Promise me that I can go home tonight.'

Solemnly, the doctor, Father and I crossed our hearts, 'and hope to die,' we intoned, in unison. Father and I added, 'We swear to you that, as soon as it's over, we will all go home.'

It was late – gone midnight – when we finally left the hospital with Valerie wrapped snugly in a blanket. Father carried her to the car and gently placed her in the back seat and I climbed in after her. I put a pillow on my lap and Valerie lay down with her head on it as we drove through the quiet, wet streets towards Surrey.

'Don't go too fast, Daddy,' said Valerie in her best, bossy voice. She was a kid who knew when she had the upper hand, and she obviously intended to make the most of it. Father and I smiled tiredly at each other. This was better, this was the Valerie we knew and loved, and who was showing a spark of her old spirit. The new blood had done its work.

Once back at the house, Valerie woke up as Father lifted her gently out of the car. To my horror, I noticed that her eyes were all wrong. They were rolled back in her head, so that all we could see was the whites. Valerie began to cry, terrified that she was so suddenly blind. We hurried into the house and put her to bed as instructed by the hospital.

'Watch her for a minute while I call the hospital and find out what the hell is going on,' said Father. I nodded. My attention was on Valerie, and, though I was terrified too, I attempted to soothe her by talking to her quietly and assuring her that we would do our very best to make it better.

I couldn't hear Father's conversation with the doctor, because he'd closed the bedroom door so as not to frighten Valerie any more than she already was. I looked at her in the dim light from the lamp and was absurdly pleased to note that the ghastly pallor had been replaced by faintly pink cheeks, but her eyes were still terrifyingly white. Father came back at last and called me out of the room for a moment. We didn't dare leave Valerie alone for more than a second or two.

'They say it may be an incipient brain haemorrhage and we've got to take her back,' he told me, tears streaming down his haggard face.

'But we promised her!' I whispered urgently.

'I know. I asked them what, if anything, we can do for her here. They said to keep an eye on her, sedate her if necessary and that if it is a brain haemorrhage, all that they could do at the hospital would be to make her comfortable and wait for the end. They finally agreed that we could do that almost as easily here. So I told them that we wouldn't be bringing her back.'

I agreed with him, because I believed then – as I still

do now – that promises to children should always be kept, if humanly possible. Kids set great store by promises, and I had experienced enough broken ones to know just how devastating it could feel. The rest of his news frightened me, though. How would we be able to comfort Gaby if her baby died while she was away? There was no good answer to that. I was also afraid of Valerie dying. I had never actually seen anyone die, and the thought filled me with dread.

'I phoned Gaby while I was at it, told her the situation, and she'll be back tomorrow,' Father whispered to me across Valerie's now quiet form.

My relief was immense. Whatever I thought of her, Gaby was Valerie's mother, and if ever a child needed her mum, Valerie did at that dreadful moment.

I looked down at Valerie. She was either asleep or had slipped into a coma. We had no way of knowing which it was without attempting to wake her, and that seemed too cruel. Father and I agreed to let her be, and to hope fervently for the best.

I even prayed to the God that I had been brought up not to believe in. 'Please,' I pleaded, 'let her live at least until her mother gets home.'

Father and I spent the rest of the night keeping our vigil, alert to the slightest sign of change. Occasionally, one of us would get up to ease our aching back and legs or to go downstairs to make a cup of black tea. The house had been closed up for the long holiday, so there was no milk or food to be had: not that we were hungry, we were way past that. It was the longest night of my life.

During that long, long night, Valerie's eyes righted themselves while she slept, and, to our relief, she awoke refreshed and even a little hungry. It seemed that my prayers had been answered after all. I was feeling faintly astonished as I nipped across the road to beg some milk and biscuits to keep Valerie going and to explain our predicament to the neighbour.

'We've had no food, Valerie's very sick and Father's the only driver,' I told the sympathetic neighbour. 'Could you possibly drive me to the shops so that I can stock up?'

She agreed immediately, and we set out straight after I'd delivered the milk and biscuits she had so kindly provided. I cooked breakfast when I got back, and we had a remarkably cheerful feast. Father and I could hardly believe the change in Valerie. Relief and the lack of rest had made us mildly hysterical, and the three of us laughed quite a lot at daft jokes and silly stories.

'What's red and squashy and goes up and down?'

'A tomato in a lift.'

'What's orange and pointy and goes at a hundred miles an hour?'

'A jet-propelled carrot.'

Valerie loved silly jokes like that, and we had a whole heap of them. We were still laughing when Gaby walked in.

Once Gaby was safely back in charge, I made up my mind to go home as soon as possible. I left Father to explain the horrors of the previous day and night, and quietly went across the road to ask the neighbour to take me to the station. I desperately wanted to get home; I was emotionally exhausted, not only by Valerie's crisis but by the tension between Father and Gaby that never seemed to let up. Even when they weren't actually fighting I was always tensed up and waiting for the explosion, and I simply didn't want to have to listen for hours to Gaby telling me what a swine my father was.

Despite Mother's best efforts, I had found myself between flats, and had gone home while I sorted myself out. She had taken it with relatively good grace, especially when she realized that I was off almost immediately to France with Father, Gaby and the kids. She was even fairly gracious when I came back so suddenly.

'I suppose you can't help Valerie being ill,' she observed. 'It must have been grim for you, darling. After all, you're only a kid yourself.'

I was grateful for the welcome and, having had a cuppa with her, I went straight to bed, and didn't wake up again until late the next morning.

Things remained quiet for a while. I can't remember quite how long; a week or maybe two. Possibly it was as much as three. I really can't remember. All I know is, life had a chance to get back to what passed for normal – and then there was a phone call that shattered all that. Mother answered the phone.

'I'm sorry to hear that, Doug. It's one thing after another

for the poor little mite, isn't it?' There was a pause. 'I don't think that's wise. She hasn't had mumps. It must be the only childhood thing she's managed to dodge, but she definitely has not had mumps.' There was another, longer pause. 'Yes, I do understand, but catching mumps now could sterilize her. I never got pregnant again after I caught the damned things from a kid at school, and let's face it, I'd never had any trouble *getting* pregnant, it was hanging on to them long enough for them to be born that was my problem.' There was another pause. By this time, Don and I were listening intently from the wrong side of the door. We glanced at each other, eyebrows raised in enquiry. What on earth was going on? 'Well, I'll ask her, but I'll advise her strongly against it. You could afford to hire a private nurse, you know. You have the money and you don't *need* to put the poor girl in this position. It's really unfair of you.'

Mother sighed loudly. 'Hang on. I'll ask, but I'm warning you, I don't think she should come.'

The receiver was put down with a clatter on the telephone table and Mother's footsteps sounded loud as she approached the living room. Don and I just had time to arrange our features into some semblance of innocence as if to say, 'Who? Us? Listening? Never!'

'It's your father. He wants you to go back to Surrey to help to nurse Valerie. Looks like she's caught mumps now. I told him that you haven't had mumps, but he's being nagged in the background by Gaby. I could hear her.' Mother lit a cigarette.

'What should I do?' I wailed. 'I don't want to go back.

301

It's awful to watch her, and those two will be fighting, and I hate that too. They're always bloody fighting.' I felt utterly wretched.

'You don't have to go, pet,' Don told me quietly. 'I've seen those two going at it hammer and tongs, and I don't blame you for not wanting to be in the middle of it.'

Mother nodded. 'Tell them you're not going. That's my advice, for what it's worth. You're too young for all this, and worse, you may want children of your own one day and mumps is a glands thing. I'm sure they put a stop to my breeding days.'

By the time I got to the phone, Father had had time to pile on the guilt. 'If you want it on your conscience for the rest of your life that you didn't help your sister when she was dying, don't come,' Father roared down the phone as soon as I'd said hello.

In one sentence Father had relayed to me just how little I actually meant to him. I was dreadfully hurt. I'd always thought he loved me, despite everything, but not caring at all what catching mumps could mean to me told me that he didn't, not really. My only value to him at that moment was what I could do for him, his wife and his other daughters, and I counted for nothing at all. That's how it felt at the time, and I was devastated.

It was only much later that I realized just how frightened he was, and I finally understood that frightened people are capable of anything. Father and Gaby couldn't seem to depend on each other, but somehow they both thought that they could depend on me, which, given the appalling circumstances, was flattering in a backhanded kind of a way. When I thought about it later, I also realized that both Valerie and Nicci probably needed me to be there as well. Despite the miserable feeling that I had been blatantly emotionally blackmailed, I didn't feel that I could possibly let everyone down, mumps or no mumps. And so I went.

Mercifully, I don't remember just how long the final stage of Valerie's illness went on, but I do remember that it was harrowing. Slowly, as the condition of her blood worsened, the systems in her poor little body broke down. Her blood was no longer able to clot properly, so her lips became covered in blackened scabs and her gums bled. Oxygen wasn't getting to her brain because she didn't have enough red blood cells to carry it there. She became delirious and spent hours and hours chanting our names, 'Mummy, Daddy, Nicci and Pippa, Mummy, Daddy, Nicci and Pippa,' over and over again. Or she'd shout, 'Push my arm to school, push arm to school.' Her impatience mounted as we failed to do as she demanded, or when we simply could not understand exactly what it was that she wanted from us.

As the days went by, she chanted less and less, then all that could be heard was her laboured breathing as her lungs tried to take in the oxygen that her blood could not carry.

One afternoon, when I'd been left alone in the house to care for her, I stood for ages with a pillow in my hands, listening to her rasping breath, willing myself to put an end to her suffering. I had reasoned that the Valerie that we knew was already gone and that she was never coming back, so the sooner she finally left us, in body as well as spirit, the sooner we could all get on with the dreadful business of mourning.

Valerie had been in the long, slow process of dying for four and a half years. Everyone was exhausted and wrung out by watching it happen and being powerless to change it. It seemed as if real life, the life outside of leukaemia, had been put on hold, and that we were all trying to hang on to a spark of hope that was fading and dying as surely as Valerie was slipping inexorably away from us.

Eventually, I put the pillow down again, unable to do the deed, because even the tiny, flickering flame of life and hope that was left was precious. I sat down beside her bed and simply listened to that awful, jagged rasping and the clock, ticking, ticking, ticking her life away.

'Wake up, wake up!'

I unglued my sleep-heavy lids and saw the dark shape of my father in the gloom as he shook me awake. 'Come quickly. Valerie's asking for you.'

Even in the grogginess that accompanies being wrenched out of a deep, exhausted sleep, I wondered that my little sister had been able to form the sentence, when she had been incapable of expressing a coherent thought for days. I glanced at Nicci, who was sleeping soundly beside me, and satisfied myself that she was OK for the time being.

'I'll be in in a minute,' I whispered.

When he knew for sure that I was awake and taking notice, Father left the room. I staggered out of bed, fumbled around for my summer dressing gown and checked on Nicci once more. I had been sleeping with her ever since she had vacated the bedroom she had shared with Valerie. Her bed was needed for whoever was on night duty, and anyway, it was too awful to leave her to witness her sister's last illness at such close quarters. However, Nicci had been having nightmares ever since she had changed rooms, and she found it comforting to have me there, ready to cuddle and soothe the night terrors away. Anxious not to wake her, and even more anxious about what I would find when I arrived at Valerie's bedside, I crept out of our room.

I pushed the sick-room door open and witnessed a heartbreaking scene. Father and Gaby were standing each side of Valerie's bed. They must have been upset beyond all measure, and were arguing about what to do for the best.

I edged round Father and looked down at Valerie's pale, pinched face. Her eyes were dark with pain.

'You wanted me?' I whispered, my mouth close to her ear so that she could hear me over her parents' voices.

'I can't bear it,' she whispered back. 'I just can't bear it.'

I nodded and turned on her parents and told them quietly, but with an absolute authority to give me a quiet moment with Valerie alone.

My voice brooked no further argument and, as one, they turned on their heel and left the room. Once safely downstairs they resumed their argument, but mercifully it was muffled by distance.

'Hold me,' Valerie whispered, for the first and last time in her life. I gathered her gently in my arms and, at last, after a few minutes, that dreadful rasping breathing finally ceased. I held on to her for some time, as tears slipped down my face, then gently laid her back on her pillows and took her small hand in mine.

How could I tell them? How could I tell them? I sat for maybe ten minutes beside the body of my dead sister and listened to the latest battle in the long war between her parents being slugged out below. I tried desperately to think of a merciful way of breaking the news to them. I could not simply say, 'She's dead.' It seemed too cruel. I decided that they would need a blessed moment or two between the words being spoken and the news sinking in. I looked at the clock, which was still ticking. It was almost four o'clock in the morning, on the day before my nineteenth birthday.

I walked slowly down the stairs, took a deep breath and opened the living-room door. Both heads turned towards me. 'She's stopped breathing,' I told them, and watched as the meaning of the words finally registered on their faces.

And then, while I stood in the doorway, feeling utterly powerless, I saw their poor battered hearts shatter, never to be entirely whole again.

21

Bye-bye, Val-Val

The doctor put it as kindly as he could.

'You will need to call a second doctor if you wish your daughter to be cremated,' he explained. 'It's the law. I know a man who will come,' he added, as he placed a copy of Valerie's death certificate on the mantelpiece. 'If that is of any help?'

Neither Father nor Gaby was able to speak, so I nodded. 'Call him,' I said.

The doctor picked up the telephone receiver. 'May I?' he asked, and I agreed that he could. He dialled, stared into space as he waited for an answer, then held a muttered and brief conversation with his colleague.

'He'll be along directly,' he told me. 'Is there anything that I can do for any of you? Sleeping tablets, perhaps some tranquillizers?'

I knew my father's view on mood-altering substances of any kind. He was very definitely against them, and had been ever since he had given up drinking. He thought tranquillizers were downright dangerous; they were addictive, he said, and as time went on, he was proved right.

I looked at Gaby. 'The doctor says can he give you anything, sleeping tablets or anything . . . ?' My voice faded to nothing as Gaby turned her haunted eyes on me and shook her head, still mute with shock and misery.

'My father won't want anything, either,' I told the doctor firmly. 'He has views.'

'And yourself? It's been a difficult time for you, too.' I remember thinking that that was the understatement of the decade, but I decided against chemical assistance none the less. The problems and heartache would still be there when the pills wore off, and I believed what my father had told me. I didn't want to be swallowing the damned things for the rest of my life.

The second doctor arrived and agreed that Valerie could be cremated, as there were no suspicious circumstances surrounding her death.

'And the sooner the better,' the second doctor added. 'The poor child has had so many drugs to treat her illness, and it's summer . . .' He allowed his sentence to drift into nothing, but we got the picture. He went on to recommend the local undertaker – 'He's a good man, considerate, efficient, he'll take all those worries off your shoulders' – and then he took his leave.

The sound of Father's voice came from a long way away; I was lost once again in the numbness that follows a terrible shock.

'Pardon?'

'I said, could you tell Nicci that her sister has . . . ?' He couldn't finish the sentence. His voice cracked as he continued. 'She'll be waking up soon, and we've got to tell her something. Gaby and I think it'll be best coming from you.'

It never occurred to me to ask them why they thought this. Even now, it seems to me that the terrible news might have been better coming from her parents; that it might have helped them to grieve together, instead of being left to do it all alone. As it was, nobody seemed to be able to help anyone else. Everyone was locked away, imprisoned by their own misery and grief.

I simply nodded and trudged up the stairs. It felt as if I was weighed down by lead boots. The short flight of steps seem to go on and on for ever.

It was still relatively early in the morning, which came as a shock. It seemed like days since I had heard Valerie breathe her last, difficult breath, but in fact it was only a little over four hours. I looked at Nicci's sleeping face for a long time, then stroked her long, blond hair from her forehead and planted a kiss on it to bring her awake as gently as I could. I can remember the smell of shampoo and warm child even now. Her eyelids fluttered open and she smiled. I sat quietly beside her to allow her to come fully awake before I spoke.

'I have something very sad to tell you.' Nicci blinked and looked puzzled. I ploughed on quickly, before I lost my nerve. 'You know that Valerie has been very ill?' Nicci nodded again. 'Well, I am sorry to tell you that she died last night.' Now Nicci looked blank, not really understanding what I was telling her. 'It means that she won't suffer any more, but it also means that you will never see her again. I am sorry, sweetheart, I'm so very sorry,' and I held my arms out to her.

Nicci didn't cry. She didn't ask any questions, nor utter a single word. She lay still in my arms, and appeared to be thinking, for a long time, before she pulled herself free to get up, wash, dress, clean her teeth, and go downstairs to the quiet kitchen to eat a bowl of cereal. Finally, still without a word, she went outside.

I watched her through the window as she walked into the middle of the front lawn and just stood for a while, staring at nothing at all, as far as I could see. Eventually, her young friend Nigel, from across the road, approached her, and then, without speaking, she punched him in the nose. It would have been funny, apart from poor Nigel's nose of course, if it hadn't been so sad.

'Why did my baby die?' Gaby asked the neatly groomed, white-haired man with the insincere, film-star smile and the expensive suit. Her voice was pathetically childlike. I forget the man's name, but he was the Christian Scientist who had been taking Gaby's money and telling her that the power of prayer would save her daughter.

'Perhaps because you didn't believe strongly enough,' he answered glibly.

I was appalled at his callousness, his complete lack of empathy and simple humanity. I felt rage build up to boiling point and for the second time in my life, the red mist blurred my vision. I wanted to kill him, or, at the very least, spread his expensive capped teeth over a very wide area. I could not believe the cruelty of his remark. He was blaming Valerie's death on her mother's supposed lack of faith, as if his answer was self-evident. Well, it wasn't evident to me. How could he say such a thing to a grief-stricken woman who had just lost her child? Where was the comfort that he was supposed to dish out? I looked hurriedly around and was relieved to realize that Father wasn't within earshot – I may have *felt* like killing the bastard, but I think Father probably would have done it. Gaby seemed frozen to the spot in the hallway, a trembling hand to her mouth, dark eyes stricken with horror.

I pushed her gently aside and confronted the so-called holy man.

'Get out,' I hissed. 'Get out of here right now, before someone hurts you.'

I may have only been eighteen years and three hundred and sixty-four days old, but something in my face told him to believe me. The swine stumbled on his way out, but sadly he did not fall flat on his face: I was fair aching to see those sparkling teeth shattered and that expensively perfect smile ruined, but it was not to be – yet more proof that there is often no justice in this world. He continued on up the drive to his car, with all the urgency of a burglar caught with his hand in a jewellery box. I think it was the first time that I ever felt such complete contempt for another human being. Any remote possibility that I would ever go against a lifetime's indoctrination and embrace Christianity died in those few moments.

I don't remember much about the rest of that day. There were a lot of comings and goings and a great many phone calls both in and out. I had had so little sleep that delayed shock and exhaustion made me go about the business of providing tea and coffee for the constant stream of visitors as if I were in a trance, which I suppose I was, in a way.

I know I called the undertaker, because he came to arrange the details of the funeral. 'What music would you like?' he asked, pen poised to take down any requests.

'Nothing religious.' Father was firm on that point. 'I don't want any hymns of any kind, or any sermons either.'

'What, nothing at all?' The undertaker looked shocked.

'Some Mozart, maybe, or some opera, or "The Dance of the Sugar Plum Fairy" from *The Nutcracker*, but no religious stuff at all,' Father repeated, when it looked as if the undertaker was not believing his own ears.

'I'm afraid the crematorium only supplies the "Dead March" and a fairly wide selection of hymns. For children and, er, young persons, "All Things Bright and Beautiful" is often the hymn of choice. I have a list of some others here.' Flustered, he held out a sheet of paper, but Father flapped it away impatiently.

'Then nothing,' he said. A slight edge had crept into his voice.

'If you don't have a pastor of your own, the crematorium can supply you with one. If you give me details of what you would like said about Valerie, I can pass that on to him . . .'

The undertaker sounded a little desperate. Things were not going to plan.

'I don't want some priest who never knew my daughter going through the motions. I said, "No sermon" and I mean "No. Fucking. Sermon".' Father's voice rose and his face took on a congested look as his fury began to build.

The undertaker, experienced in the vagaries of grief, finally got the point. 'Right,' he said hastily, 'no music, no sermon. Perhaps one of you would like to say a few words?'

We looked at one another, but none of us felt equal to the task. If there had been more time before the death and the funeral, one of us could have managed it, but the ceremony had been arranged to take place on the day following Valerie's death: on my birthday, in fact. Speed was of the essence, both doctors and the undertaker were agreed on that.

'Flowers?' the poor man asked, and, to his relief, my father and Gaby agreed that flowers were a good idea – but no wreaths, nor crosses either. A coffin was chosen from photographs of a selection usually reserved for children and, eventually, the undertaker and his attendants went upstairs to prepare Valerie's body to be taken away.

Gaby asked me to place a posy of roses that she had picked in her dead daughter's hands, but I could not face going back into the sick-room and seeing her again, so I knocked on the door and asked the undertaker to do it for me.

It was only when everything quieted down, late that night, that it occurred to me that, for the first time ever, Grandma and I would not be spending the birthday that we shared together. In past years, I had either gone to France after our birthday, or returned before it, but we had always, always shared our day.

It was then, when I lay beside the sleeping Nicci, that I began to cry. I cried for Valerie, I cried for Father, Gaby and Nicci, and I cried because I would be attending my little sister's funeral instead of a birthday tea with my grandma. I cried for everything and everybody and I thought that I would never stop.

'Bye, bye Val-Val.xxxx' read the note on the little posy.

'Val-Val' was the nickname that Nicci had given her sister almost as soon as she could speak. It was the nearest that her infant tongue could get to saying 'Valerie'. It was what she had always called her sister, and the rest of us often followed suit. A lump formed in my throat and tears threatened again as I read the little note, so carefully written in dark blue crayon.

Nicci had walked around the garden all by herself, choosing the flowers she wanted. She had carefully selected the summer blooms, pink Elizabeth roses, white, yellow and rusty-coloured snapdragons, pink and white cosmos, blue love-in-a-mist, blood-red geraniums, orange marigolds and the last of the blue Canterbury bells. She had wrapped the flowers very carefully in a white, lacy paper doily, tied it with pink ribbon, and, to finish off, had tucked her note between two rosebuds.

'Will you give them to Val-Val, please?' Nicci's large blue eyes glistened with the tears she still could not shed. I nodded and smiled wanly down at her, speechless. I put the posy in a cool place, ready for Valerie's last journey.

The big, black hearse proceeded at a stately pace, as hearses are wont to do, but it didn't take Father long to get fed up with our slow progress behind it. Finally, in a fit of irritation, he put his foot down and sped past the hearse, which dwindled, very rapidly, to a black dot behind us. I had just enough time to note the shocked expressions on the faces of the black-clad, frock-coated figures that accompanied my sister's coffin as we purred alongside the hearse, then left the funeral procession in our dust.

Naturally, we arrived at the crematorium long before the hearse and the more reverent members of the funeral party, but others had followed Father's example and arrived shortly after us, so that when the coffin finally got there, we had all been waiting for it for some considerable time. One of the things I remember most clearly was the strained laughter at something Father had said as the hearse drew up. Even at the time, I recognized Father's compulsive need to entertain as a reaction to intolerable misery and strain, but it was still a little shocking. People were not supposed to be rocking with mirth at a funeral. It just wasn't done. Even with my limited experience, I knew that.

We all lined up and filed into the building to be met with absolute silence. It was forty years ago; crematoriums just didn't run to anything but religious music in those bygone days, and, as the undertaker had warned us, it was hymns or nothing. So there was nothing to muffle the sound of our footsteps and the shuffling as the congregation found their places.

In the gloom, Valerie's white coffin stood out, so small and lonely on the dais. The sight made me begin to cry, and I was not alone. Soon, quiet sobbing, sniffles and blown noses joined the shuffling of feet as the only sounds to be heard. As there was no service, we just had time to get in, find our places and to stand, heads bowed, for a few moments, before there was a whirr of hidden machinery and the coffin began its slow, steady descent into the bowels of the building. Dark red, velvet curtains swished closed just before the white casket finally disappeared from view. The funeral was over almost before it had begun. Nobody spoke and there was a stunned pause before everyone began the slow shuffle out into the sunlight once again. It was a beautiful day.

The silent ceremony, if it could be called that, was both incredibly moving and somehow wrong, all at the same time. It was as if Valerie's life had been so short and so filled with sickness and pain that there was little more to say about it, but that wasn't true. Valerie had been a gifted artist, and had been interested in so many things that she had made herself a small museum, with each exhibit carefully labelled and displayed in such a way as to bear witness to her sense and need for order. She was funny, sensitive, secretive, very bright and, occasionally, very difficult, in an arch and curiously adult way. Before her illness really took hold, her dark, delicate, elfin looks made her striking and beautiful rather than pretty. There had been, in fact, a great deal that could have been said about Valerie at her funeral, if only one of us could have borne to say it.

There was a gathering at the house afterwards. Father, Gaby, me, Father's friends Frank and Ron the artist, and a few neighbours were there, plus one of Valerie's teachers from the days when she had been able to attend school. Towards the end, she was so liable to catch infections that school had become impossible, but her teachers remembered her; they had sent flowers, a note of condolence and a representative.

My mother and Don had elected to spend the day with my grandma, partly to make up for me not being there, but also because there was no real place for them at the funeral, except, perhaps, as a comforting presence for me. As it was, I busied myself pouring teas, coffees and drinks and handing around plates of sandwiches, which was comfort of a sort.

22

All My Fault

'He says to tell you that he couldn't help it. He fell in love. He couldn't help himself,' my ex-boyfriend's pal explained, not even trying to keep the smile from her broad, freckly face. She had always been a funny one, but not in a ha-ha kind of a way.

It seemed that while I had been away in Surrey, burying my sister, I had been dumped by my boyfriend with absolutely no ceremony at all.

Mother had been both delighted and appalled when I had finally found myself a boyfriend. She was delighted because I was showing signs of growing up at last and she was looking forward to passing responsibility for my well-being on to some husband or other; as far as she was concerned, a proper boyfriend was the first real step on that desirable route. She was, however, appalled at my choice of man. He was a singer with a folk band, and he led an itinerant kind of life. He was a good deal older than me – a father figure, some might say, and I expect they would be right. That would explain why my mother was so wary, of course: he was *far too much* like my father for comfort, and certainly not good husband material.

After Valerie's funeral, I had tried really hard to return to my everyday life, but I found it impossible. My boyfriend had upped and gone in a particularly lame and pathetic fashion. I thought I loved him and was desperately hurt. I also felt, in some obscure way, that he had been right. That I wasn't lovable, and that it was *all my fault*. Of course, a swift, and very large, boot up the bum would seem a more appropriate response to my ex's profound shabbiness, but I was too young and inexperienced either to know that, or to have the nerve to apply the giant footwear.

More painful, in a way, was that the small gang of friends that I had hung around with, in that claustrophobic way that teenagers have, began to avoid me. They were uncertain what to say or to do in the face of such a huge loss, so they decided to say and do nothing at all. Nobody had had the experiences that I had had, and they simply did not know how to handle them, or how to handle me. It was so very hurtful not to have my calls returned, to see familiar eyes slide away from my face when we met by accident in the street, to be told that their social calendars were too full to fit me in. It was a very lonely time. It taught me something, though – two things, in fact: never, ever to trust a silver-tongued charmer, and never to ignore or avoid the recently bereaved.

I made frequent visits to the Surrey house in the weeks,

months and years that followed Valerie's death, largely to keep an eye on my surviving sister and to try to offer some sort of comfort to Father and Gaby, but I don't think I succeeded very well in any of that. Although Father was grateful that his little girl had not died alone. I always felt that Gaby was never able to forgive me either, because I was their when Valerie died. She was never able to acknowledge my birthday again, for example, and I think that's an indication of just how hard it always was for her. Me too. Ever since, even after all these years, my birthday has been tinged with an awful sadness.

Meanwhile, Gaby and Father seemed unable to help one another or their remaining little girl. It was a truly dark, bleak time for everyone. I didn't know what to say, I didn't know what to do and there was absolutely no one to tell me.

Mother and Don also avoided talking about Valerie. My mother was a stoic, one of the war generation, who had learned to 'put up and shut up', and she did this very well. Instead of unseemly outbursts of emotion, Mother expressed herself in a dry, often caustic way. When the situation was too serious for graveyard humour, she kept quiet, but busy. She expected everyone else to do the same, and was nonplussed and rather shocked when they didn't. Mother was more inclined to offer little acts of kindness as support, rather than the lend of an ear, so the only indication I had that she was sympathetic to my plight was that I enjoyed quite a lot more of my favourite meals for a while and, for a few weeks, she stopped reminding me that it was high time I found somewhere to live other than her spare room. As for Don, the whole thing must have been a very sad reminder of his own lost little girl, Diana.

I reasoned that, if I felt so isolated and lonely in grief, then Nicci must have felt herself virtually abandoned, which is why, despite the wretchedness of it, I tried to visit her as often as possible. I felt sorry and worried for her; she was only a scrap after all, just about school age.

Apart from my worries about Nicci, I think that I visited so often because I needed to touch base with others who had been present when we had all lost Valerie. Although I don't think I was aware of that aspect at the time, it was more of an instinct than anything. There was always this underlying anxiety about the family, particularly Nicci, that nagged away in the back of my mind, however hard I tried to dodge it – and I often tried very hard indeed.

Because I had been the one who was with Valerie when she died, I felt responsible – even, in some obscure way, as if I was to blame. For a long time afterwards, I felt guilty that I had made no attempt to resuscitate her, even though I knew that all the oxygen in the world would be useless when her blood could no longer carry it to where it was needed. But I felt I should have tried, that I had given up too easily, that all I wanted was for her suffering – and ours – to end. In fact, in a way, it had been a relief when Valerie's terrible, rasping breathing had finally stopped. It took many years before I could forgive myself for that.

23

Dr Kingdom's Special Trial No.13

The interviewing panel at the teachers' training college decided to take a punt on me, and I was duly enrolled in the History Department of the Polytechnic of North London. I had got tired of the dead-end and very boring jobs that punctuated my much more interesting travels around Europe and North Africa, and had finally decided to try to get to grips with a proper, grown-up life by entering into one of the family professions – well, the respectable side of the family, anyway: Mother's lot. They were all teachers and headteachers on Grandma's side, and Methodist ministers on Grandfather's. Working on the theory that the Church – any church – was not for me, I plumped for teaching.

By the time I started college, I was living in a flat in Kilburn and had two new flatmates. Peter had followed his marriage by becoming a father – twice – then moving to Canada in very rapid succession. And I moved out to Kilburn. It may be a bit of a stretch of the imagination to suggest that Mother and Don's next move, to the Outer Hebrides, was meant to ensure that once I was fully fledged, I 'stayed bloody fledged', but let's just say that distance lent a good deal of enchantment to my mother's view of me.

At first, I enjoyed the teaching course. There were elements that I found difficult and stressful, but I turned out better at it than I would ever have imagined possible. I also made some new friends while I revelled in the student life. I had had enough experience of the real world to know what a privilege higher education was for me. I had never expected to get any, and I was both incredulous and grateful when I did. There was nothing I liked better than lounging about in a North London greasy spoon, drinking strong tea, eating artery-clogging nosh and chatting with pals about Life and the meaning of everything. I can't remember what conclusions we came to, if any, but I really enjoyed trying to reach them.

Along with the odd artery, I had also managed to block the final exams from my consciousness. I had driven all thought of them from my mind for two years and more, so that when they eventually forced themselves on my attention, I was very frightened and ill-prepared. Looking back, I can see that there had been clear signs that all was not well with me for some considerable time, but I didn't recognize them then, and neither did my friends and flatmates.

I began having a series of minor accidents: a twisted ankle here, a sprained wrist there. I often took to my bed, sometimes for weeks at a time, apparently chirpy enough but unable to face the world outside my duvet and occasional runs to the bathroom and the kettle. And all the time those terrifying exams loomed in front of me, and Valerie's death, and the terrible wounds it had inflicted on my poor, benighted family, haunted my memories.

'I don't want the pills,' I told the doctor flatly.

I was at the doctor's yet again, and yet again tranquillizers were being offered as a cure-all for everything from fractured toenails to fractured lives. The trouble was, they wiped away everything, all joy as well as pain, and that never seemed a fair trade-off to me. I had a close friend who had been reduced to a zombie by the things, and I can't say I fancied it one tiny little bit. The really big advantage of being brought up with no faith at all was that I knew that life was for living, not for 'getting through', and that deadening things by popping the docs' little miracle pills until the old 'pie in the sky by and by' saved me from it all wasn't an option. I was certain that there was no pie.

'I wasn't aware that you'd gained a medical degree since last we met.' The doctor looked over his half-moon specs in his best intimidating manner. 'What do you suggest we do with you?' The doctor did almost as good a line in world-weary as he did in heavy-handed patronage. He had a gift for saying little but implying much. He was able to convey, by the merest inflection, just what a pain in the arse I was being.

'It seems to me' – I tried to keep the pathetic whine of pleading out of my voice, but I felt weedy and it was hard to hide it – 'that treating the *cause* of my troubles might be cheaper in the long run, and more productive too.' It's hard to put across just how bone-weary I was of having the symptoms of my distress treated, but none of its fundamental causes. I was forever tearing up prescriptions for Librium, Valium and various other 'ums'. As time went by, I became so demoralized by the total absence of any kind of official support for my point of view that I fell into a deep despair.

The whole thing came to a head just before the dreaded exams, when in an incident that seemed agonizingly familiar and terribly personal, Father shot another dog that I loved. Print was a white springer spaniel with orangey-brown splodges dotted about here and there. The splodges were reduced to freckle size by the time they reached his nose, and scattered themselves across his muzzle in the most fetching way. He also had great lugs, long dangly things with curls. Print and I had had a special relationship ever since I'd rescued him from one of Father's rages when he was a pup. So I was devastated when he failed to bound up to me when I arrived one day on a visit and was told that Father had shot him. I never knew why.

Thus it was that, a few weeks before my finals, I finally suffered the full-blown nervous breakdown that had been threatening for so long, and I was carted off to the local psychiatric ward late one night after being stuffed full of Largactil – the so-called 'liquid cosh' – liberally administered by a locum. According to the nurses, I had had enough to knock out a stable full of cart-horses, and I was still going like a train when I was admitted into the ward. Apparently, I was literally begging someone, anyone, to cut my throat and put me out of my misery. I meant it too.

The ward could once have been some official's house back in the day when the grim, red-brick general hospital was built. It was situated in the substantial grounds, tucked well away from the main buildings. There was a large room that was meant to be used by the patients as a lounge, but it was too institutional to be cosy. I remember that it had black and white lino tiles on the floor, and a big, bile-coloured rug in the middle. Upright armchairs were placed in a circle around the bilious-looking rug. The chairs were covered in either dark red plastic or battleship grey, and were always cold to the touch. One or two tired cushions were scattered about, in a futile attempt to bring a homely touch. Nobody really used the lounge except at coffee time at eleven in the morning, and again at four in the afternoon for tea. We only ventured in then because we didn't get a drink unless we presented ourselves there at the appointed hour.

Occasionally, a patient was called for a 'review' in the lounge. This was a terrifying ordeal for a person suffering from acute anxiety, because the entire staff sat in a large circle around the patient as if he or she were an exhibit in a zoo. Each member of staff then gave their assessment of the condition and progress of the hapless patient, whose job it was simply to sit and listen.

Some inmates slept in small, single-sex wards of twelve, while others, like myself, were blessed with rooms to our-selves. The men's quarters were on one side of the building and the women's on the other. Separating the two were the administration offices and the cheerless lounge. The idea was to discourage midnight creeping by those patients whose condition might include sexual obsession. The manic depressives were considered fairly notorious for that kind of behaviour, although I have to say that most people were so drugged up to the eyeballs that raising an eyelid was an effort, let alone anything else.

I was allocated a room because I was studying for my exams and it afforded me some privacy, as well as much-needed peace and quiet. The room was how I imagined a nun's cell would be, with just the bare essentials – a narrow single bed, covered in a worn, well-washed, white cotton bedspread, a small chest of drawers and, as a special dispensation, a table and chair for studying. The curtains had once been patterned chintz, but were so washed out as to be almost white.

The whole building smelt of disinfectant, floor polish and – surprisingly, because no cooking was done there – over-boiled cabbage. That combination of smells seemed to follow me around to every miserable institution I had ever been in, starting with the Rest Centre, through various hospitals and all of my many schools. Fancifully perhaps, I have always associated that smell with quiet, and not so quiet, desperation.

Dimly, I was aware that a lot of my problems, at that precise moment at least, stemmed from being convinced that I wasn't at all bright. The crunch had come: the examinations were about to find me out. Worse, they'd expose me to all the world, as if the world would be interested, as an idiot. The problem was – the really tricky, sticky bit was – that if I didn't try to take those bloody exams, then I'd never know for absolute, certain sure that I was, in fact, utterly useless. And I would regret not finding out – I knew I would – if I dodged the issue altogether. Anyway, it would make facing the next set of tests even worse. So, reluctantly, I decided to plug on and sit the papers, even though I was still in the bin.

Being actively engaged in revision meant that I was excused a lot of the usual stuff like occupational therapy in favour of studying time, which meant that I was a bit cut off from the other inmates. Perhaps that would have been the case anyway, as everyone was so drugged all the time, we were all isolated in our own little worlds. We had no choice in the matter. Or, at least, it didn't feel as if there was one. The nurses were wise to tricks with pills, and everyone was either dosed in liquid form or watched really closely as they swallowed.

Mostly I kept close to the hospital, but I did occasionally venture out to get the books I needed for my college work. I have vague memories of visits from friends, and in my mind's eye I can see them in the sunny grounds, but I have very few clear memories of that time. It is hardly surprising. I was on prodigious doses of strong drugs and the whole world seemed hazy.

I was very quickly allocated a psychiatrist. He was a young Australian chap with a stammer. He decided that visits from my father would be unsettling for me, and banned them. He also pointed out that it was unwise for me to attempt to share flats with a couple (one of my flatmates had moved her boyfriend in), because I was over-sensitive to domestic strife, and I was unlikely to grow out of it.

He dished out advice along with the tranquillizers. 'What you need is a good husband,' I can remember him saying, a shade testily, one day.

'And do you supply them on the National Health?' I asked, wide-eyed with innocence.

'Th-there's n-n-no n-n-need to b-b-be f-f-facetious . . .' The poor man's stammer was really bad.

My next shrink was a tiny Austrian lady, youngish, skinny and intense. We didn't do too well together, either. It was the long silences. I hated those. After I'd horrified myself by gabbling non-stop into them a few times, I decided to keep schtum. I'm not sure why; perhaps I needed more encouragement than I was getting. The long silences had begun to get up my nose, and I was blowed if I was going to flog myself to fill them all on my own.

Meanwhile, I beavered away revising for my exams, and one day it became necessary to go to a book shop in the West End to fill some gaps in the material I had to study. I decided to visit Father at his office while I was at it, because he would literally be within spitting distance from the shop I needed to visit, and it seemed churlish not to.

First, I went to Dillons and, to my relief, was met by a member of staff who knew their stuff and was able to find a whole load of relevant texts in no time at all. My general state of being was so very shaky at that point that I was suffused with gratitude that someone could be so good at her job. Making decisions, even the smallest ones, like which knickers to wear that day, had become such an effort that I often gave it up in a fit of frantic wobbles or, worse, uncontrolled sobbing.

The next part of my trip was not so easy. I was anxious all the way to Father's office, and when I arrived I was shivering with fear at the reception I'd get. Father didn't disappoint. The swine kept me waiting in the outer office for three hours before sending someone to tell me that he couldn't see me after all. I was being punished for allowing the hospital to refuse to let him see me when I was so ill.

By the time I crawled down the stairs to the street I felt completely wrung out and fuddled. Everything was such very hard work, even putting one lead-booted foot in front of another. I could not face the insurmountable obstacle of planning a tube and bus journey back to the hospital. My brains simply weren't up to it, and neither were my watery knees. Eventually, I managed to hail a taxi and sank into the back seat with a whimper of relief. I was so grateful to be off the street and enclosed in a safe space for a while.

'Where to, love?' the cab driver asked.

I told him the name of the hospital.

'Where?'

I repeated the name of the hospital.

'But that's bloody miles away!' His tone was accusatory. 'That's out Harlesden way, that is. Further, even,' the cab driver said, incredulous that I should suggest venturing so far out of the West End. 'I don't do Harlesden, love,' he told me, as if I'd suggested Outer Mongolia. 'T'aint worth me while, 'cause I won't get a fare back, see? You can bet your life on that.'

Just as red mists can descend, so can emotional dams burst, I discovered. Mine burst in that cab in Oxford Street in front of a horrified cab driver. I told him everything. I told him about being in the bin. I told him about my terror of exams and not having 'the family brains' to fall back on. I told him about my father keeping me waiting for three hours and then refusing to see me. I told him that I simply could not get on that damned tube because my brains were scrambled and my knees were rubber.

'Have a fruit drop,' he said softly when I finally ground to a halt. 'Take two.' He carefully selected one in an unlikely shade of purple and unwrapped it in meditative silence as he absorbed the torrent of information I had poured over him. He came to a decision. I could tell by the way his mouth set and he squared his shoulders slightly.

'Seems like a lot for one day. I'll take you back to the hospital, don't you worry,' he smiled. 'I've got a daughter about your age, lives in Sydney, Australia. I'd like to think that if she was in trouble, some Ozzie cabbie'd help her out. So sit back and relax, love, I'll deliver you safe and sound.'

When we arrived at the ward, the cabbie helped me out of his cab and handed me my bag of books. 'There you are, love. Now, you hurry up and get well quick, despite that dad of yours.' He smiled sadly. 'I don't understand the man, meself, I'd give me right arm to see my girl . . .'

He eyed me a little blearily. 'You're a nice kid, a good

kid, and don't you let that miserable old beggar make you feel otherwise! Get well really quick, just to spite the old beggar.'

He wouldn't take the fare. 'I didn't put the meter on, you see, so I've no way of knowing.'

'Well, can't you make an educated guess?'

He shook his head. 'Nah, I never come out this far. These is foreign parts, these is, couldn't even begin to guess. Have it on me, love. It's good ju-ju in case my little girl needs a helping hand one day, eh?'

Along with the staff at Dillons, that cabbie lives in my mind to this day.

'Alone' did seem to characterize the way I was during this period. My mother said that she was unable to visit me because most of my stay coincided with her term time. She was teaching on the Outer Hebridean island of Harris. By half-term, her exhaustion made the trip south out of the question. Gaby came once, which was kind of her, but I don't remember much about her visit.

I was in the hospital for a little under twelve weeks. I took all of my exams from there and passed the lot, after a fashion, except an oral, which I flunked by coming over all wobbly right in the middle and rushing out of the room sobbing. As I had done really well in my final teaching practice, which I had completed before the breakdown, I think they kindly overlooked that awful oral.

Eventually, I was let out of the bin. I had gained a friend – an alcoholic priest called Derek, who made me laugh – a drum of downers large enough to snuff out most of London plus a healthy chunk of the Home Counties, and a feeling that I had failed some vital test and that I was a marked woman for life.

I'd also gained my Teaching Certificate, but I would not find out about that until later. Funny thing was, facing up to the exams had not had the desired effect at all. I remain terrified of tests and examinations. To this day they seem to represent abject failure – despite the fact that, looked at objectively, they could be seen as achievements. I had, after all, passed my A levels and my teaching qualification – I'd even managed to gain a distinction in my teaching practice – but the fact remained that I always felt as if I should have done better, and without misplacing my marbles while I was at it.

'Dr Kingdom's Special Trial Number 13' said the label on the tub of downers. I didn't like the look of it, not one little bit. I didn't like the look of the bomb-shaped pills behind the label, either. I had an awful feeling they'd blow my brains out if I took them. So I didn't.

I had been let out of the bin on three conditions: I should take the doobs (pills) as per instructions on the label; I should be released into the care of my mother until I settled down and could face life again; and in the fullness of time – in other words, when they could get it organized – I should attend group therapy sessions, weekly on a Saturday morning, at the hospital. We'd all given up on the one-to-one sessions quite early on.

I was not going to take the pills, and as for being released into the care of my mother, nobody said what I was supposed to do if my mother, care-giver *extraordinaire*, had legged it. I had done my best, but when I turned up in the wilds of the Scottish Isles, my mother had buggered off on an arts and crafts course somewhere on the mainland. Poor old Don was left to deal with his nutty stepdaughter all by himself. I can't remember anything at all about that period. I seem to have blotted it completely from my memory banks.

What I do remember is getting back to London sharpish, going to group therapy sessions as soon as they started up, and attending religiously every Saturday morning for a couple of years thereafter. It was at these therapy sessions that I first began to hear the horror stories of the women and men who were trying, in vain, to get off their tranquillizers. I couldn't understand it. Didn't you just stop taking them? After all, I had.

But listening to those sad stories, I thanked God for my stubbornness. I had always held out against the downers until they were more or less forced on me in the hospital, then dumb luck dictated that I was held there for a shade less than the number of weeks that can lead to addiction. Apparently, it takes a minimum of twelve weeks or so for many of these substances to get a real hold on a person.

My refusal to take the pills the doctors prescribed for me may have been due to a form of displaced rage at my parents for not being there – or, indeed, anywhere handy – in my hour of need. Or I may just have been bloody furious at being used as a guinea pig without so much as a polite enquiry as to whether I minded.

Be that as it may, I had never liked Dr Kingdom, the head honcho of the Ward. I had never liked the way he'd swan through the narrow room, stolen from a corridor, where we inmates ate our meals, without even the briefest glance left or right, as if we were not present. I suspect that he was embarrassed at barging through our mealtimes, but it came over as arrogance. Everyone else – the nurses, the other shrinks, porters, admin staff – all said hello with varying degrees of chirpiness, and some stopped to chat, but Kingdom never did.

I didn't like the notion of any 'Special Trial Number 13' either, and the fact that no one had consulted me before doling out what looked like an experimental drug. That also smacked of breathtaking arrogance, and I was cross, very, very cross about it.

'May I ask what "Special Trial Number 13" means?' I asked, keeping my teeth gritted against the seething fury that was just aching to be unleashed. I was at my three-month review with the great man himself. 'Does it mean that you have been dosing me with drugs that are, in fact, still at an experimental stage?'

He was guarded. 'You could say that, but none of the compounds in question is experimental in itself. Number 13 is a cocktail of Librium and Valium. The experimental part comes in the dosages of each drug.'

'But the fact remains, there is an experimental element. It is a kind of trial?'

'Well, I suppose you could put it like that.'

'So, I'm right in thinking that you experimented on me, like some kind of two-legged lab rat, without either my knowledge or my permission. Is that the size of it, Dr Kingdom?' My teeth were virtually rattling in their sockets, I had such a head of steam up. I could tell by his eyes that he didn't like where my questions were leading.

'Well I suppose you could view it that way . . .'

'What other way is there to view it?' I knew my voice was trembling, so I forged on before I could let myself down with hysterical yelling. I was literally shaking with pent-up fury. My sense of self, my basic humanity had been denied, insulted and abused, and I wanted to choke the bugger.

'Why didn't you consult me? Why didn't you ask my permission?'

He actually snorted, let out almost an incredulous chortle. 'Because you were in no condition to ask, that's why,' he said, as if any moron could work that one out.

I shot out of my chair. 'Then you should have waited until I was,' I spat. 'You take your pills, mister, because I won't. I'm a person, not some lab animal for you to play about with and I won't have it, do you hear me, *I will not have it*!'

I shook the lid off the vat of Doctor Kingdom's Special Trial Number 13 and hurled the tub at him. For some seconds, the world slowed, pills hung in the air then scattered and landed everywhere – in his hair, over his jacket, in his lap, all over his desk and the nice bit of carpet that showed his exalted rank; the lesser shrinks got little bitty rugs to brighten their lino if they were lucky.

Dr Kingdom and I surveyed the scene with wildly differing feelings. Judging by his bewildered eyes and slack jaw, Dr Kingdom was somewhat taken aback, shocked even. He was used to servile deference at work, not flying pharmaceuticals. I surveyed the wreckage with a deep satisfaction. My self-esteem had always been rocky at best, and being carted off to the bin and used as a laboratory animal had done nothing to improve it. But making a stand and telling Authority, in the shape of the good doctor, where it could shove its casual indifference to my humanity did wonders for it. Triumphantly, I smiled down at the shaken man, picked up my handbag and stalked to the door, head held high.

'Goodbye doctor,' I said, and walked out to face my future.

Epilogue

After my grandfather died, Grandma moved to the Outer Hebrides to be near Mother, who, after years of restlessly moving, finally settled on Scotland's remote Western Isles. As I was teaching, I was able to visit regularly in the school holidays.

I loved the Hebrides and the Hebrideans. I loved the seabirds, otters and seals that were a part of daily life. I marvelled at the lazy flight of a golden eagle riding the thermals over the hills and ignoring the darting attacks of the 'hoodies', or hooded crows, that objected so noisily and aggressively to an eagle in 'their' airspace.

The contrast between those wild, rocky islands in the Atlantic and the crowded streets of Soho in England's capital could not have been greater, but both took up significant parts of my heart and have stayed there. The inhabitants of both places are tough in their different ways. The Hebrideans quietly go about their business of eking a living out of thin, rocky soil and unpredictable seas, while coping with everything that the Atlantic can throw at them – storms, howling gales, towering seas and crashing waves. The Soho-ites, with their live and let live attitude to all comers, bustle about selling cakes, running up suits and theatrical costumes and knocking up plaster saints or mouth-watering pasta, while side-stepping gambling joints, porn shops, gangsters and booze hounds with a cheery smile of acceptance. In the Hebrides, the harsh, croaky cry of the corncrake, invisible in the hummocky grass of the machair, sometimes fills the twilight air: in Windmill Street, the croaking comes from the fag-laden throats of clip-joint hustlers, inviting the unwary in 'to see the show'.

In stark contrast with the quiet peace of Mother's Hebridean home, life in Father's Surrey house went further downhill, as did my relations with Father. His behaviour became more and more bizarre as his brain injury progressed. On one occasion I made the mistake of intervening in yet another monumental domestic, when it looked as if Father would strangle Gaby. Enraged, Father chased me out of the house and pursued me round and round the car in the driveway. Luckily, I was nippier on my feet than he was and came away very shaken but unscathed. The Rover, however, was a mess when he finally ran out of breath and steam and gave it up.

'You should have let him kill her. It would have saved you a lot of bother in the long run,' Mother observed drily some time later.

The phone rang one evening in December 1980. 'What

the fuck do you mean by giving my wife a few lousy chocolate biscuits for her Christmas present, you c***?' Father
screamed in my ear. 'We've got you a Fortnum and Mason's
hamper.' They hadn't, of course, but to prove that they had,
Nicci was dispatched a few days later to deliver their own
Christmas hamper in the boot of her car. Pauper that I was,
even I realized that Fortnum and Mason delivered in a smart
liveried van.

Father hadn't allowed me to explain that I had walked all
the way from my flat in Kilburn to Finchley Road just to
buy him his favourite, handmade marzipan fruits and Gaby
her favourite Bendicks handmade chocolate mints. It was
snowing, I remember, and the pavements were slick with
ice. I'd walked because I couldn't afford to buy their gifts
and pay the tube fares. It is difficult to buy presents for very
wealthy people when it's coming to the end of the month
and one's salary hasn't yet found its way into the bank.

I sent their hamper back to Father with a quote from
Oscar Wilde about Father and Gaby knowing 'the price of
everything and the value of nothing'. I'd also added that the
next time I heard from him, I wanted to hear that he was
dead. I was desperately hurt that he'd failed to appreciate
the effort I had made to please him and I lashed out blindly
in retaliation.

On a wet, cold day the following month, I woke up so
depressed that I simply could not get to work. This was
unusual for me, as I had found ways to combat my
depressions and anyway, I loved my work – by this time I

was a peripatetic teacher working with children with learn-ing difficulties in London's East End. But that day was different, and I could not, for the life of me, work out why I felt so dreadful.

All day I was obsessed with fire. I kept moving restlessly from room to room, lighting gas fires and then turning them off again, irrationally convinced that the minute I left a room, the damned things would explode. It made no sense at all, but that was how it was.

Finally, for no reason that I could figure out, I decided that I really had to have a bonfire in the garden, despite having nothing to burn. In the end, I nipped down to the off-licence to pick up some empty cardboard boxes to fuel my fire, and a can of lighter petrol to get it going in the incessant, sleety drizzle. At the moment I lit my fire, my father suffered a massive heart attack in his office, keeled over and landed on a three-bar electric fire. When he was found, he was ablaze, and the heat was so intense, his face had begun to melt.

As Father and I had not been on speaking terms when he died, I wondered if I should attend his funeral. 'Oh I should, dear,' Mother advised, 'if only to make sure the old bastard's dead.'

I did as Mother suggested, and went to the ceremony at the same crematorium where Valerie's funeral had been held. So many people attended, it was hard to get them into the room. One after another, men and women stood up to give their eulogies. These friends and strangers (at least to me) had loved the man: it was obvious. I wondered, at one point, if I had strayed into the wrong funeral. It dawned on me, as I listened, that the way to get the very best out of my father was not to be related to him in any way. It made me so very sad and angry that it took me a long, long time to get over it.

Don also died of a heart attack, not all that long after. His death could not have been more different from Father's, and it illustrated the stark contrast in their natures. Don died quietly in his favourite armchair. As Mother said, 'He couldn't have been more considerate. If he'd died in bed, we'd have had the hell's own job getting him past the bend in the stairs – I would have had to get the darling man lowered out of the window, like a giant sack of spuds.' His funeral was very small, and no one stood up to tell us how wonderful he was. But those few of us who were there knew it anyway.

Mother died in 1987, of lung cancer. I travelled up to Scotland to nurse her after the operation to remove her lung and again, almost a year later, for the final month of her life. Just before she died, I was finally able to persuade my brother to come to Scotland, and he was with her for her last moments.

Peter and his wife didn't stay for Mother's funeral, or indeed, send any flowers. I was desperately hurt, partly by Pots's apparent lack of respect for our mother, but also by his lack of compassion for me. If Ray, my future husband, and Nicci hadn't come for the funeral, I would have been alone among strangers, yet again.

Peter died of brain cancer a little under a month after his fiftieth birthday in 1993. I travelled to northern Ontario to see him as he began his gruelling radiotherapy. Ironically, I arrived on Mother's birthday. I hadn't realized, until he told me during that visit, just how hurt and bitter he was about our mother's drinking, promiscuity and lack of motherly instincts. It explained why he hadn't felt the need to attend her funeral. Before I left to return to England, Pots thanked me for making the effort to see him before he died, and added, 'I didn't think I was worth it.' That last sentence haunts me to this day. Of course he was worth it, he was my brother and I loved him.

Shortly before he fell ill, Pots had been made redundant from his job as chief laboratory technician at his local hospital. He was looking forward to being able to concentrate at last on photography, something he had always wanted to do. Tragically, he died before he was able to realize his dream.

It was after coming home from that visit that I finally plucked up the nerve to begin my first novel, *Not All Tarts Are Apple*. I was terrified that, like my brother, I'd never live to fulfil my dream, and I was also desperate to memorialize the time and the place that we shared the most, before he was sent away to boarding-school.

I am often asked if the narrator of the book, Rosie, is me, and whether the book was based on my life. All I can answer is 'Yes', but then again, 'No'. Yes, I remember Soho, and some of the people who lived there in the 1950s, in my work, but no, Rosie's family life bears little resemblance to mine. Maggie and Bert, Rosie's adoptive parents, are the Mum and Dad that I wish Peter and I had

had. On mature reflection, I realize that another character, Luigi, is a heavily disguised Pots, that Sharky Finn, the bent solicitor, bears an uncanny resemblance to Father in some ways, and that the Perfumed Lady is our mother, except Mother was nowhere near as posh.

One of the most flattering things a fan ever said to me about my novels was that 'when I get inside that café, I feel like one of the gang, and I love that'.

And I have to say that, when I am writing one of my novels, I feel pretty much the same way. I feel happy in the company of the motley crew who make up my cast of characters: from Rosie, Maggie and Bert, T.C., Madame Zelda and the Campanini clan, to the waspish Bandy and her sweet-natured sidekick, Sugar Plum, I love them all. But revisiting my own past life was nowhere near as cosy for me.

Writing this memoir has been a really painful and difficult process. Sometimes it was so hard, I would have to walk away from it for a few days. On other occasions, I'd find such a flood of tears dripping on to my keyboard that Noah would be letting down his gangplank. I would hastily mop them up, for fear of imminent electrocution or, worse, losing the work and having to start again – a truly dreadful prospect.

Over the years, it has been suggested to me several times that writing about my childhood would help me to come to terms with it, but every time I tried, I fizzled out after just a few paragraphs. When this project was first mooted, I was against it, but, to my astonishment, my husband and many friends thought that writing a memoir might, in fact, be a cathartic experience for me. I was doubtful myself but, in the end, despite my better judgement, I decided to give it a go.

'You're a writer, why aren't you fucking writing?' Father once asked me. Anglo-Saxon curses always featured large in Father's speech, even simple, everyday utterances, and although it may not appear so, I've *toned it down* for this book.

It was difficult to reply to Father's question, because it was many years before I knew the answer, and it was my dear husband, Ray, who finally supplied it. I had just seen my first article in print – a non-fiction piece about preschool education – and was reading the editor's very flattering letter when I remarked that I wished my mother had lived to see it, because 'She would have been absolutely thrilled for me.'

There was a long, pregnant silence from my old geezer until finally he shook his head. 'No she wouldn't. She would have been jealous of you.' And, with a painful lurch of the heart, I realized that what he said was true.

Every time I sat down to write in the past, I had heard this sneering voice in my head, saying, 'Who the hell do you think you are? Whatever made you think *you* could be a writer?' And that voice was my mother's.

Sadly, my mother was always envious of me, and I've spent quite some time trying to fathom why. All I can come up with is that, after a brilliant success in her school years, she set out on her road to womanhood with high hopes and high expectations, but wound up being bitterly disappointed. She never did become the great writer that she had hoped to be, largely because she frittered away her best years on my father and booze. She had to work full time in order to pay for both of her obsessions, and when she'd done her day's work, she came home to a demanding husband and 'whining brats' and was simply too exhausted to think, let alone write.

Besides, pounding a typewriter would have got in the way of the boozing, the brawling and the making-up that so characterized the early years of her marriage to Father. They were both highly competitive when it came to writing, as well, and Father was merciless in his criticism. Thus, it was no accident that I didn't start writing until both of my parents were dead.

Although it's been a very painful and often wretched business, in a strange way writing this memoir has provided some catharsis. It has given me an overview that I didn't have before. With the benefit of adult eyes, I have come to see that my poor father bore all the hallmarks of an undiagnosed, untreated manic depressive, and I can, at last, feel compassion for him, now that he's not frightening me any more. I can also understand my mother better, and I feel sad for her blighted ambition and expectations. It was sad for both of us that she allowed envy to colour her relationship with me to such an extent that she was often unkind, competitive and apparently uncaring.

I have discovered, by writing about my parents, that the poor old darlings loved me in their fashion: they just weren't cut out to be parents, because they never really grew up themselves. Best of all, I have at last come to understand that everything we all went through – the terrifying rows, the tears, the bitter partings and all the heartbreaks that followed – wasn't *all my fault*.

THE END

OUT OF THE DARK
One Woman's Harrowing Journey to Discover her Past
By Linda Caine & Dr Robin Royston

Life for Linda Caine should hold no fears. As a contented wife and
mother, she should have everything to live for. Yet a blackness has
started to leak into her thoughts. Images flash through her head
leaving her stunned and breathless. On the face of it, there is no
rational explanation for the way she feels.

But Linda believes there is something bad inside her. At the back of
her mind a voice tells her over and over again that everything will
be OK. When it finally gets too much, she can always simply die.
*'How shall I die if that time comes? I need to know these things.
They have to be planned.'* It must look like an accident. She will
drive off a cliff on her way home from her weekly shopping trip.
After all, who commits suicide with a load of groceries in their car?

The raw and powerful journey that Linda takes with her
psychiatrist Robin Royston to discover what lies at the heart of her
depression will leave you breathless. The secrets in her African
childhood and adolescence are buried so deep that to reveal them
may destroy her completely. Nothing is what it seems, no-one is
above suspicion. Together Linda and Robin race to unravel the
clues, before it is too late . . .

**'Reads like a psychological detective story . . . Linda's passage
back to health and sanity makes for compulsive reading'**
Mail on Sunday

9780552148696

A PIECE OF CAKE
A Memoir
by Cupcake Brown

The number one bestseller

From beloved daughter to abused foster child to crack addict, this
is the heart-wrenching true story of a girl named Cupcake Brown.

Following her mother's death, Cupcake was just eleven years
old when she entered the child welfare system. Moved from one
disastrous placement to the next, like so many, she was neglected
and sexually abused. She developed a massive appetite for drugs
and alcohol – an appetite fed by hustling and turning tricks – and
before long, stumbled headlong into the wild, notoriously
dangerous world of the gangsta.

But ironically, it was Cupcake's rapid descent into the nightmare of
crack cocaine addiction that finally saved her. After one crack
binge she woke up behind a dumpster. Half dressed and more than
half-dead, she finally knew she had to change her life or die.

Brutally frank, startlingly funny, *A Piece of Cake* is the
remarkable true story of a resilient spirit who took on the worst
of contemporary urban life and survived it. It is also the most
genuinely affecting rollercoaster ride through hell and back that
you will ever take.

**'A story that is poetic in its simplicity.
Beautifully stripped to the basics'
*Washington Post***

9780553818178